Born in a Bookshop

Chapters from the Chicago Renascence

Born in a Bookshop

Chapters from the Chicago Renascence

by Vincent Starrett

UNIVERSITY OF OKLAHOMA PRESS : NORMAN

Some Books by Vincent Starrett

Arthur Machen (Chicago, 1918)

Ambrose Bierce (Chicago, 1920)

Buried Caesars (Chicago, 1923)

Coffins for Two (Chicago, 1924)

Seaports in the Moon (New York, 1928)

Penny Wise and Book Foolish (New York, 1929)

Murder on "B" Deck (New York, 1929)

The Private Life of Sherlock Holmes (New York, 1933; Chicago, 1960)

Persons from Porlock (Chicago, 1938)

Books Alive (New York, 1940)

Bookman's Holiday (New York, 1942)

Autolycus in Limbo (New York, 1943)

The Case Book of Jimmie Lavender (New York, 1944)

Books and Bipeds (Chicago, 1947)

Best Loved Books of the Twentieth Century (New York, 1955)

Book Column (Chicago, 1958)

Library of Congress Catalog Number: 65–24204

Copyright 1965 by the University of Oklahoma Press, Publishing Division of the University. Composed and printed at Norman, Oklahoma, by the University of Oklahoma Press. First edition.

Dedicated to
HARRY HANSEN AND ROBERT CROMIE
Friends and Colleagues
Old and New

Foreword

When I first meditated this long reminiscence I planned to call it *Somnambulist*, but I no longer like that title or the sort of philosophy it projects, although it still haunts me. The significance of the word will become clear to readers of the book. I have been a sleepwalker in certain important things all my life—religion, politics, economics, and other troublesome matters. Indeed, that is still my happy predicament.

Other titles considered, either frivolously or prayerfully, were *Three Star Final, Reasonable Facsimile, Once Is Enough, From Shakespeare to Sherlock, Innocent Bystander*. I find them all attractive still, each in its own way, and all admirably descriptive of the immodest time-capsule I have labored to produce.

There are serious omissions in this book. Except facetiously, little has been said about my liking for music; but I have no words to describe what music has meant to me. And I have no words to speak my gratitude and affection for two little animals who have honored me with their friendship—Whisky, a wire-haired terrier, and Wing Lee, a black and white cat. Perhaps I shall have to write another book.

Many friends and colleagues have helped me to write *Born in a Bookshop*, with reminiscences and reproaches, congratulations and corrections, and just by asking from time to time how my book was coming along and who was going to publish it. I am grateful to them all; but my warmest gratitude goes to Stanley Pargellis, curator of the Newberry Library, and the officers and trustees of that institution, who made it possible for me to write this garrulous life-and-times on a Newberry Fellowship.

One final note may be in order. If there appear to be gaps here and there in the narrative, and the reader wonders what I was doing at those secret moments, it may be assumed that I was somewhere in a corner reading a book.

V. S.

Clarendon Island
February 18, 1965

Table of Contents

List of Illustrations

Born in a Bookshop
Chapters from the Chicago Renascence

"*I will talk of things heavenly, or things earthly; things moral, or things evangelical; things sacred, or things profane; things past, or things to come; things foreign; or things at home; things more essential, or things circumstantial.*"

BUNYAN: *Pilgrim's Progress*

Born in a Bookshop

I WAS BORN IN A BOOKSHOP or so close to it as to be able to claim the distinction. It was in a bookshop that I first learned the odor of books, first read the immortal works of George Alfred Henty, and felt the first vague stirrings of envy, admiration and authorship. If I were not a writer of books, I would be a bookseller, selling the dreams and solutions of other writers across the counter. Preferably, I think, an antiquarian bookseller. Books to me are the most important things in life after food, water, dogs, cats, girls, and the usual catalogue of imperatives. As a sort of literary religion I would be willing to subscribe to the attractive hypothesis of Pierre MacOrlan that all the great figures of history—kings, queens, travelers, and outlaws—were born into the world, and lived and suffered and died, only to furnish material for the good writers that were to come after them.

I have written about books and bookmen because I, myself, like to read about books and bookmen. I am fascinated by books and their fortunes along the years; what happened to them and their authors in consequence of publication; what effect, if any, they had upon their times; what people have said and thought about them; by their adventures and misadventures in every period of history. I am interested in their contents, in their physical appearance and typography, the paper on which they are printed, and their speculative values in the antiquarian market. My curiosity about books and authors is insatiable, and writers to me are the most interesting people in the world. I like the good, the bad, and the in-between, but on the whole I prefer the good and the bad, meaning both books and authors. And I like the authors best in their books; that is to say, as God loves all His children, at a distance. In perspective, as it were.

Superficially it may appear that I am more interested in books than in people; but I think it nearer the mark to say that I am more interested in people as they are revealed to me in books than as they reveal themselves to me in daily contact. "The children of the brain become to us actual existences," as Alexander Smith observes in *Dreamthorp*. "More actual indeed than the people who impinge upon us in the street, or who live next door. We are more intimate with Shakespeare's men and women than we are with our own contemporaries and they are, on the whole, better company." Nevertheless, although this will be in large part a book about books, you will find it also a book about people.

It was Margery Allingham's Mr. Campion who said that the "main thing to remember in autobiography is not to let any damn modesty creep in to spoil the story." This admirable dictum encourages me to open my own narrative with a faintly immodest story, told me by my mother, in which I have always taken great pleasure.

It appears that when I was born I was so impassive and improbable a specimen of the human animal that I was written off as "dead on arrival." As my mother's life was in some danger, my supposedly lifeless carcass was wrapped in a convenient newspaper and thrust under the bed to be disposed of at greater leisure. Subsequent inquiry by the physician in charge, prompted I suppose by some slight movement on my part—possibly a gentle rustle of protest—revealed the pleasing fact, since verified, that I was not dead at all but living, albeit feebly and with difficulty. (It has been suggested by friends that I was reading my first headlines.) At any rate, I was haled from my concealment and spanked into life after the startling fashion of obstetricians in that day and perhaps in this. I have lived after a fashion ever since, and persistent rumor has it that I am still living.

If the point of this shameless anecdote is not clear, I call attention to that fortuitous newspaper—the Toronto *Globe*, if I am not mistaken. It was my first garment in a strange new world and in effect I have never taken it off. Can any of my colleagues of the typewriter point to an earlier appearance in print?

It was the early morning of Tuesday, October 26, 1886, and the scene was No. 26 Oxford Street in the City of Toronto. In its prime it was a handsome enough middle-class dwelling, I have been told, but I have no memory of it whatever and no particular affection for it. I saw it consciously for the first time about thirty years ago and was not impressed.

The date is more important. Indeed, October 26 must surely be one of the more important dates in the history of the world, for it was the week of October 23–29 (B.C. 4004), according to Archbishop Ussher, that witnessed the Creation. I have been reading his *Annales Veteris et Novi Testamenti* (1650–54) with understandable interest, and certainly that was an eventful week in which God created Heaven and Earth and made all things possible. If the Archbishop's calculations are correct, it was on October 26 that the sun, the moon and "the rest of the stars" were created, two days before man himself appeared. I once consulted my old friend Edgar J. Goodspeed, the eminent theologian, on the subject and it is only fair to include his comment. "I really cannot find anything to support the very attractive view that the universe was, on so good an authority as Abp. Ussher, launched in anticipation of your so auspicious birthday," Dr. Goodspeed wrote me, "but I have access here only to minor works."

Of my earliest years I have no memory at all, but two other stories told me by my mother may be worth repeating. When I was quite a little boy, she said, I used to embarrass her by remembering —sometimes in front of strangers—being present at her wedding. This was neither a fact nor a precocious prenatal memory. It was simply that I had heard the story of Mother's wedding so often, and so often had seen the yellow satin dress in which she was married, that the event was as clear to me as if I had been there.

The other story concerns my father. It is the earliest and most illuminating story I know about a simple, kindly, and courageous man who was obviously, in his youth (as indeed he was to the end of his life), a hell of a fellow. He and Mother had been visiting friends one evening and were walking home a little before midnight. They were cutting diagonally across Bellevue Square, near their home in Oxford Street, when an officious police constable demanded to know their business. "Now, now," he said reprovingly, "where have you been until this hour of night?" It was an idiotic question, since they were obviously a young married couple homeward bound and were creating no disturbance. The constable was simply showing his authority.

Dad was carrying me in his arms, but at the question he stopped and handed me to Mother. "Hold the baby a minute, Mag," he said; and then he smote the Toronto constable so swiftly and so hard on the point of the jaw that the policeman went down with a crash and lay spread-eagled on the path. No other words were spoken. Mother, terrified, passed me back to Dad and they continued on their way, leaving the constable where he had fallen.

That is the end of the story. The policeman did not pursue them. I suspect he didn't feel like it, for in those days a blow from my father's fist was something to be remembered. He was a powerful fellow and he was also an expert boxer who had once knocked out the champion middleweight of Canada in a friendly bout at one of the Toronto gymnasiums. Kind as he was, his temper was

6

swift and terrible and he had a fine sense of justice that sometimes led him to take the law into his own hands. His name was Robert Polk Starrett. He was then about twenty-three years old and employed somewhere as a bookkeeper, a profession that he followed to the end of his life.

My mother's name was Young—Margaret Deniston Young. She was as Scotch as my father was Irish, although both were born in Canada. She had been a schoolteacher (a good one, I believe) but after her marriage she devoted herself exclusively to Dad, who needed a lot of looking after. Her father, John Young, was a bookseller, a circumstance for which I have always been grateful, for it was in his bookshop that I was, in the best sense, born.

Victorian Toronto in the last years of the old century was an interesting place to be born, for the old Tory capital was like a bit of old London itself. To Grandfather Young, who had arrived from Glasgow in 1847, it was a bustling metropolis of excellent business opportunities, of noble churches and pious Christian homes, of good government, good schools, and kindly courteous people like himself; altogether a desirable place in which to beget and rear his numerous Presbyterian children. But to me, in the four years of my infancy there, it was largely a city of soldiers. It was also, of course, a city of delightful, adoring aunts and uncles, for I was the first child of an elder daughter and a younger son; but in a more cosmopolitan sense it was a city of soldiers. One might meet the colorful creatures in the street at any moment of any day and worship them with shining eyes.

For more than seventy years British soldiers had been in garrison in Toronto; but in my time, so to call it, the troops were all militiamen. There were three notable regiments of them: the Queen's Own Rifles (to which, I later learned, my father had once briefly belonged), the 10th Royal Grenadiers, and the 48th (Gordon) Highlanders. The uniform of the Queen's Own was a handsome dark green, the tunics frogged in black. The Grenadiers wore the scarlet coat and tall black busbies of the traditional

British soldier. The Highlanders, who were my favorites perhaps for inherited reasons, wore the flashing kilts of the Gordons and they, too, as I recall them, were jacketed in bright scarlet. It was still a day of scarlet and pipeclay, and I loved it all as only a small boy can love a soldier. One or another of the gorgeous regiments seemed always to be on view; there were drills, parades, jubilee celebrations, and similar spectacles that can only be called tremendous. The bands played, the pipes skirled, the tartans blew in the breeze—and it was altogether one small boy's idea of a perfect universe.

II

MY HAPPIEST RECOLLECTIONS of books and reading are the hours I spent in Grandfather Young's bookshop in Toronto. In retrospect it seems to me that *all* my early years were passed there, so vivid are my memories of the dear old place; yet I know that actually most of those early years were spent elsewhere, for I was only four years old when my parents left Toronto to make their home in Chicago. My fondest memories of the old shop are a sort of montage of the numerous return visits I made between my fourth and fourteenth years. Until I was ten or twelve, most of my school vacations were spent in Toronto, a city that I passionately preferred to Chicago.

It was the bookshop that drew me back, the bookshop and two of my father's sisters yet to be introduced. Together they influenced my early years more than my school companions or even my parents. This is not rodomontade or sentiment, but a simple statement of fact.

I call it Grandfather Young's bookshop, but in reality he was only the manager. Once he had had his own shop, but that was before my time. When I began to know him he was and had been for some years depository, as it was called, of the Upper Canada Bible and Tract Society, a position that he held until his death in

8

1904. What interested me was the retail book shop operated in connection with the other work of the society. It was of course a religious bookshop for the most part, but broadminded enough to carry the latest books, fiction and nonfiction, that it was proper for a religious bookstore to carry. Hundreds of theological works and other pious volumes were imported from London every month, and these with the Canadian product populated the shop up front, together with a vast number of Bibles. One whole section was devoted to Bibles in all sorts of bindings and at all sorts of prices; but there were tables of English novels, including a line of current fiction of a sort that threatened no peril to the human soul.

But not any of this is what I have in mind when I say that my happiest recollection of books is my grandfather's shop. My particular playground was at the back, a small room given over exclusively to children's books, where on bright days the sunlight fell through a back window in a warm blaze of friendliness such as I have never experienced elsewhere. It fell across the backs of hundreds of books in red, blue, green, and gold bindings that contained (as they still do) some of the greatest stories ever written on this planet.

That was a wonderful period for boys' books; perhaps for girls' books too, but I know less about that. In that magic cubicle were all the latest tales of adventure, and many of the old ones, by some of the finest writers for boys this world has known. Nearly all of Henty's books were there, for he was then living and at the peak of his fame; and so also were the tales of George Manville Fenn, his only comparable rival. Their predecessors, W. H. G. Kingston and R. M. Ballantyne, were only recently deceased and were still enormously popular. Lovers of *Treasure Island* will remember Stevenson's tribute to "Kingston and Ballantyne the Brave," in the stanzas he wrote to introduce his enchanting island story. They, too, were there, to say nothing of such lesser lights as David Ker, Gordon Stables, Robert Leighton, S. Whitchurch Sadler, Arthur Lee Knight, C. W. Whistler, Talbot Baines Reed, Ascott R. Hope, Alfred St. Johnston, and so many others that, with only a slight effort of memory, I could fill a page with their names.

All these books were arrestingly bound in the primary colors to catch the eye of a child, and all were admirably illustrated by the best black-and-white artists of the time. It is impossible to describe the radiance of that little room as the sunlight picked out the titles of the books and brought out the illustrations on their spines—soldiers, horses, cowboys, Indians, gold diggers, frigates, ships in full sail and ships sinking beneath the waves, a stirring panorama of all the traditional scenes of peril and adventure.

The upper shelves were too high for me to reach; they were too high, indeed, for an adult to reach, and so there had been provided a delightful little ladder of three steps, hinged somewhere in the middle in such a way that, by turning over the top half, it could be converted into a low seat. I had never seen anything like it before and I have never seen anything like it since. I often wonder what became of it and I would pay a pretty penny to have it in my library today. To whatever limbo it has been consigned these many years, it was in that little convertible chair that I first read such books as *With Clive in India, With Lee in Virginia, With Wolfe in Canada,* and some hundreds of other books that I still remember with greater affection than I remember *Daniel Deronda* and *Adam Bede.*

Everybody was very kind to me and, more to the point perhaps, everybody knew exactly where to find me when I was wanted. I venture to think that the happiest hours of my life were spent in that little back room that was actually the juvenile stockroom of my grandfather's shop. I shall have more to say about the books I read there, in another chapter.

I have read many books about children who were born on farms and of the wonderful times they had, but I have never been able to believe that any youngster had a more delightful childhood than mine, living as I did (at least part of the time) in the very heart of a great city—in its busiest district—with a houseful of aunts and uncles upstairs and the happy possibility that at any moment the Gordon Highlanders might swing past my private balcony.

These were my mother's people and they were very kind to me in their somewhat reserved Presbyterian way. The fact that I was more attracted to my father's people, whose Irish humor and more informal (not to say reckless) manner of living appealed to me strongly, does not weaken the respect and gratitude and affection I still hold for those warmhearted and pious Scots.

But the truth is I cared more for my father's people than my mother's, and from the first to last more of my time was passed with them. It was the bookshop that took me to Yonge Street. There were books at 153 Denison Avenue, too; but better still there was talk of books, for my Irish aunts were quite as literate as my Scotch aunts and more sympathetic to my uninhibited personality. With the Starretts I did more or less as I pleased, while with the Youngs I seemed always to feel a constabulary eye on my activities. Family prayers and grace before meals made me restless even then, and Sundays at Grandfather Young's could be trying. There was little piety in my Irish aunts and Sundays at Denison Avenue were almost as lively as week days; sometimes they were livelier because on Sundays my schoolteacher aunts were at home to make a fuss over me. In brief, as Mother never ceased to remind me, I "took after" my father's people rather than hers.

For a time my Grandmother Starrett was there, too, but my memory of her is slight—only the sense of her kindness remains. It is pleasant to remember that she was an American, Harriet Johnson of Ohio. But it was Aunt Lilian and Aunt Bella, as I called them for sixty years, who made Toronto exciting for me; who seemed to me so uniquely wonderful that of all my numerous relations they still stand first in my affection. I was their first nephew and they spoiled me for sixty years.

It was a dark old house in which we lived; but the many angled attic was bright and enchanting. My Grandfather Starrett, who had gone West to make a fortune years before and never returned, had left behind him a collection of fishing and hunting tackle (to indicate the sort of fellow he was), and this was all at the top of the house for my divertissement. There were also two or three hundred old volumes, discarded over the years, a miscellaneous lot representing the curious tastes of my two aunts, who were nothing if not catholic readers. They had been notable book buyers. I can still remember some of the titles I turned over in the course of my explorations. Two in particular seemed to me very attractive, although to this day I have not been able to get very deeply into them. These were Maxwell Gray's *The Silence of Dean Maitland* and Beatrice Harraden's *Ships That Pass in the Night*. Miss Harraden's famous book, I quickly discovered, had nothing to do with ships, and I was never very clear about what occasioned the silence of Dean Maitland. There were a number of E. F. Benson's novels too, including the then notorious *Dodo*. Everybody read *Dodo* in the eighteen-nineties, I don't know why; my Scotch aunts had it also. Then one day—a day of gilt and glory—I found a battered copy of *The Adventures of Sherlock Holmes*.

I have no idea what "edition" it was. I don't remember what it looked like. I didn't recognize the author's name. I turned a few pages tentatively, reading at random, and felt my heart begin to thump under my ribs. It was a warm sunny afternoon, possibly in July or August, and I was perhaps ten years old, a small boy in an old attic in Toronto. I carried the book outdoors and sat down with it on the front steps in a blaze of summer sunshine. My aunts came and went on the porch above me but, in the words of the old Biblical writers, I heard them not. I was still reading Sherlock Holmes when the lamps were lit inside the house and I was called to dinner. "Oh yes," said Aunt Lilian when I told her what I had been reading, "we read that last summer at Muskoka. Isn't it exciting!" And then, as her sister entered the room, she added, "Charlie's discovered Sherlock Holmes and thinks he'd like to be a detective."

I had indeed discovered Sherlock Holmes; and it seems

strange to me now that so many years were to pass before I pursued the discovery and read the other available titles in the great saga of the Detective and the Doctor. It did not occur to me, I suppose, that there could be another such book in the world. Probably I accepted it as something unique and miraculous that could never happen again.

Later I came to know that both my aunts were prodigious readers. But, although the house was filled with books, neither of them was a collector. Rather, they were accumulators of books. Years afterward, when I looked over their shelves for "first editions," I was appalled to discover how few there were. Apparently they had always just missed the first edition of an important book from England, but they had the finest collection of second printings I have ever seen. Aunt Bella was the extravagant member of the family. It was unsafe to send her downtown alone for towels or table linens, for she would return invariably with an armful of books—purchased at a shattering bargain at Eaton's or Simpson's—and sometimes without the things she had been sent for. Her weakness was neat little English reprints published at two shillings and reduced by the department stores to nineteen cents. Aunt Lilian kept a watchful eye on her younger sister when they went to Simpson's together, and tried to keep her out of the book department. But Aunt Lilian, alone in a book shop, was often in need of watching, herself. Several times a year she would slip away alone and purchase anything new that Toronto had to offer about Sir Henry Irving, her secret passion. Two shelves were needed to hold the books she had brought together about the handsome English actor.

My bedroom on the second floor of the house was a narrow little cubicle at the back and just across the hall was the bathroom, a curious old-fashioned place that seemed to me forever out of order in some of its more important functions. But the most curious feature of the bathroom was a perfectly round hole in the floor. Presumably it had been intended originally to enclose a stove pipe, but it seemed never to have been used and usually it was kept covered by a square of heavy linoleum. It looked down into the kitchen and was my favorite peep hole. Sometimes, as a very small boy, I spent hours on my stomach just peering down into the kitchen below, where my grandmother was preparing the meals. As the hole was immediately over the stove, all the odors of her cooking were wafted up to me as I pushed my face into the opening in the floor. I could, of course, have occupied a chair in the kitchen while my grandmother prepared luncheon or dinner, but somehow it was more fun to spy on her through the hole in the floor. She always knew I was there and occasionally she spoke to me. At such times I either answered or failed to answer, depending on my mood.

I should say at this time that, although my brother Stanley was sometimes with me, for the most part my memories are of solo visits. I was the favorite nephew, a circumstance well known to my parents, and a visit from Stanley and me at the same time was an affliction that even the delightful Starrett aunts did nothing to encourage. My memory of other children in the neighborhood is slight. I had no boon companions.

One of the clearest memories of my early years in Toronto is the Salvation Army band that used to come to Bellevue Square, which was at the head of our street, only a quarter of a block away. It came on Sunday evening, and then the little square would be filled with people from all the neighboring thoroughfares. Sometimes the band played lively music that was pleasing to me, but much of the time it played old-fashioned hymns that even then struck me as being unnecessarily melancholy. There was one piece in particular that tore the heart out of me. It was called "Almost Persuaded," I believe, and I know now that it was the sort of song that ought to have been stopped by an act of Parliament. Mother used to sing it sometimes too, playing her own accompaniment, in our home in Chicago; and I would stand it just as long as I could, then rush from the house.

Probably there was little love lost between my Irish aunts and my Scotch aunts, although individual members of both families

14

were friendly. But the Youngs were pious God-fearing Presbyterians and the Starretts, bless their hearts, were not. They were Irish Protestants, which is all that can honestly be said about their religion. Probably Grandfather Young thought them frivolous at best; at worst, perhaps slightly blasphemous. Both were sentimental to an absurd degree, a circumstance that seemed to contradict their satirical opinion of the world and its inhabitants. They held reckless notions about other people, in high places or low, and spoke their minds with devastating wit. In short, they were two very remarkable women. Thackeray would have loved them. Neither ever published a line, to the best of my knowledge, but their conversation was always a delight and I regret that no Thackeray was available to put it into covers. They looked Irish and they *were* Irish, although both were born in Canada. Aunt Bella, indeed, looked remarkably like a leprechaun and was in many respects precisely like a leprechaun.

When I first knew them they rode bicycles to and from school, and to the end of their lives that was about the extent of their derring-do. They distrusted automobiles in the early years of the century and continued to distrust them to the end of the chapter. Occasionally they drank a little wine, a literary thing to do, making a very small quantity seem a veritable debauch, and in later years even ventured a cocktail and a cigarette; but these were only gestures to put their friends at ease. I was never allowed to taste anything alcoholic in their home.

Dear old ladies! They were the salt of the earth and they meant more to me than I shall ever be able to say.

These, then, were the two households in which as a child I spent so many months, at one time and another, that in retrospect they seem like years. For the most part I lived with my father's sisters, but the bookshop drew me like a lodestone, so I visited back and forth, sometimes sleeping for a few nights over the bookshop, but always returning to my preferred headquarters. In general, I tried to avoid spending Sunday with the Youngs, for on that day the bookshop was closed and there was always a chance that I would be urged out of bed at an early hour and taken off to church with the family. As the Youngs were a large family, they made a brave showing in the streets of Toronto on a Sunday morning. Often there were as many as a dozen of us tramping the quiet squares to Erskine church, with the heads of the family leading the procession.

Early in my reading, and in discussion with my several aunts—for in some matters my Scotch and Irish aunts were united—I had discovered that American and Canadian history told different stories about the same events, a circumstance that puzzled me a great deal. My Scotch aunts explained this very simply. They said that obviously the American histories were in error and the Canadian histories told the truth. When I discovered that they could be annoyed by my insistence on the American version of such conflicts as the Revolutionary War and the War of 1812, I raised the issue frequently for the pleasure of seeing their eyes flash. They were very patriotic Britons. My Irish aunts, who did not take their history so seriously, only laughed and said, "My, what a little American he is becoming!"

Not far from my grandfather's place, in the years of my Toronto childhood, lived two young men who, I like to think, came sometimes to the shop to purchase books. Both were already bookmen, in a small way, and later both came to prominence in the book world. Their names were George Doran and Stephen Leacock. Doran, a native of Toronto, was employed as a salesman by a rival book house, the Toronto Willard Tract Depository, Ltd., one of the numerous religious publishing houses then doing business in the city. I have no doubt that he visited the Yonge Street establishment many times and that I sometimes passed him in the aisles on the way to my private lair in the back room. Leacock was first a student, then a teacher, at the Upper Canada College, only a short walk from King and Yonge streets. I am certain that he, too, came frequently to my grandfather's shop and that I saw him many

16

times. But if my grandfather knew him I never heard him mention his name; and how was I to know that I was looking at one of the great humorists of the future?

I never met Stephen Leacock in later life. It was only when I read his autobiography, *The Boy I Left Behind Me,* after his death, that I learned he had lived so near us in Toronto; but it is a little surprising that I did not meet George Doran earlier than I did. Several years were to elapse before his brother Fred became a member of the Young family by marrying my mother's pretty sister May; and ten years before I suddenly found myself George Doran's reluctant errand boy in Chicago. But that, as the novelists say, is another story.

III

S o MUCH, for the moment, for Toronto. It will be clear to any-body reading these pages that for ten years, from approximately my fourth to fourteenth years, I practically commuted between Chicago and Toronto, and the fact is that some of my memories of the two cities are inextricably mixed. It is clearly of record, how-ever, that I was brought to Chicago at the age of four when my father accepted a position with Carson, Pirie, Scott & Company and brought his family with him.

My earliest memory of the city is a dingy flat over a shop on Van Buren Street near Loomis—a memory so vague that it almost eludes me. Directly across the street, I remember, stood a cigar-store Indian clutching a handful of wooden cigars, whose name (my father said) was Rain-in-the-Face. And the first book I con-sciously remember as such was a copy of *Peter Pindar's Poems* that I attempted to read with little pleasure. It had belonged to a man named Rowan who rented a room with us for a time. He went away owing Dad some money, I believe, and left this one book—an eighteenth-century edition—possibly in payment of his debt. It was always called "Mr. Rowan's Book," and that is all I remember about it except that it contained a series of illustrations, one or two of which showed naked women. Years later when I encountered John Byrom's ballad, "The Three Black Crows," in a school reader, I remembered that I had first read it in Mr. Rowan's Book, and this led to the discovery that Peter Pindar was a pen name used by John Byrom.

Another early memory is of being taken by Dad and Mother to the Moody Bible Institute on the north side of the city, a long streetcar journey, and hearing the famous Dwight L. Moody speak. I say hearing him, but actually I remember only a small stout gentleman with a beard who walked back and forth on a platform brandishing his arms.

After several removes we were all located in another dingy flat near Douglas Park where we were visited—the year would then be 1893—by a procession of aunts and uncles from Toronto who came to see the World's Columbian Exposition, a notable event. My clearest memory of it is a tin sardine fork that was given away as a souvenir by some fish company.

Only one friend of that period remembered happily is Monty Marshall, who read books and collected autographs. He was several years my senior and perhaps he came along at just the right time to keep me from developing a nasty little inferiority complex. Already I had begun to note the many ways in which I was unlike other boys and to wonder about it. Always there seemed to be some boy in our changing group who was gifted beyond his fellows—some kid who could wriggle his scalp so that his ears flapped, or dislocate his shoulder with a sudden easy movement that was irresistably attractive, or do extraordinary things with double-jointed fingers. Whoever he was, I always envied him. I could never do anything. I was not even left-handed. It was very discouraging.

Montgomery Marshall helped to end all that. He was so much like myself that we might have been brothers: a born collector who collected not only autographs but stamps and mineral curiosities, bird feathers and arrowheads. Best of all, he liked books and com-

18

municated his enthusiasm. It was Monty who started me on autographs and soon I had the signatures of all the celebrities in the neighborhood including Mother's clergyman, the Rev. John Brokenshire. To Monty Marshall, wherever he is, I owe many happy hours at a time when his companionship was unique.

Meanwhile there had been an addition to our family. In the winter of 1893 my brother Stanley and I were sent to Toronto and when we came back my brother Harold was there. Although he will deny it hotly, he was a good little boy; and again, as twice before, Mother began to dream that one of her boys might become a clergyman. But, although a few years later there was yet another addition to the family, let me say at once that none of Mother's four boys ever did become a clergyman.

Throughout all the years of which I have been writing I was reading furiously and my small library was growing. I kept it in Mother's china cabinet, where it filled a number of shelves. Travel and adventure had continued to be my favorite subjects and Henty and his kind had continued to be my favorite writers. Both my parents were happy that I was a reader. They encouraged me to buy books, and I needed little encouragement.

Bookish boys, except for Monty Marshall, had not been common in my life, so it was a piece of great luck about this time to meet Raymond Henderson who, as I look back on our acquaintance, was an exceptional mixture of the introvert and extrovert. Although he read books and enjoyed them, he also liked being a boy and living in the traditions of boyhood. The most interesting thing about Ray Henderson, when I met him, was his part-time profession. He was a lamplighter, like so many of Alger's heroes. The street lamps then in use were gas lamps and Ray had what was called a "route." Every evening a little before dusk he fared forth with a long pole in the head of which was concealed a pinpoint of flame enclosed in a miniature lantern. The district he served was perhaps a quarter of a mile square, and it became my greatest happiness to be allowed to accompany him on his expeditions. For a time, indeed, I longed to be a lamplighter myself; it

19

seemed to me a romantic and profitable profession. Sometimes I was permitted to thrust the torch up into the lamp with my own hands, and when this happened my happiness was complete.

Ray's father had been a newspaperman, another romantic profession. Sometimes he talked to us about books and once he traded me a copy of *The Great Shadow*, by a certain A. Conan Doyle, for a copy of *Ben Hur* that had been given me by my aunts, a swap that pleased us both. Sometimes on Saturdays, after school, his son and I foregathered in the Henderson back yard and played such stirring games as "Saint George and the Dragon," taking turns at being Saint George. Sometimes we played more dangerous games. There was an old cavalry saber in the family that fascinated us, which we borrowed when the ex-newspaperman was not around. One afternoon while fencing with the heavy weapon, taking turns with saber and scabbard, Ray—in possession of the saber—made a savage thrust that I failed to parry, and the point of the weapon entered my right thigh. Although small, the wound was painful and bloody—I lost half an inch of flesh and more blood than I had thought I possessed. No estrangement resulted from this episode, but I still carry on my thigh a minute saber scar that is becoming increasingly hard to find.

Possibly it was about this time that I saw my first professional baseball game. There is good reason for remembering it, for out of the experience indirectly came one of my most popular books. My father was a baseball fan and one day, when he happened to be in funds, he took me with him to the old Cubs' Ball Park at Harrison and Wood streets. It was only a few years afterward (or so it seems) that I was going to ball games by myself. Frank Chance was then manager of the club, and a mighty man was he. That was in the great days of Mordecai Brown, the famous three-fingered pitcher, and "Big Ed" Ruelbach, and the phenomenal combination suggested by the phrase "Tinker to Evers to Chance."

I mention all this because it was then I first became aware of a superlative pitcher named Jimmie Lavender who, for some reason, became a favorite of mine. Possibly I was attracted by his

20

III

name; at any rate I borrowed it many years afterward, with his permission, and gave it to a private detective I had created for the pulp magazines. And that is how it came about that the name of the famous old baseball pitcher appears in large letters on the cover of one of my books.

Something, I suppose, should be said about my early schooling. It was at John Ericsson grammar school that I began my lifelong struggle to acquire a rudimentary understanding of mathematics. I was graduated, without that understanding, either in 1899 or 1900. Only one teacher of the period remains in memory. Somehow, miraculously, I reached the eighth grade and came under the influence of Elizabeth Waldt, one of the kindest persons I have ever known and one of the finest forces in my life.

Miss Waldt was a bookish person herself and my passion for reading delighted her. She encouraged me to read some of the books that pleased *her*, and having done so I was surprised to find that they pleased me, too. My school compositions were beginning to be somewhat individual, and she urged me to write more and more of them. Occasionally I drew pictures to illustrate them. She predicted a brilliant career for me some day. I would write stories, she said, and illustrate them myself. However, I still had to be helped with my compositions at home, for Mother—a frustrated writer herself—would not allow my essays to reach Miss Waldt until she had been over them. Together Mother and I wrote stories and essays that delighted my teacher and also the principal of the school, an elderly graybeard who wrote inspirational poetry and sometimes read it to the class. Ultimately Mother and I collaborated, if that is the word, on a prose masterpiece that brought me undeserved distinction. In those days Victor F. Lawson, the editor of the Chicago *Daily News*, offered medals annually for the best essays on patriotism written by eighth-graders in the Chicago schools—a silver medal for the best essay, a bronze medal for the second best—and Miss Waldt and Mr. Wood, the principal, were enormously pleased when I was awarded the silver medal at

21

Ericsson. I remember how the great work began. These were its opening words:

> A crisis in the affairs of a nation always brings forth men who rise to meet the occasion. There are in every land men who are so filled with love of country that they are willing to sacrifice even life itself to serve the country's best interests.

I am sorry I don't remember more of it. It was one of the best essays Mother ever wrote.

But to get back to Miss Waldt: It was her pleasing practice to read aloud to the class on Friday afternoons, using whatever time was left between the end of the last lesson and the closing bell. She read full-length novels, a chapter or half a chapter at a stretch, as time allowed, and kept up the suspense admirably by ending her reading on a note of high entertainment. The class loved it and could scarcely wait for Friday afternoon. In this way I heard some excellent stories that I shall never forget, among them *Arthur Bonnicastle*, by J. G. Holland, and *Winning His Way*, by Charles Carleton Coffin, two books that remain vividly in memory to this day.

Miss Waldt lived a long time. She became a very old woman before she died, and I used to see her occasionally in after years. She was much pleased when I entered newspaper work and continued to predict a brilliant career for me. From first to last she was a cripple who walked grotesquely with a stick for support; and from first to last she was an admirable human being.

One of my classmates at Ericsson was Jack Chandler, who lived in our street. He, too, was a great reader and, as luck would have it, we liked the same books; that is to say, we liked books of travel and adventure. And he, too, had a highly personal collection of titles that he had brought together over the years. We borrowed each other's books and made impossible plans for a joint future career of peril and prowess. There were other boys in our block, but I took little part in their games. My brother Stanley was their crony and a little later my brother Harold; but Jack Chandler and

22

I preferred to take long walks in the evenings and talk over the many things we would need for our projected journey to the headwaters of the Amazon.

A long time was to pass before Jack confessed the reason for his first interest in me. Then it came out: in the give-and-take of neighborhood gossip, after our appearance in the little red cottage on Flournoy Street, he had heard that one of my brothers was a "nigger." Naturally, he was filled with curiosity; so he slipped into our yard one day, when Stanley and I were together, and was disappointed to find the interesting rumor a canard. We were dark complected, that was all—Stanley, perhaps, a little darker than I. This would appear to have been the origin of our neighborhood nicknames, "Big Nigger" and "Little Nigger," which clung to us for years.

But our real interest, Jack's and mine, was books. Our tastes were surprisingly similar, for his background like my own was largely British. It was almost miraculous to have found another boy who not only knew and appreciated Henty and Manville Fenn but was addicted also to such earlier giants as Cooper and Kingston and Ballantyne. He even owned some of their books that I had not read and, as my Irish aunts were always sending me English juveniles from Canada, we traded books constantly. Jack also knew American writers for boys who had been little more than names to me; it was through him, I think, that I first came to know and read the tales of Horatio Alger, Jr., "Oliver Optic," "Harry Castlemon," and the enchanting Edward S. Ellis. We talked books endlessly in our homes and on the streets, but a favorite spot was a bench overlooking the lagoon in Garfield Park, where we actively meditated a series of unparalleled journeys of exploration as soon as school days were over. We even prepared long lists of the necessary equipment for such voyages—sleeping bags, rifles (there were to be two rifles, an express rifle for tigers and elephants and a lighter weapon for less formidable encounters), canteens, cameras, compasses, beads or similar gewgaws for the natives, a joint medicine chest, and of course innumerable maps—and we thought we could manage it on a thousand dollars apiece. My own preference was for South America (I had been reading Manville Fenn's *Nat the Naturalist*) and the jungles of British Guiana, but Jack rather favored Africa, entering at Capetown and working northward to Alexandria. We were never entirely in agreement and so the discussions went on and on like Texas. It wasn't just day-dreaming either; there came a day when we actually started.

Meanwhile, at the beginning of the long summer vacation that preceded my last term at grammar school, Aunt Lilian picked me up in Chicago and took me with her to Vancouver, British Columbia, to visit her sister. (This is a third sister who has not previously appeared in the narrative.) According to family legend, I traveled half-fare and was challenged by a train conductor who thought I looked pretty large for the age assigned to me. My aunt agreed courteously and the man grinned and added: "He needs a shave!" We got through, however, and two stirring memories of Vancouver remain to me.

Uncle Otto, my aunt's husband, whom I had never met, was an amiable German. He was a handsome fellow with an eye for the ladies. One day, by way of entertaining me, he took me to a "street fair and carnival" where, in addition to the usual Ferris wheel, merry-go-round, and similar divertissements, there were a number of "side shows" of a sort pleasing to adult males. My uncle visited all these, towing me in his wake, and in one of them I witnessed for the first time the famous solo dance known as the hoochee-koochee. It was performed by a half naked girl with tremendous breasts and a revolving stomach; probably it was a thoroughly revolting exhibition. Uncle Otto liked it, however, and I was not displeased myself, although precisely wherein my pleasure lay I could not have said.

Vancouver offered other educational features, however. Once I accompanied the whole family to the home of a friend whose private library filled the house. I never had seen so many books in a home. A houseful of books! It was what I dreamed of for myself. In spite of the difference in our ages, my new friend was a sympathetic man and we talked only of books until refreshments came on. There was no suggestion of condescension. We knew each other at once as kindred spirits. He had graduated from Henty and the other writers of my private stable not too long before and still retained many of his early books. We tramped upstairs to a book room to look them over. That night I read S. K. Hocking's *Story of Andrew Fairfax* in bed until I fell asleep.

But at this point it may be useful to summarize my early reading in a comprehensive chapter that may be read or skipped at discretion.

IV

T HE FIRST BOOK I remember reading by myself, that is to say, without adult assistance, was a pious little tome for infants called *The Peep of Day*. I remember only its title but assume that it was a history of the Creation in words of one syllable.* It was followed almost immediately by another work in the same series, *Line Upon Line* and by a third called *Precept Upon Precept*. All these were gifts from my Grandfather Young, and all were attractively illustrated. My only other clear memory of early books (other than "Mr. Rowan's Book") is of a huge family Bible by which I was sometimes raised to table level at mealtime.

But I didn't just sit on it; I read it with close attention, here and there, notably the more stirring events in the Old Testament when the pictures aroused my curiosity. The big book was wonderfully illustrated with hundreds of old woodcuts, some of which were as exciting as any pictures I have ever seen. Such scenes as "David and Goliath" and "Samson Pulling Down the Temple" could not have been more inspiring if they had been drawn by Frederic Remington or Charles M. Russell, and the picture of Queen Jezebel being thrown from a window could not have been improved by any

* A rare book catalogue informs me that it was by a Mrs. Mortimer, who died in 1878 (aet. 76)

artist who ever lived. She was shown falling headfirst onto the spears of the soldiery in the street, her garments billowing behind her and terror in her eyes, while from the casement above leered the evil faces of her executioners. This masterpiece remained vividly in my imagination for years and, to tell the truth, it still fascinates me in retrospect.

I must have graduated from Biblical stories early, however, for the next books that come to mind are three mawkish little tales that I always think of together: *Miss Toosey's Mission, Jessica's First Prayer* and *Probable Sons*. I don't remember who wrote the first, the second was by Hesba Stretton, and the third (I think) by Amy Le Feuvre. I suspect all three were written under the influence of Dickens at his sentimental worst, although of course they were miles behind Dickens. I blush to think there was a time when they caused me to laugh and weep even after repeated readings. Obviously my taste had begun to slip for after the Bible stories these were poor stuff. It picked up again when my Irish aunts, who probably suspected the sort of literature coming to me from Yonge Street, countered the insidious propaganda with such classics of childhood as Kingsley's *Water Babies* and Hawthorne's *Wonder Book*, and with a slim twelvemo that was for long a favorite. Who now remembers *The Robber Kitten*, and who but I could tell you that its author was Robert Michael Ballantyne? I read this picaresque fable of crime and its consequences about the time I began to read fairy tales and rated it almost as high as the stories of Andersen and Grimm, although of course I was mistaken; I have relegated *The Robber Kitten* to limbo while Andersen and Grimm remain on my shelves. I hope there may never come a time when I shall fail to put "The Tinder Box" and "The Musicians of Bremen" (to say nothing of a dozen other tales) on my list of the great short stories of the world. From Denison Avenue came also *The Adventures of a Brownie* by the excellent Miss Mulock, whose *John Halifax, Gentleman* bored me so intensely a few years later. And never, never, let me say at once, was I inspired by or even interested in the pedantic little prigs in *Sandford and Merton* or

Harry and Lucy. My taste, I am happy to think, was fairly sound even in infancy. To such improving fiddle-faddle I preferred *The King of the Golden River* and *The Nuernberg Stove*, those outstanding masterpieces of (need I say?) Mr. Ruskin and the lady who wrote as Ouida.

My orgy of fairy tales and similar children's classics included one book that I am glad I read in childhood since, alas, I have not been able to read it since. *The Pilgrim's Progress* should be read in childhood as a fairy story, since no harm can possibly come of it and its simple singing narrative may even lead one to an early appreciation of good literature. But, however it may bore me now, there is no doubt that once I thought Bunyan's parable the most wonderful fairy tale of them all. It was succeeded, I can't think why, by an orgy of animal stories of a more humane temper than *The Robber Kitten*. First came *Black Beauty*; then a poor second, *Beautiful Joe*, and ultimately the early stories of Ernest Seton-Thompson,[1] who was just beginning to seduce my aunts on both sides of the house—a notable feat—so that I received copies of *The Trail of the Sandhill Stag* and *The Biography of a Grizzly* in duplicate and almost in the same mail.

There were early books of history and adventure, too, during that first fine frenzy of reading when my taste for the good and the bad was inextricably mixed, among them Dickens's *Child's History of England*, a glorious entertainment, and *The Scottish Chiefs*, by a Miss Jane Porter, the high-flying style of which enchanted me as much as the melodramatic narrative. Her other book, *Thaddeus of Warsaw*, I found to be unreadable. However, she led me to Sir Walter Scott, although a little too early for appreciation, I am afraid. In only two of his many novels did I find the requisite enchantment until later, although I could recite reams of *The Lady of the Lake*, beginning with "The stag at eve" and carrying on through several cantos. The two novels that, even in my tenth year, held me breathless were, of course, *Ivanhoe* and *Quentin Durward*. There are chapters of each that I still read with all the old enthusiasm.

[1] Later Thompson-Seton.

For a time I was seduced by English school stories, notably *Tom Brown's Schooldays*, by Thomas Hughes, an admirable yarn for all its somewhat obtrusive morality, and a revoltingly sanctimonious tale by Canon Farrar: *Eric, Or Little by Little* it was called. I used to weep buckets over Eric and possibly it did me a lot of good; but when I found an old copy a few years ago I stood it on my juvenile shelf determined never to look inside its covers. Then, in a nostalgic moment, I did look into it and ultimately reread it, weeping copiously at every chapter. Poor Eric, he was given every chance, but the implacable Canon Farrar saw to it that he muffed them all. It was necessary to his theme that Eric's weaknesses should be pointed up so that the attractive lad might repent in the last chapter and die a Christian death. The moral lessons of *Tom Brown's Schooldays* are inoffensive, even manly, and they are so placed in the narrative as to be easily skipped; but the sentimentality and religiosity of *Eric* are constant, overpowering, and as morbid as the depressing stanzas of "Almost Persuaded."

Better than either of these books I liked the jolly stories of Talbot Baines Reed which were packed with incident and misdemeanor at once humorous and exciting. I hope they are read today for it would be hard to beat such yarns as *Tom, Dick and Harry, Fifth Form at St. Dominic's, Follow My Leader,* and *The Cock House at Fellsgarth*. These, too, are stories of school life in England and it was long before I found an American school story to stand beside them. In point of fact, I never did find an American school story to stand beside them, unless it was *Little Men*, which is a school story of a sort but not the sort I have in mind. All three of the immortal Alcott books celebrating the March family, *Little Women, Little Men,* and *Jo's Boys,* were huge favorites with me at that time and remain so to this day. So were, and are, a few other American classics, notably Aldrich's *Story of a Bad Boy* and Mark Twain's *Tom Sawyer*, which contain excellent school chapters, and Mrs. Lothrop's *Five Little Peppers* and Mrs. Burnett's *Little Lord Fauntleroy*, which do not. The two latter volumes pleased me most,

28

IV

at the time, although it is the Aldrich and Clemens tales to which I now return. The sweetness and light of *Little Lord Fauntleroy* didn't offend me; I loved it. At that time, indeed, I must have somewhat resembled Ceddie Errol, for my mother and all my aunts dressed me for the part, possibly without realizing the literary connotation. I didn't know that I looked like a "sissy" until some of my American companions mentioned it to me. Dad agreeing, I had my first professional haircut. But I liked only the first of the Pepper books, *Five Little Peppers and How They Grew*; the several sequels bored me. It is still a charming story for the sound reason that it is simple and sincere, and quite without the cloying sentiment of, say, *Little Lord Fauntleroy*. And, when I first read it, we too were almost as poor as the inhabitants of the "little brown house." It sentimentalized poverty for me and helped to make it appealing.

Last but not least of this special group was *Sir Toady Lion* by S. R. Crockett, which I read almost to pieces in one summer, with Jack Chandler's help. Why this superb juvenile is not better known —why it is not an acknowledged classic of childhood—I can't imagine. In my opinion it stands near the top of any list of the great stories for children. It is English, to be sure, but even in England it is by way of being forgotten. For me, Hugh John Picton Smith stands foursquare in my affection with Tom Sawyer, Tom Bailey and Teddy Laurence. Too many years elapsed before Samuel Rutherford Crockett attempted to repeat the first success of *Sir Toady Lion* and the result was unhappy. *Sir Toady Crusoe* may safely be disregarded by historians.

At all times, however, my reading diet consisted largely of books of adventure. As it was my good fortune to be born in the last quarter of the nineteenth century, I was in effect a contemporary of many of the finest writers for boys the English-speaking world has known. There have been great "periods" in juvenile literature, just as in more adult fiction, and the years from the eighteen-fifties to the turn of the century, and even a little beyond, mark one of the greatest of those periods. I know now that writing standards among boys' authors were high in those days, but I knew little then about standards. I knew only that the books I read were delightful. I have mentioned the "giants" of the time—Henty, Fenn, Ballantyne, and Kingston—who were the "big four" among writers for boys. But there were other writers of adventure who stood only a little lower in my affection, notably David Ker whose stories I first encountered in the *Boy's Own Paper*, a delicious English weekly that I used to receive at Christmas when all its fifty-two issues had been brought together in a handsome annual. It was as well for my nerves, perhaps, that I did not have to wait from week to week to follow the exploits of David Ker's adventurous boys, for every installment ended on a high note of suspense. A dozen or more of Ker's novels for boys already had appeared in hard covers when I began to read him, and I went through all of them at a tearing gallop. Another dozen at least were lost in the files of the B.O.P. and most of these I managed to read also, since the old annuals were not then difficult to find in Toronto.

Little is known today about David Ker but curious readers may be referred to my nostalgic essay on the occasion of his death, in a book called *Buried Caesars*. He was a war correspondent who traveled extensively in the then almost unknown continents of Asia and Africa; although, indeed, there was scarcely a foot of the globe that he did not visit at one time and another. Many of his stories were based on his own experience and these were perhaps his best. In nearly all of them appeared a genial bearded adventurer (sometimes he was a war correspondent, sometimes an explorer, sometimes even a writer of books for boys) whose name approximated his own; at any rate, his initials were frequently D. K. Usually he was in charge of two lively English boys who in some fashion found themselves vacationing in the wildest parts of the earth. Sometimes, when an adventure was a particularly tall one, he certified it with a footnote as something that had happened to himself in the spring of 1883 or the winter of 1887; he had been shipwrecked eight times. I had only one fault to find with David Ker; he was addicted to punning and frequently carried the vice over into his names. In one of his tales, I recall, he introduced a Russian physician whose remarkable name was Dr. Poisonsoupoff, an occupational jest that even then struck me as a bit excessive. Once, years ago, I owned nearly every book David Ker ever wrote; but that, as I say, was years ago. I wish I had some of them today for I would like to read again such tales as *Cossack and Czar, Lost Among White Africans, The Boy Slave in Bokhara, Prisoner Among Pirates, The Lost City or the Boy Explorers in Central Asia*. They were capital stories.

Among Kingston's fifty or more books for boys my two favorites were *Manco the Peruvian Chief* and *Salt Water; the Sea Life and Adventures of Neil D'Arcy the Midshipman. Manco* and *Salt Water* descended to me from my father's ragged library and have remained my favorites—possibly because they were the first I read of this author's long list of titles. The others, all that were available, I read furiously throughout an entire winter by courtesy of the Chicago Public Library. Once I lost one on a street car; for two weeks I was in despair. The cost of the book, which I would have to pay if it were not recovered, troubled me a little; but, far worse, a dozen rifles had just "spoken" when, for a reason I do not remember, I laid the book aside, and every rifle was leveled at Our Hero's breast. At the end of a fortnight of agonized conjecture the book was returned to me by a grownup friend who, by an interesting coincidence, had found it. My library card was in its pocket and he knew that it was mine; but he had opened the volume to see the sort of thing I read, he told me, and had been himself lost. He offered to pay the fine I had piled up, but I declined the offer, got rid of him as quickly as possible, and discovered what I should have known—that the hero of a boy's story is never killed, whatever the number of weapons leveled at his heaving breast.

Would you care to know how the dauntless lad escaped those rifles? He watched the lips of the officer directing his execution and, at the first letter of the fatal word *"Fire!"*, leaped high into the air so that the bullets whistled around his legs. By great good fortune

31

a river ran immediately behind him and, before the astounded marksmen could recover from their quite natural astonishment, he had plunged into the stream and to safety. My hat is off to W. H. G. Kingston. There may have been too much preaching in his stories for boys, but he had the proper imagination for a dime novelist. Another jolly thing about Kingston—William Henry Giles Kingston, to give him all his names at once—was his talent for titles, although, indeed, all the boys' writers of that day were good at that. Among other pleasing notions, Kingston had a passion for the word *three*. I don't know how many of his titles used the word, but four of them come quickly to mind: *The Three Midshipmen, The Three Lieutenants, The Three Commanders, The Three Admirals.*[2] All these I read with gusto and reached the perhaps reckless conclusion that all "Three" stories were first-rate. However, it worked out very well in practice and I am still foolishly attracted to any title in which the magic word is involved.

Having mentioned my father's library, the handful of thumbed and tattered books that I found in his old home in Toronto, let me say another word about it. At no time can the boy who became my father ever have been bookish; he was too fond of what were then called the "manly sports." But his taste in books appears to have been sound and it was his battered old copies of Kingston and Ballantyne that got me off to a good start. He can not have had many books at any time and obviously he read the few he liked over and over again. "Oh, yes," said my aunts when I came upon these volumes at the bottom of an old trunk one day, "those were Polk's books." (His middle name was Polk because the eleventh president of the United States had been his father's cousin.) I can remember only one other title that carried his flowing signature on its fly. It was *The Life of a British Soldier*, by Thomas Faughnan, the only copy I have ever seen of this curious autobiography. I learned a lot of history from it and, on the whole, enjoyed it almost as much

---

2 Incidentally, the triad of heroes almost invariably were English, Irish and Scotch, for patriotic reasons, and the Irishman (or boy) was always a humorist with a notable brogue.

as Henty's *Jack Archer*, which dealt with the same scenes and adventures.

It was Stevenson, was it not, who said that he would sacrifice something very valuable—perhaps his entire list of writings—to have written *The Coral Island*. I would not myself exchange it for *Treasure Island*, but I know how he felt. *The Coral Island* is the magnum opus of Robert Michael Ballantyne of the Hudson's Bay Company. The astonishing experiences of his delectable band of shipwrecked adventurers on a coral reef in the Pacific are among the most moving and memorable episodes in juvenile literature. The adventurers themselves enjoyed it, for old inhabitants will remember that the irrepressible Peterkin sought out his erstwhile companions of the coral strand and took them upon adventures equally perilous, in a sequel called *The Gorilla Hunters*. Those two were, I think, my favorite Ballantynes; but *The Red Eric* was a close third on my list. When I visited the Protestant cemetery in Rome, in 1937, to view the graves of Keats and Shelley, I found there also the grave of Ballantyne, my old writing hero, and was more moved by it than by the graves of the two poets.

Island books, after *The Coral Island*, so stirred my imagination that for a time I read almost nothing else. What a wonderful lot of them there were even then, and there have been no better ones since. With Dr. L. P. Jacks I can say: "No philosopher has ever had a clearer conception of the true end of man than I had at the age of twelve." His father had given him a copy of *Robinson Crusoe* and his one desire was to get himself cast away on a Desolate Island. He ransacked libraries for the literature of islands, and the more desolate they were the better he was pleased. Little islands, of course. I suppose nobody ever seriously wished to be cast ashore on Ireland or Australia, unless it might be to visit the bookshops.

So also it was with me. I don't remember who first directed my attention to *Robinson Crusoe*, but the old story performed its traditional miracle; and thereafter I read all the great tales of shipwreck and island adventure. Some of them I liked even better than *Robinson Crusoe*, outstandingly the *Swiss Family Robinson*, surely "one of the dearest old books in the world," as Howells called it. Here was Robinson Crusoe in the bosom of his family, for in the *Swiss Family Robinson*, old inhabitants will remember, a clergyman, his wife, and four growing sons were cast away upon such an island as never existed save in an author's imagination. The enviable Robinsons became the first human inhabitants of a tropical Eden in which everything was provided by a beneficent natural goodness. Through this enchanting story strides good Father Robinson, a natural scoutmaster, shepherding his remarkable family, finding new wonders of nature at every step, commenting on the Divine Goodness that made possible this perpetual Lutheran picnic. At any moment one expects the precocious boys to stumble on a field of growing musical instruments with which the happy castaways will start a family band. But the charm of the old tale is beyond dispute; and there is a quality of busy kindness in it that I have never encountered to the same degree in any other book. It projects a philosophy of contentment that is perhaps the most sentimental and seductive in island literature.

Hard on the heels of the *Swiss Family Robinson* came half a dozen other island stories of varying merit: *Masterman Ready*, by Capt. Frederick Marryat; *The Mysterious Island*, by Jules Verne; *Gulliver's Travels*, by that astonishing clergyman, Jonathan Swift; *The Pirate Island*, by Harry Collingwood; *Perseverance Island*, by Douglas Frazar; and, greatest of them all, Stevenson's *Treasure Island*. I don't know in which order I read those six; *Gulliver* may have been earlier in my reading than I now think; but *Treasure Island* is the masterpiece, of course. In it Stevenson synthesized all the best of what had gone before, with completely satisfying results. John Silver's parrot was borrowed from Crusoe, and Robinson himself was lovingly caricatured in Ben Gunn, the marooned seaman found by the treasure seekers on the island. I suppose it is the best boy's book ever written.

I look into all these books occasionally, when the impulse

seizes me, and *Treasure Island* I reread once a year. The island mood needs no explanation. Next to coming into an unexpected fortune, man's dearest wish is to be cast away on a desert island. That is his wistful answer to the problems presented by the civilization he has himself created. To get away from them.

I think there is something to be said for the theory that the first book one reads by an admired author remains the special favorite thereafter. My first "Henty book" was *The Cornet of Horse*, which was a present from my Irish aunts and which remains today the Henty by which all others are measured. Certainly it is a glorious story—a tale of Marlborough's wars—and I need not remind admirers of this writer that its youthful hero was one of the first swordsmen of his time. (All Henty heroes were the first swordsmen of their time, when swords were permitted by the historical background.) Few tales of history and adventure stirred me as did this one. After reading it, I went on a Henty binge that lasted for years. In quick succession I read every Henty I could find and in the end, I think, I read every one of the hundred and fifty or more titles that comprise his bibliography; but the earlier ones were the best. I could name every title on the list if I wanted to, but the six I like most are *The Cornet of Horse, Bonnie Prince Charlie, With Lee in Virginia, Under Drake's Flag, Orange and Green,* and *By Pike and Dyke.*

Several of these, including *The Cornet of Horse,* are now on my shelves in handsome first edition copies; I value them above gold and rubies. Do I ever take them down and reread them? Not precisely. I look at them, I gloat over them, I pat them gently on their backs; and sometimes, when the world is too much with me, I take down *The Cornet of Horse* and read a few chapters of the old magic. It never fails to cheer me.

I have fewer favorites among the books of Manville Fenn, but three are outstanding and I own them all in sparkling first editions: *Nat the Naturalist, The Golden Magnet, Bunyip Land.* The number of times I have read certain chapters of these magnificent tales appalls me when I think of certain immortal works I have never read at all.

Most of the books I have mentioned above were admirably illustrated by draftsmen of considerable competence; I remember many of the illustrations with almost as much pleasure as the stories they depict. In particular, I admired the fine black and white drawings of Gordon Browne, who illustrated yards and yards of Henty and Manville Fenn. Browne was an ideal illustrator for boys' books of adventure, who somehow managed to pack as much action into his pictures as the authors did into their stories. He was, I came to know, a younger son of Hablot K. Browne, Dickens's "Phiz," and years afterward it was my privilege to meet him in London and tell him of the pleasure his pictures had given me.

It is not possible to mention all the books I read and liked at this time, but certain old favorites still clamor for attention. All were cornerstones, as it were, in the small private—almost secret—library I was even then building. For I was not a particularly generous boy; it pleased me to think that these unparalleled entertainments were peculiarly mine. I shared them with reluctance, and I was always a little annoyed to learn that some other boy already knew and liked a book I had mentioned as something pretty special. Even my crony, Jack Chandler, had difficulty coaxing the loan of a book that I rated absolute tops and therefore beyond his appreciation. When my Irish aunts sent me a green-and-gold copy of Henty's *Condemned as a Nihilist* for Christmas one year, I put him off for a couple of weeks before I could bear to let it out of my possession, although he tempted me with Harry Collingwood's *The Log of the 'Flying Fish,'* a superior job.

But about those old favorites: at this minute I could walk to Mother's china cabinet, in the dark, and pluck any book I then owned from its place on the shelves. Let's see: there was *The Final War*, by Louis Tracy; *The Braes of Yarrow*, by James Grant; *Mr. Midshipman Easy*, by Captain Marryat; *The Rajah's Fortress*, by William Murray Graydon; *Michael Strogoff, the Courier of the Czar*, by Jules Verne; *Perilous Seas*, by S. W. Sadler—with a colored frontispiece that would make your hair curl—and a

36

strange and wonderful tale called *A.D. 2000*, by Lieutenant Alvarado M. Fuller of the United States Army. Those among others. Tracy's novel was my first hint of Armageddon, and I read and reread it with fearful delight, thrilled and enchanted by its thesis that England and America would ultimately fight side by side against Germany and the rest of the world in the last of all earthly wars. My first copy of this stirring fable got away from me but I have now replaced it with a handsome copy of the first edition. *The Rajah's Fortress* is not Graydon's best book, but it was the first of his dime-novel fictions to come my way and I liked it well enough to hunt up all the others I could find. When I learned that he was an American living and writing in England, I became so interested in him that I wrote him a fan letter. He replied courteously and a brief correspondence ensued as a result of which, years later (in 1924, to be exact), I called on William Murray Graydon in London, considerably to his surprise, and talked with him for an hour about his many, many books for boys. He was then writing "Sexton Blakes" for an English syndicate, and I shall have more to say about him when I reach that point in my narrative. *A.D. 2000* was, as far as I can remember, my first experience of what is now called science-fiction and it is still a high spot for me in that field. This was Fuller's only work of fiction, I believe. It is difficult to explain the fascination the tale held for me and, indeed, still holds. A story of an "airship" voyage of discovery to the North Pole would seem tame to the boys of today; but, when I read Lieutenant Fuller's pioneer opus, the North Pole was the most inaccessible spot on earth and airplanes had not yet been invented. That's why he had to put his hero and heroine to sleep in eighteen-eighty something and wake them in the twenty-first century. . . . But don't get me started on *A.D. 2000*. At one time it was the most secret and most precious of my discoveries.

America, in the general period of which I am writing, had a fine lot of writers for boys, with much of whose work I became acquainted, but having been brought up in the English tradition, I preferred the writers of England, generally speaking. Nevertheless I read with pleasure the books of Edward S. Ellis, James Otis, Harry Castlemon, and a little later, Kirk Monroe, all admirable story-tellers. Ellis, I think, pleased me most. I liked his Indians better than I did Cooper's, and I still do.

For a time, too, although with less enthusiasm, I read the stereotyped tales of Horatio Alger, Jr., and Oliver Optic, whose "Yacht" Club series also pleased my younger brother; but "Optic" didn't register at all and my Alger period, I am happy to report, was brief. I quickly discovered that his stories were all alike, that in reading one of them I was reading them all. I am afraid I didn't make that discovery, however, until I had read some twenty of them in rapid succession, beginning with *Tom Temple's Career*. I ought also to confess that I read at this time a number of novels written (I learned later) for adults, but not altogether beyond the comprehension of a child. Possibly I was attracted by their titles— e.g., *Lady Audley's Secret, Under Two Flags, The Smuggler of King's Cove, The Wandering Heir*—but the fact is I liked them, in spots, and incidents from all of them remain in memory to this day. For the information of librarians who may recognize only two of the titles, *The Smuggler of King's Cove* was written by Sylvanus Cobb, Jr., and *The Wandering Heir*, by Charles Reade. Better than any of these was *The Spy*, by Fenimore Cooper, which is still the only one of Cooper's novels I can read; even his "Leatherstocking" tales were only so-so after Ellis's Deerfoot stories.

It was inevitable that sooner or later I would encounter a "dime novel" and explore fresh caverns of delight in that weird underworld of popular literature. It was a neighbor's son, a Western Union telegrapher, who introduced me to the new mythology. Visiting his home one evening, I found him preparing to leave for work; in the very act, indeed, of thrusting into his overcoat pocket a handful of quarto pamphlets with highly lithographed covers, which excited my curiosity. I asked him what they were, and he replied: "You mean to say you've never read any dime novels? Boy, have you got a treat ahead of you! Here, take a look at this—" and he snatched one from a drawer and gave it to me. It was one of the lurid adventures of a folk hero called Diamond Dick, Junior, written by one W. B. Lawson; and I felt a strange new excitement steal over me as I looked at it. I sat down at once in the kitchen of his mother's home and began to read for the first time one of the exploits of young Diamond Dick and his partner, a fantastic giant called Handsome Harry. An hour later I had to be sent home, but I took my new sin with me and finished the glamorous tale in bed. What a story! I wish I could remember its title; but subsequently I read so many just like it that now it is impossible to guess which one of the many it was.

Through this fortuitous accident, I came also to read and know the adventures of other extraordinary heroes who were once, it seems, detectives and justice-doers of the Old West. And not only of the West, for the East had its Nick Carter, its Old and Young King Brady, and a dozen others. But although I came to like Nick Carter and the Bradys very much, Diamond Dick Jr. remained my favorite, and I still think of him first among the paladins under whose spell I fell in that moment of my reading career. I have read of boys who had to read dime novels in secret, "behind the barn," out of eyeshot of their parents—George Ade and others brag of it in their memoirs of boyhood—but I brought them into the house and read them in the living room while Mother read her Bible and Dad rustled the pages of his newspaper. After a time, it is true, Mother became suspicious of them—their very appearance was sinful—and spoke about them to my father.

"Bobby," she said, "I wish you would take a look at those things your son is reading. They don't look wholesome." "All right," he soothed her, "I'll read one of them tonight, before I turn in." He did so and came to me for more, and then more, until Mother protested again. She said he was getting to be as bad as I was. "Oh, they're not so bad," he told her seriously. "They're just stories of slick detective work. No harm in them." *Slick* was one of his favorite words. But he never really convinced her; and once when I found Dad prowling about the house, looking under sofa pillows and feeling in behind the books in the china cabinet, I knew he was looking for my dime novels and thought that Mother or I had hidden them.

My orgy of dime-novel reading ended, however, almost as suddenly as it began; I don't quite know why. I simply tired of them, I suppose, after the first hundred or two, or something new and equally alluring came along. They were a passing infatuation, a violent love affair that failed to last, and when I was done with them I was done with them for keeps. I now preserve a few specimens of the genre in my historical survey of the detective story, which fills about eight bookcases, but I seldom look at them. Oddly, I did not as a boy read any of their English counterparts— they were not available in my grandfather's bookshop certainly— and I was quite grown up and only academically interested in dime novels before I knew Jack Harkaway and Sexton Blake ever had been created.

The first hint of realism in my reading that I can remember was a long story called *What Necessity Knows*, by Lily Dougall, which ran serially for a year in some English magazine. Every Christmas, Mother received from Toronto a number of bound volumes of the less lively British journals of the day, among them the *Galaxy*, *Leisure Hours* and *Good Words*, and it was in one of these that I read Miss Dougall's novel, with all the chapters conveniently in one set of covers. It was a grim tale, for all its sentiment, and what particularly wrung my infant heart was its depiction of grinding poverty and injustice. I couldn't put it down and its effect on me lasted for months; indeed, as long as the old annual held together, I used to go back to it every now and then to reread some especially harrowing scene. Ultimately it was published as a book, I believe, but I have never seen a copy and I have never heard anybody mention it. It is one of the many obscure titles that lurk somewhere in the back of my mind, and I still hope to find it some day in a bin of old books. If and when I do, I suppose I shall find it unreadable.

My first experience of Dickens, other than his *Child's History of England*, was *Oliver Twist*, in which also I found considerable realism of a sort. I remember vividly the pages describing Bill Sikes's dreadful death, and for a time that scene was the touchstone by which I tested other tales. I have not reread *Oliver Twist*, and many scenes have stirred me similarly since that far day, but I shall never forget Bill Sikes dropping over the edge of the roof in his effort to escape the police, and hanging himself with the rope that was intended to assist his escape. The emotion is long forgotten, lost in later excitements, but memory or imagination calls back the picture of a small boy reading the incident for the first time, shocked to his vitals, his eyes bursting from his head, convinced that he was reading the most horrendous event in history or literature.

Some years were to elapse before I read another of Dickens's novels and then it was *David Copperfield* that kept me awake when I should have been asleep. I read it in bed and it literally kept me up all night. Perhaps I was seventeen at the time, perhaps I skipped a little here and there to see what happened next, but it was after four o'clock in the morning when I put out my light. I had read *David Copperfield* at a sitting. A little later I was to read *Great Expectations* at one sitting, and after that I don't know in which order I read Dickens's novels or how I rated them. In point of fact, there are still half a dozen of them that I have yet to read. My two favorites came late; that is, they were read in my young manhood; and these—the *Pickwick Papers* and *The Mystery of Edwin Drood* —are the two novels in which I can still browse happily whenever the impulse takes me. I don't know why I have never read *Our Mutual Friend, Dombey and Son*, and *The Old Curiosity Shop*. Other enthusiasms came along to interrupt what might have been a blissful lifetime devoted exclusively to Dickens—which, perhaps, was just as well. Somehow, I believe, without actually reading the books myself, I learned most of their contents, for I seem to know parts of the unread novels almost as intimately as if I had read them. I have lived a lot among Dickensians, and no doubt I have heard the unread novels discussed in such detail that I have acquired a working knowledge of their contents by a sort of osmosis. Just now my feeling is that Dickens should be read in youth and, just possibly, never reread. I don't insist on this; it is just a notion that sometimes crosses my mind.

I have said nothing about poetry, partly because there is little to say. I came late to poetry as a "synthesis of hyacinths and biscuits," but ballads pleased me as, indeed, they still do. At first they were songs, sung to simple melodies, calling my infant attention to a "little brown thrush" or a "dear little moon" that resembled a cradle. Then they were brisk stanzas narrating the misadventures of minor animal life, including "Brer Fox." Ultimately they were narrative ballads about heroes and villains of legend and ladies in distress. High on my list of early favorites were Southey's "The Inchcape Rock," Campbell's "Lord Ullin's Daughter," and Tennyson's "Charge of the Light Brigade." A little later there was Kipling. I first heard his remarkable name, which struck me as very funny, as the author of a Boer War ballad about an "absent-minded beggar" whose weaknesses were great. We all sang it to an attractive melody about the year 1899. That was in Toronto, where the song was enormously popular among admirers of the Empire. I sang it myself and loved it, and its refrain of "Cook's son, duke's son, son of a hundred kings" seemed to me poetry at its highest level. Thereafter all Kipling ballads enchanted me and I could recite, and did recite, such popular masterpieces as "Gunga Din" and "Danny Deever" with appalling gusto. In "Mandalay" I had my first glimpse of poetry, perhaps, in the picture of dawn coming up "like thunder out of China 'cross the bay," a line that struck me as being a little bit of orl right. Indeed, I thought it terrific, and judged most other poetry of the day by Kipling's. It was a long time, however, before I read any of his prose and then I didn't greatly like it.

This, then, or something like it, was my reading (the remembered part of it) until the turn of the century, when I graduated from pure adventure to adventure plus something called love, and opened a new and even more wonderful chapter of "reading for pleasure." Thereafter for a time my preferred reading became such romances as Miss Johnston's *To Have and to Hold*, and *Richard Carvel*, by the American Winston Churchill. These highly colored, dazzlingly unreal, and altogether satisfying fictions of our colonial period came along in my teens, and for some years I was not a boy at all but a romantic adolescent—and magpie—who lived only for the sentimental costume novels he could acquire and add to the growing collection in the family china cabinet.

All these titles I once owned. They were part of my first library; and, to tell the truth, I miss them. One should be wary of becoming too sophisticated, for that way one loses a lot of happiness. Early enthusiasms should not be too recklessly discarded in maturity, particularly when one is a collector. Today I am looking again for some of the books that gave me pleasure in my youth, and having a hard time finding them. Most of them now are rare books. It annoys me to remember that once I owned beautiful copies of some fifty books I now want, and foolishly got rid of, when (as I ignorantly supposed) my taste had improved. I think now that I had very good taste as a boy. But, however that may be, I am now endeavoring in some part to replace my first library, and few of the books as they come to light disappoint me. They are still grand stories, just as I knew they were when I first read them; and if I now read with equal pleasure the "greater" books of the world, including some of the good books of this day, that is not a valid reason for dismissing my early enthusiasms. All have gone to the making and are still a part of the book inebriate who walks around in my shoes.

V

I WAS GRADUATED FROM ERICSSON without honors and Dad thought a spot of work would do me no harm. Mother agreed and thought an ideal place for me would be the Fleming H. Revell firm, publishers of religious books, whose headquarters were then in Chicago and who, like my grandfather, operated a retail bookshop. As the manager of the company was George H. Doran, recently of Toronto, whose brother Fred had recently married one of my Scottish aunts, it seemed a perfect setup for a bookish boy.

So it fell out that I visited Mr. Doran one hot morning in July, carrying a letter from Mother, after reading which he looked me over thoughtfully and said, "So your mother was a Miss Young, was she?" I agreed, and he was thoughtful again—a tall handsome gentleman with a short brown beard (an Imperial, I think) and twinkling eye glasses. After a time he made me a startling offer. He said he would give me a job as office boy and pay me three dollars and a half a week while I was learning the business. Then he introduced me to a young man named Hurd and left me to the mercies of his subordinate. Fortunately Hurd was a friendly fellow; we got along admirably. He was in the production department, therefore I was in the production department, where my duties were numerous and sometimes fairly heavy. I was called on at times to carry packages of considerable weight to and from a number of printing houses. Perhaps it was only proofs I carried, possibly it was plates; but either way I had a hand in the production of Ralph Connor's *The Man from Glengarry*, which became a best seller. Another book on which I worked, so to speak, was *My Host, the Enemy*, by Franklin Welles Calkins, a book of short stories about Indians.

The high spot of my employment was a visit made to the establishment by Ralph Connor, the firm's most successful author, who was really (I was told) the Reverend Charles W. Gordon. I held no conversation with the Reverend Gordon but I liked his looks. He had a noticeable cast in one eye that gave him a wicked, albeit jolly, piratical look that was very attractive.

As the summer neared its close and there was talk at home of sending me to high school, the question of a possible salary advance at Revell's came up and Mother stipulated that, if I stayed, I should get more money. This was embarrassing, for I had read

44

enough of Horatio Alger Jr. to know that such advances should come unsolicited from the head of the company with a few well chosen words of commendation. However, I approached the office manager—Mr. Doran was out of town—and reluctantly confessed that my mother thought I ought to be getting more than three dollars and a half a week. "How much does she think you ought to get?" he asked, and I took a chance and said, "Five dollars!" Then we parted on good terms, my job ended with the summer, and I went back to school, which may be the reason I never became a figure in the publishing world, like Mr. Doran; but I doubt it.

At John Marshall High School, as at Ericsson, I had great good luck with one teacher. Her name, and I wish I might put it in caps, was Georgia E. Bennett, and I was in her English classes from first to last. This cultured and attractive young woman took me in hand at once and did more to encourage my writing than any other early influence. She began by asking me to write something for the school paper, *The Quill*, and not long afterward I first saw my name in print. Thereafter for a time I published stories, essays, and occasionally poems—I called them poems—in *The Quill* that won the approval of the school's principal, Louis J. Block, himself a minor poet. Mr. Block also contributed to *The Quill* and sometimes we appeared together in the same issue, a circumstance that pleased one of us immensely.

My first published work of any kind was a pair of stanzas inspired by the death of Queen Victoria, a fatality that had struck deep into our home life. Of course Mother wrote practically the whole poem, although I may have contributed a word or two, and great was our delight when it appeared in *The Quill* over my signature. I should be glad to plead that I have forgotten this first item in my bibliography; but I am afraid I remember it—and here it is:

> *The Queen has passed to the unknown;*
> *No other had such fame.*

King Edward reigns on England's throne,
The seventh of his name.

Mourned as a woman and a queen,
The fairest of her race,
Down through the ages rings the paean
Of her immortal grace.

I received many compliments on this masterpiece and some criticism, too, but as the criticism came from boys in the class who could not have composed a poem on the death of Buffalo Bill, I knew they were just envious. I believe this was the last time Mother and I collaborated. Somehow I got away from her literary influence about that time and began to write poems and stories of my own. Stories of the court and camp seduced me, and so it was stories of the court and the camp that for the most part I wrote. One imitated the manner of the elder Dumas, whose *Three Musketeers* I had just read, but was—I think—an original story; although to steal from Dumas is not a sin, of course, since the old gentleman himself stole from nearly everybody else. That was the way I learned to write: by "playing the sedulous ape" (in Stevenson's words) to the great writers whose work I admired and reverenced. All this youthful stuff pleased Miss Bennett and Mr. Block enormously, and they predicted a brilliant future for their talented student. Both, I am happy to remember, lived long enough to see me publish better work in better magazines.

I had already begun my career of Conan Doyle idolatry, although at that time I preferred his historical romances to Sherlock Holmes: *Micah Clarke, The White Company, The Refugees* and three or four others. Indeed, I read so much of Conan Doyle in connection with the book reports we made once a week that ultimately Miss Bennett called a halt. "Remember now," she would say to the class, "you may read and report on any book you like— all except Charles, who must not report on any more Conan Doyles." I had reached Doyle, I think, through Dumas and Walter Scott (and of course Henty) and thereafter for a time I went back to Dumas. It was Miss Bennett, however, who turned my mind to other writers than the writers of romance and adventure, and led me into the suburbs at least of the greater kingdom of books. Her constant sympathy and encouragement helped me at a time when it counted most and her influence was so important to me that I shall never cease to be grateful to her. I dedicated my *Bookman's Holiday* to her, some time after her retirement, and was shocked when her sister wrote to say that she had been dead for several years; I had waited too long.

In all my other classes I was pretty much of a duffer, and in mathematics I was so appallingly bad that my teachers gave me up in despair. Happily, nobody minded except my math teachers, and I was shoved ahead somehow. Years afterward Miss Bennett said to me, at tea one afternoon, "You were a very dreamy boy, Charles. You never seemed to know what was going on around you; but Mr. Block and I didn't worry about you. We knew you were going to be a writer and that it wouldn't make any difference whether you knew algebra or not." She knew more about me than I knew about myself, for at that time I had just about decided to be an illustrator. I had always been able to draw pictures fairly well, without any training, and the life of an illustrator seemed to me in anticipation to be a very pleasant one. As it happened, I never improved; I can still draw pictures about as well as I could at fourteen.

Except for the English classes, and the wonderful opportunity to print my stories in *The Quill*, I disliked school life. I didn't particularly dislike my schoolmates but certainly they didn't interest me and as Jack Chandler was no longer a classmate—he had gone to a business school—I had no boon companion with whom to foregather after hours. According to a legend of the institution, I was graduated from Marshall High in 1904 but I have no memory of graduating, and it doesn't matter either way.

Throughout all these years of school life I had been in a small way a theater-goer. At first it was a very small way, indeed, for as a small boy I went only when my father took me. Although once we reveled in an adaptation of Jules Verne's spy story *Michael Strogoff* it was at the old Hopkins' Theater that I saw my first motion picture. That was in the very early days of motion pictures; the instrument used for projection was called a kinetoscope and the pictures were very juvenile. Still, a railroad train rushing directly out of the screen at the audience was pretty thrilling.

My professional theater-going, however, commenced when Jack Chandler and I began to visit the old People's Theater in Van Buren Street, a mile or two from our homes. There a stock company produced standard plays and did a very good job of it. We always walked to the theater and walked home, to save our pocket money, and we always occupied seats in the top gallery. The company was headed by May Hosmer, who had been a good comedienne in her time and now, middle-aged and plump, continued to play all the heroines herself. Her several leading men, during the years of my attendance, were enormously popular among the women and girls of the community. My own favorite was a tall, good-looking young man with a romantic name: to wit, Rodney Ranous. I thought him magnificent and one of my warmest recollections of the period is of Rodney Ranous in *Old Heidelberg*. Years later, when I was a young reporter, I met him on the street one day and recognized him at once. The encounter was in Clark Street outside Mangler's bar, where newspaper men gathered to drink. The glorious Ranous had just emerged from the bar. I touched his arm, introduced myself as a reporter for the *Daily News*, and told him of my early admiration. Without a word he put both hands on my shoulders, spun me about, and walked me into Mangler's where we talked for several hours about the old days at the People's Theater.

It was at the People's Theater also that Jack and I saw such memorable oldtimers as *Charley's Aunt*, *When We Were Twenty-One*, *East Lynne*, *Camille*, and *The Two Orphans*. We saw more ambitious performances, too, for I remember a very fine production (as I then thought) of Shakespeare's *Othello*, in which an

48

elderly actor named James Nelson, once a player of repute, set a standard by which I have judged all subsequent Iagos. But all the plays were wonderful, we thought, and for a time the theater almost supplanted books in our affections. Every experience was magical and every play a masterpiece. I was thrilled long before the curtain went up and long after it came down. And that in large degree has been my emotional response to the theater ever since. It took me years to acquire a critical temperament, to know whether a play was good or bad or just somewhere in between. I did learn, of course, but sometimes I feel that this education was a waste of time. Sometimes I miss the old uncritical rapture of those early days.

After a time, Jack and I thought it would be fun to visit the larger theaters down town, but melodrama continued to be our favorite fare. Occupying seats in the top gallery, as always, we managed to see James O'Neill in *The Count of Monte Cristo* long before he was remembered only as Eugene O'Neill's father; Blanche Bates in *Under Two Flags*, and Mrs. Leslie Carter in *Du Barry*. Occasionally we took in a musical comedy, although on the whole we preferred costume drama, and I remember with pleasure *King Dodo*, the *Prince of Pilsen*, and *The Student King*. Ultimately—O frabjous day!—we made two of an enchanted audience that succumbed to the soul-stirring impersonation of Mr. Sherlock Holmes by William Gillette. Fortunate, indeed, are the boys of America whose birth dates made possible this historic experience. Only one other memory of those days approximates that of Gillette in Sherlock Holmes; it is my memory of Kyrle Bellew in *Raffles*. How admirably the handsome English actor brought the glorious cracksman to life in the theater is known only to those aging citizens who witnessed his performance. Like Gillette, Bellew was born to play the part by which he is remembered and a fortunate few were born to see his triumph. He was wonderfully supported by E. M. Holland, in the role of a Scotland Yard inspector; I can still close my eyes and see them in their stealthy parts.

49

Involved somewhere in this period was another spot of work. The winter of 1903 found me a stock boy in the carpet department of Carson's wholesale house, where Dad was employed in the business office. The date is clear in my mind because it was while I was hustling carpet samples for the road salesmen that the Iroquois Theater fire occurred. The day was December 30, and I remember the excitement the fire caused in the carpet department. Somebody came in and told us about the shocking event going forward in Randolph Street. After hours that day I hurried to the scene of the disaster, where a cordon of police still held back the crowds of spectators. The fire was then over but the bodies of many of the six hundred victims were still lying in rows on the sidewalk. In after years, as a newspaper reporter, I saw death in many forms and later, as a war correspondent, saw men dying in battle; but except for the *Eastland* disaster nothing to touch the Iroquois fire in shuddering horror.

I have said little of church affairs and shall say as little as possible now, since proverbially they make for dull reading; but the fact is some of my most vivid memories of this period center around an old Methodist church in Sacramento Avenue at the head of Adams Street. It was Mother's church, of course, but at one time and another we were all involved in its convivial enterprises. We were now living within half a block of its inveigling doors, which seemed always to be open for one purpose or another. By helping out in the Sunday school library, I was enabled to miss classes and putter for an hour among books, and ultimately I was able to mitigate the tedium of morning and evening service by joining the choir, where the liveliest and least pious of the young people had already preceded me. It was a jolly enough church, however, as churches go; even my father, who usually disliked clergymen, had found one he could like. The Reverend T. K. Gale, surprisingly, was an ex-jockey and so a man after Dad's heart, and as the Reverend Billy Sunday, the ex-ballplayer, came sometimes to preach at his friend's church, the whole atmosphere of the place was often pretty breezy. I once saw Billy Sunday race for a streetcar after service at a speed that suggested his earlier profession. "That's the way he used to go down to first base," said Dad admiringly. The only family matter of interest not yet recorded is the birth of my brother Robert, which had occurred three years earlier. He was the last of Mother's boys and thereafter, I take it, she gave up the idea of ever having a daughter.

In this atmosphere I lived for some years and took more pleasure in it than you might think. Indeed, one episode of the period undoubtedly marked me for life; I relate it in some detail to get it out of my subconscious. Among the more charming visitors to the church was a young deaconess who came occasionally on whatever missions a deaconess performs. She was very pretty in her little black bonnet edged with white and perhaps I was a little in love with her. Possibly she was about twenty-seven years old. Sensing my adoration, she traded on it shamelessly and urged me to give a "chalk talk" to the Junior Leaguers; and in a vain moment I agreed. It was her idea that I might speak briefly on the Solomonic text about the "lilies of the field," making pictures on the blackboard as I went along. Under her blue gaze I became enormously interested in the project and, with Mother's assistance, worked up a pleasing little essay on lilies. For some days I practiced drawing lilies of every description, which was no great feat since they are easy to draw.

When the day came, however, I was so nearly petrified that I could scarcely enter the church. I had never spoken in public before. The ordeal went forward in the Sunday school room, where a huge blackboard dominated the rostrum, and a flattering number of my friends were on hand to see me perform. Everybody applauded politely when I was introduced and for a moment a warm glow of pleasure flooded me. While thirty or forty young people and a scattering of oldsters watched my every movement, I read the text assigned to me and rapidly sketched the first lily on my blackboard. "This," I said, "is a calla lily. It is one of the field lilies, too." Then a cold hand squeezed my heart and I stopped, appalled. The word *too* was not in the script and was of course quite inac-

51

curate since I had not previously mentioned any other lilies. I blushed hotly and every word of the bright little talk I had memorized vanished from my mind. I stood trembling for what seemed a very long time, knowing that I could not possibly proceed. In an effort to regain my composure, I slipped around behind the blackboard where my box of chalks reposed on a concealed lectern, and there inspiration seized me. The folding doors leading to a smaller classroom behind the rostrum stood ajar only two or three steps from the lectern. It was a God-given opportunity and I slid quietly into the back room, leaving my audience to wait nervously for my reappearance. But I did not reappear. I continued my flight through the back door of the church and out into the street; and that was the end of my first and last chalk talk.

I stayed away all afternoon and only appeared at home in time for supper. The whole miserable episode colored my life for years. I have no doubt that a certain self-consciousness which still afflicts me in public dates back to that unhappy first experience.

Ultimately, as I have hinted, I was singing in the choir. Some time was to elapse before I achieved my ambition to become a soloist while the collection boxes were being passed, but in the meantime it was pleasant to sit high above the audience while the preacher droned through the morning service, and next to me sometimes sat a red-haired young woman named Helen who made the whole experience more attractive. She was several years my senior, but a jolly girl with a pleasant singing voice and a nice smile. And, too, there was Nellie Hamilton, who came into my young life about this time and troubled my peace of mind for a number of years. As I remember her, she couldn't sing a note, but she looked well in the choir and was happy there. Our attraction for each other was Art; she, too, was fond of drawing and hoped to be an illustrator. She was my first love and on my side it was quite a maudlin affair. Nellie took it more coolly, but she liked my admiration and encouraged it. Not to drag this experience out until it becomes a bore, I loved her wildly and suffered torments in the belief that she walked and talked also with other boys. My intentions were honorable; I would have married her at sixteen. But she was a born coquette and my tender passion became a mounting and miserable jealousy. It is painful for me now to remember what a dance this charming girl led me before I escaped her curious fascination.

VI

MY SEVENTEENTH BIRTHDAY was some months behind me when my childhood dreams of adventure came to a boil. I had been thinking about foreign lands ever since I was in kilts and it was always the wilder parts of the globe that attracted me most, preferable tropical areas where there was still plenty of jungle and an alphabet of strange animals running wild. By this and by that, it was South America upon which Jack Chandler and I settled when the moment of decision came. *Nat the Naturalist* had come to be our *vade mecum*, if not our Bible; we determined to seek the headwaters of the Amazon or the Orinoco—perhaps both. We knew the difficulties that lay ahead of us for we had seen them illustrated in Gordon Browne's pictures. There would be desperate adventures with snakes and jaguars and leopards and we would come down with a variety of fevers, possibly even with bubonic plague. For these latter emergencies we planned to take with us certain surefire remedies that we jotted down in notebooks. The whole undertaking was so clear in our minds that we could have lectured on the expedition. But about this time—in the early summer of 1904, to be exact—we suddenly decided to visit the World's Fair at St. Louis first.

Our overall plan now was to work a passage from St. Louis to New Orleans on one of the river boats, then catch a tramp steamer for British Guiana. The sum necessary for our South American adventure had proved a mirage of course. We had figured it at a thousand dollars apiece; actually Jack had twenty-five dollars when we left Chicago and I had fifteen. Our parents confidently looked forward to our return within a fortnight, and their prescience was amply borne out by the fact. After a day or two at the fair we were close to bankruptcy. And as the river boats tied up at Saint Louis were unanimously in no need of our services,[1] the day came when we had to choose between returning to Chicago or continuing our expedition on foot. To our credit, let it be noted, we chose the second alternative and started off one morning, intending to walk the length of Missouri. Two days of railroad ties and farm wagons, however, somewhat dimmed the high romance of the adventure, and a freezing night in an exposed cave completed our discomfiture. On the last morning of the journey we struck out along the river for Ste. Genevieve, where we understood Jesse James had once robbed a bank, and waited for the first train back to St. Louis. It had not yet dawned on either of us, perhaps, that we were strictly armchair geographers, but the seed had been planted and in spite of the adventures that lay ahead for both of us, we were slowly growing up.

That was the situation midway between my seventeenth and eighteenth birthdays. The expedition to the ends of the earth had been halted in its first stages and for the usual reason, an acute lack of funds. But suddenly, as our favorite novelists so often observed, something happened. Somewhere I had heard that it was possible to visit England on no money at all. The altruists who made this possible were the great Chicago meat packers who, as the story went, liked to send young men to England on their cattle boats. In high excitement I hurried to the offices of Armour & Company in the Loop and learned that the sensational rumor was true. Simply by working one's passage one could voyage to Liverpool or London on an ocean liner. I signed up at once for the first available sailing and hurried home to tell my parents. Of course Jack had to be informed too. He had elected to remain in St. Louis for a spell. I wrote immediately urging him to hurry home, that we were going to Europe; but, before he could arrive, Mr. Armour or somebody

[1] A number of years were to elapse before we learned that a boy named Sam Clemens had been similarly turned away at St. Louis when he offered his services as pilot to shipmasters of an earlier day.

54

telephoned to say that a cattle shipment for England was leaving Chicago the next morning. In twelve hours I was on my way to Philadelphia in the caboose of a cattle train and in forty-eight hours I was being tossed like a chip on what poets have called the bosom of the broad Atlantic.

Poor Jack! Many times during the weeks that followed I wished that he were with me and would have traded my whole collection of Hentys for his companionship, for it was a lonely and disillusioning adventure on which I had embarked. For ten days I helped to feed, water, and bed down three hundred and ten head of American cattle bound for extinction in England. It was a gruesome trip. The food was dreadful, I thought, the work revolting. Sometimes at night, while the professional cattle hustlers were drinking in our forecastle, I would steal up on deck for a sight of the moon and stars and wonder what in the world had ever induced me to leave a decent home in Chicago for this nauseating voyage. And I wondered even harder when I was at work in the cattle pens. On the whole, this experience is not one of my happiest memories; but it was a salutary error. It took a lot of the sticky romance out of me quickly and effectively, leaving me a less confirmed adventurer early in my career.

Eventually we reached London, inching up the river through a tangle of Joseph Pennell shipping, and disembarked at the West India docks. I had no money coming to me, of course, and I remember selling my tobacco pouch to a sailor who admired it. The shilling he gave me was precisely all the money I had in the world as Bill Clark and I sauntered up Commercial Road in quest of lodgings. Happily, Clark knew a place where we could get a bed and a meal for a shilling. That one night, at any rate, was provided for. For the rest, I was sanguine—and I was in London. We had arrived early in the morning. A whole day was ahead of me and I made the most of it.

It is difficult, so long after the fact, to reconstruct the London scene that morning in the summer of 1904. The day was warm as I strolled away from my hotel and headed into the heart of the great city about which for years I had been reading. Tower Bridge and the great dome of St. Paul's loomed in the distance. Historic names appeared on every street corner. Historic pictures filled my mind. A costermonger and his donkey were having an altercation assisted by a knot of strident gamins. The shop signs were enchanting. I remember stopping for a cup of tea and a sugar bun, and I remember counting the British coins that remained to me after I had paid my bill. I had that morning sold the handsome leather belt from around my waist to Bill Clark for two or three shillings, and that was all I had. . . . So at last I came into Fleet Street, where it had occured to my innocent mind that I might find employment on a newspaper.

I can not now remember how many newspaper offices I visited that morning—several, I think—in whose anterooms I must have cut a strange figure. I do remember the amused glances I received and the courtesy with which I was treated. But I got no work. The harried men who listened to my story urged me to write an account of my cattleboating, if I cared to, and offered to consider it. I went to a stationer's and laid out a few pennies on a pad of paper, intending to begin that evening. Somewhere in the roaring Strand I asked for work in a prosperous bookshop, where again I was courteously turned away, and in Charing Cross Road I sought employment with the antiquarian booksellers. It was, I'm sure, the only time I ever visited Charing Cross Road and came away emptyhanded.

All this went forward on foot. I spent no money that day for transportation; and toward evening, tired and hungry but curiously happy, I trudged back to the drab little sailors' hostelry near the docks and was glad to bed down for the night. Clark was still there and I sold him something else—a scarf he had admired—and so acquired another pair of shillings: I suspect now that he was only being kind. That night, however, he told me something that was to be immediately useful. He said: "When you're up against it, kid, look up a Salvation Army hotel and they will take care of you."

As matters turned out, it was the best piece of advice I received in London.

In the morning I was abroad early, determined to make the most of a visit that might be terminated abruptly, and this time I managed to see more of the city. I spent some time admiring the Tudor houses in Holborn and looked in at Staple Inn, where Mr. Grewgious of Dickens's *Edwin Drood* once had a set of rooms—quite dark ones, I imagine. And eventually I reached the Edgeware Road, stopping to ask for work when the idea took me—occasionally stopping for a cup of tea—before finding a new way back to the Sailor's Rest through a labyrinth of little streets, in which for a time I lost myself. But this sort of life could not continue. Clark was not there when I returned. He had moved on and I never saw him again. There was no one else to buy my scarves and handkerchiefs for a shilling or two. I was on my own at last and it colored my thinking. That evening was spent trying to write an account of my cattle boat experience for the newspapers. Probably it was not a very good piece of journalism for it was rejected on my third London day by the first and second editors to whom I showed it. There was no third, and ultimately I mailed the thing to my parents in Chicago, suggesting that they offer it to a local paper. Nothing ever came of this either, but the manuscript was among my father's treasures for some years before it vanished. In my accompanying letter I told my parents that London was wonderful, that I was having a glorious time, and that I expected to find work shortly. Try as I would, however, I could not stretch my shillings and pence beyond the third day and the evening of that day was my last at the sailors' hotel.

It must have been on the afternoon of my fourth day that I visited the Dean of St. Paul's. Why I made this remarkable visit I have never been able to understand, nor do I understand now. Possibly I was hungry and thought I might be fed, but there was more to it than that. The name of the great cathedral stood for something in my mind and the sight of the adjacent dwelling, where the dean resided, was curiously appealing. At any rate, as I passed the old place I turned in at the gate on an impulse, mounted the steps, and made known my wish to see the dean. My wistful appearance may have touched the maid, for she smiled and asked me to wait, and after a time I was led into an old-fashioned living room and invited to have a chair. The dean came in a few minutes afterward, looking exactly (I thought) as he should have looked. From head to foot he was in clerical black, except for his white collar, and he wore black gaiters buttoned to the knee—a bent old man, quite elderly, with thin white hair and a fringe of white whiskers round his face. So I remember him. His smile was singularly attractive and friendly. He shook hands with me and looked me over with dancing eyes, while I told my story. Then he asked me a great many questions that I answered as best I could, giving him, I hope, an attractive picture of my home life in Chicago. When we had talked for a while, there was a rustle and a rattle in the corridor and my friend, the maid, came in with a tea cart. The dean and I ate heartily, I am happy to remember, and after a time he wished me well and I went on my way considerably cheered. His name was Robert Gregory, a name I shall always hold in affection.

After this first success, I made other surprise visits in London, selecting my victims with some care from the telephone directory. They were all celebrities of a sort, although possibly some of them were surprised to hear it. Five were illustrators, whose spirited drawings I had followed in the pages of the *Strand Magazine*. Ernest Prater was the first and working with him in the studio was his friend George Soper. They were immensely gracious and, I like to think, pleased by my youthful admiration; I carried away with me original drawings selected from their portfolios. Later Paul Hardy, Alfred Pearse, and the admirable Stanley L. Wood received me with startled eyes and sent me away with gifts. Indeed, Stanley Wood—so long associated in juvenile minds with the adventures of Captain Kettle—repaid my visit. Years afterward he surprised me by dropping in on me at the *Daily News* office in Chicago. Such were my choices. London in the year 1904 must have been filled with greater names, but the men I elected to visit were men whose stirring pictures I had come to know in the pages of a favorite magazine. My outstanding favorite, Gordon Browne, lived somewhere out of town, to my regret, and so I did not meet him on that trip. The visit to Dean Gregory, however, was pure inspiration and remains with me as one of the happiest memories of my life.

But thereafter my life in London was of another and quite different sort, and Bill Clark's advice was all that kept me from starvation. This was the way it came about. Before the end of the week, in the most dismal circumstances—I remember that it was raining hard and I was suddenly desperate—a man gave me a few coppers. All day I had gone hungry and the weather made it impossible to sleep outdoors. Somewhere in my wanderings I recalled passing a small Salvation Army hotel, and late that evening I tried to find it again. It was called The Ark and it was somewhere on the south side of the river. I crossed Blackfriars' Bridge and lost myself for a time in the maze of streets around the waterfront; but my sense of direction stood me in good stead and I found The Ark again. Soaked to the skin, I paused for only an instant, then slipped inside and stood shivering before an open fire. After a time a man approached me and asked if I intended to stay the night. I answered that I was without money and offered to do whatever might be required of me if I were permitted to stay; and he nodded and said he would get me some coffee and something to eat. Then he introduced me to a man named George and asked him to look after me.

Thus I met W. T. George, and I have met no better fellow since. He looked after me so admirably that for several days he was my constant companion. That night, however, I merely dried myself before the fire, drank several cups of hot coffee with the food that was given me, and went immediately to bed.

I should have caught my death of cold; but I was young, and in the morning I was quite all right. George was waiting for me. If I were an artist, I could draw you his picture from memory. He looked a little like H. G. Wells—a fairer, sandier, smaller H. G.

Wells. We had breakfast together in the common room and I was told I might stay until my circumstances improved. When George learned that I was in love with London, at any rate the London I had been reading about in books, he offered to show me round, an offer that I accepted gratefully. For a time I believed him to be connected with the personnel of the hotel but in fact, I learned, he was a paying guest who by long residence had become a trusted aide. He was a kind, clean-living little man whose few shillings were ever at my service, and I came to like him very much indeed.

In George's company I really saw London. It was with George that I explored Westminster Abbey and the Tower of London, the British Museum, and the picture galleries. It was with George that I wandered the famous streets of London and made bus-top pilgrimages to outlying districts almost mythical in their literary significance. In a burst of gratitude I invited him to visit me if ever he came to America, and that is precisely what he did; but that is another story. I shall never forget the incredible kindness of this English working man—for occasionally he appeared to have tasks to perform—who for a few weeks was my guide and companion. I can still see him standing beside me in the Abbey before a flagstone lettered with an illustrious name. "The gryve of Charles Dickens," he said proudly. His air was that of a genial shopkeeper showing me the finest item on his shelves.

One night he took me to another Army hotel, one of the divisional headquarters, where some sort of revival was going forward, and we sang so lustily that we called attention to ourselves. Just above me on the rostrum was the leader of the band, who also led the congregational singing. Suddenly, at the end of the first verse of one of my favorite hymns, he held up a hand for silence. "You have a nice voice, my boy," he said, looking directly at *me*. "Won't you sing the next stanza for us alone?" So I sang the next verse alone, a bit shakily at first but with mounting enthusiasm, and everybody came in on the chorus, and George was so pleased that he pinched my elbow.

Later, when the singing and speaking were over and refresh-

60

ments were being served, the band leader came down to me and said, "Look here, my boy, what are you doing in London? You're an American, aren't you?" I said yes, I was an American; and then George and I fell all over each other trying to tell him my story first. A thoughtful look came into his eyes. After a moment he continued: "So you want to see London, do you? We of the Army cover a great deal of London. If you were to go around with us now and then—say evenings and Sundays—there wouldn't be much of London you wouldn't see." He added quickly, "Singing, I mean, just singing the old songs as you did tonight." George was delighted, and slowly it dawned on me that perhaps this strange offer was the very job I had been looking for. Thus it came about that for a number of weeks I sang on the street corners of London for the Salvation Army and, as my friend the bandmaster had predicted, there was little of London that I didn't see.

I am glad all this happened in 1904, for one of the many streets that George and I explored was Baker Street, and it was in 1904 that Sherlock Holmes and Dr. Watson gave up their Baker Street lodgings. I was not then thinking of Holmes and Watson, it distresses me to recall, and years were to elapse before I became an incurable Sherlockian; yet I am happy to remember that I walked up Baker Street in that final year of their residence. I like to think that we passed the detective and the doctor on the street that day. They may have been in one of the carriages that rattled past us. If only I had thought to ask George about them, I am sure he could have taken me directly to their door.

Some years ago, and some forty years after that first visit to London, I encountered W. H. Davies' *Autobiography of a Super-Tramp* and read Chapter XXII with unusual interest. That chapter is titled "The Ark," and relates the vagabond poet's experiences at the Salvation Army hotel whose personnel had been so kind to me. I can't place the date of Davies' stay there—he is curiously vague about dates—but it was some time after the Boer War and probably a year or two before my own adventure. He was there for six months and had little good to report of the place. He asserts that no charity was dispensed on the premises and that the food, although cheap, was "such food as was not fit for a human being." Certainly this was not my experience, and as I read Davies' almost nauseating account of the hotel's accommodations and the sort of transients who used them, I am inclined to think important changes had been effected before my arrival. He hints, indeed, that certain officers were subsequently dismissed. Perhaps it was then that the friendly atmosphere I encountered came in. And I wondered, too, as I read the poet's strictures, how many other vagabond poets had found sanctuary there before his time—and after mine.

But I became homesick, inevitably, and could not wait to get back to Chicago to tell Jack Chandler of my adventures. The problem was to arrange a passage without benefit of legal tender. Then one day I encountered one of the cattlemen who had made the voyage with me and learned that he was returning at once. A company ship was leaving in a few days, he said, and all I had to do was join up. The Atlantic Transport Company was obligated to return me to America; it was part of the contract, he said. And so there came an evening when George and I clasped hands, swore eternal friendship, and I said goodbye to the best friend I had made in England. The ship sailed from Tilbury, some miles out of London. I joined the other cattlemen who were returning, at a convenient rendezvous, and we walked all night, reaching Tilbury a little before dawn. The gangplank was out, and at daylight we were on our way to Boulogne, where some sort of cargo—we vaguely understood—was to be picked up.

What a cargo it turned out to be! In the early hours of a French morning I looked over the ship's side, with a sense of nightmare in my veins, and heard it come aboard in a discord of animal sounds that must have startled the crews of other vessels in the harbor. Howls, roars, snarls, screeches, barkings, bellowings—caterwauls of every description—filled the darkness and blew out across the water with curious effect. Bostock's Wild Animal Circus, which had been showing somewhere in France, was returning to America in crates and cages; it was being derricked into the hold and distributed along the runways and cattle pens in preparation for eight days at sea, and the star performers were protesting the indignity in their several ways. It was Noah's Ark all over again. Then the dawn came, the whistles blew, the ship sailed for New York, and I was afloat with a wild animal show.

At first the cattlemen would have nothing to do with this outfit; but curiosity lured us to the dismantled circus and ultimately some of our fellows signed up with the show for the duration. The wage was seventy-five cents a day. It was hard work and the odor between decks was terrific; but on the whole it was a well-behaved collection of animals. There were no outbreaks, and I have only good to report of them. My own earnings for such casual assistance as I rendered were slight, but the money I acquired by my curious labors was all I had coming to me when the ship docked at New York. I landed in my own country with little more in my pocket than when I landed in England.

Remembering my predicament in London, I went at once to the famous Bowery, where I assumed the cheaper hotels were to be found. I knew quite a lot about the Bowery, having read about that dangerous section in some of Alger's stories of New York, and of course I knew the old song. Such information as I possessed, however, proved to be inaccurate. I did not save a banker's little daughter from beneath the wheels of a roaring fire engine; and no millionaire's son, slumming in the district, was attracted by my innocent face. I was as desolately alone as I had been for a time in London. For a few days, when there were only pennies left in my pocket, I slept on a mattress on the floor of a malodorous flophouse, surrounded by derelicts as broke as myself. Memories of that first experience of New York are unhappy and I have buried them so deep that they do not readily emerge; but one episode might have furnished a story plot to O. Henry. For one whole day and part of a second I went hungry. Then late in the afternoon, sick and desperate, I found myself standing outside a bakery, sniffing the delicious odors that poured from the shop every time the door was opened.

Suddenly I became aware that I was standing on a sidewalk grating that communicated with the baker's basement. The shop was close to the corner, and several persons were waiting for a streetcar. Inspiration seized me. Every day, I thought, workers stood on that grating, waiting for streetcars, reaching into their pockets for change before the car arrived. Many persons leaving the bakeshop with purchases must have crossed the grating, stuffing their change into their purses. A dozen ways occurred to me in which small change might have been lost down that grating over the years. I wondered—idly at first, then acutely—how much treasure the black hole in the sidewalk concealed. After a few moments of feverish thought I dropped my fountain pen, an inexpensive gift from George, through the iron bars. At first the shop keeper was reluctant to let me recover it, but I was persuasive about my pen and finally he said I might try. He took me down to the basement, indicating the old crates and cartons I would have to clear away, and hurried back to his duties. When he had gone I made a path to the window giving onto the aperture beneath the grating—an oblong hole littered with paper, cigarette butts, chewing gum wrappers, and miscellaneous filth. It seemed never to have been cleaned. This was all to the good, however, for after about ten minutes of intensive research I uncovered seventeen cents—not all at once of course—a dime, a nickel, and two pennies. My fountain pen I had recovered at once, and I showed it triumphantly to the baker when I went back to the shop. In a burst of gratitude and affection, I spent nearly my entire wealth in the bakeshop.

That night I sought a Salvation Army hotel and again met people who were humanely, preposterously kind. A visiting social worker, who questioned me at some length, was particularly kind. She held me at the hotel for two days, then told me that she had communicated with my parents who were sending money to bring me home. And thus it came about that, while my journey to

64

Philadelphia had been made in the caboose of a cattle train, my return journey from New York was made in a comfortable day coach. For a number of years my wanderings were over.

One final word about George. I had been home barely two weeks when Mother answered the bell one night and found a strange man on the stoop. She reported that my friend, Mr. George, about whom I had told her, had arrived from England. It appeared that my account of the altruism of our cattle companies had inflamed him with immediate desire to visit America. I gathered also that he was eager to see *me* again. He had reached Chicago some days before, but had put off his visit until he had found a job. He was working as a dishwasher in a small restaurant somewhere in South State Street. It sounded unattractive and George agreed that it was, indeed, unattractive. An open sewer close by gave off such foul odors, he said, that he was thinking of reporting the place to the city's health authorities. George had a civic conscience that he had brought with him to Chicago.

He declined to stay with us that night but promised to return when he had found another job. Then he thanked Mother for the dinner she had prepared for him, told her she had a fine son, wrung my hand affectionately, and vanished from my sight forever. We never saw him again; we never knew what happened to him. We made what inquiries were possible, but there was no trace of the little man to be found. I hope he did not come to grief in our wicked city. It is possible that he simply sickened of Chicago in a few days and caught the next ship back to England. I hope so—but why did he not write me?

VII

ABOUT THIS TIME I acquired another grandfather in curious circumstances, and Dad for the first time met his father. Even quiet lives have their moments of high drama and surely this was one of them. Grandfather Starrett had long been a legend in the family and might have remained a legend if it had not been for Mother. He had left home to make his fortune in the Canadian West, leaving his family behind him in Toronto. Later his eldest son had followed him and neither had returned. Dad had been then a babe in arms and had reached the age of forty-odd without ever knowing his own father. Learning that the old man was alone, Mother offered him a home with us in Chicago; and one memorable day he arrived.

I witnessed his arrival from the front window. He came down Adams Street in a city hack drawn by a single horse, his long black sea chest, like a coffin, upright on the box beside the driver. The cab window was open; his lean old face was half out of it. I saw a dominating nose and a fringe of white hair. When he disembarked I saw that he was more than six feet in height. He looked like what he was, a frontiersman. I rushed out of the house to greet him. "Grandfather!" I shouted; and the old man—he was nearly eighty —answered timidly, "Is it Bobby?" and put his arm around my shoulders. He had mistaken me for my father.

Then Mother came bustling out of the house, and we hustled him inside and established him in the living room. But he would not be left alone. He followed Mother to the kitchen where he sat and talked while preparations for tea went on around him. Suddenly he whipped out a little black bottle. "Will you have a nip, Maggie?" he asked, and chuckled at her shocked refusal.

He was not much of a drinker, however, in spite of this frightening introduction. He was a simple and delightful old man and, although he sometimes scandalized Mother, he settled down with us like a friendly puppy and gave no trouble to anybody until he began to die.

It occurs to me that, throughout all the years of which I am now writing, Mother must have all but dominated the church. She was that kind and, on the whole, it was probably good for the church. At one time and another she was president of everything that required a president. Sometimes she played the piano at Sunday School and, although I never saw her do it, she was quite capable of taking over the organist's duties at morning service. She played both piano and organ acceptably. As far back as I can remember, there was always a small upright piano in our home on which she played us hymns in the evening. Sometimes she played and sang old Scotch songs she had learned as a child in Toronto. They were mistful, melancholy things for the most part, and they used to depress me at times with an unfathomable sense of sadness and longing.

Mother was a good woman and a brave one, and frequently she was an unhappy one. But much of the time, too, she was a happy woman who found her happiness in her church. She had several churches. Although born a Presbyterian, in Chicago she attended first a Congregational church, then a Methodist, and finally an Evangelical chapel, where for the first time, I believe, her troubled spirit found something it had been seeking. She had the missionary spirit and would have been a missionary in foreign lands if opportunity had permitted. For a time, in her last years, she was actually a missionary among the Indians in western Canada, and at the time of her death, in 1935, was on her way to a waterside mission in Vancouver, British Columbia.

God, as I first learned to think of Him, was a fine old gentleman with a noble beard, rather like Santa Claus; and that is still the only way I can think of him. He is big, of course, and Anglo-Saxon. Grant Allen once said that an Englishman's idea of God was another Englishman twelve feet high, and I suppose that is more or less everybody's idea of God—with the necessary geographical adjustment. Zenith Brown, who writes delightful detective stories under several names (e.g., David Frome, Leslie Ford) and who invented the enchanting Evan Pinkerton, has an idea about God that pleases me. She explained it to me one afternoon a few years ago at Mortimer Adler's home in Chicago. "God," said Mrs. Brown, "is obviously a friendly enough Old Gentleman most of the time, Who wishes us well and tries to see to it that we are reasonably happy. It is equally obvious," said Mrs. Brown, "that He has an idiot brother who takes over the reins whenever God Himself goes fishing. It is when the idiot brother is in charge of things that the world goes wrong and we have wars, famines, pestilences, and New Deals on earth."

But Mother, that grand old force of nature, was very humble toward the end. She told me once that she would be very happy with whatever the Lord gave her to do; even, she said, if it were only to tend a toll gate somewhere. That, I suppose, is the proper spirit and I am willing to go along with her on that, substituting a bookshop for her toll gate.

But to resume the chronological narrative: after my return from London, I found myself in the choir again and enjoying it. My English experiences had proved immediately valuable and shortly, to my pleased surprise, I was being asked to sing some of the baritone solos. On such formal occasions I rose on signal and stalked slowly down to the rail, just behind the preacher's head, as the offertory strains began. While the collection boxes were being passed, I leaned out into the auditorium and gave forth with such pieces as Dudley Buck's *My Redeemer*, Wagner's *Hymn to the Evening Star* (with new and appropriate words), and such old favorites as *The Holy City*, by Stephen Adams, and Schubert's *Ave Maria*. My voice had improved, I was told, and for a time I toyed with the idea of becoming a professional singer; but this notion did not last. Sometimes I sang at funerals, with a stout contralto whose voice blended well with my own. And, not to be reticent about it, the redhead named Helen was still there. Her clear soprano bubbled at my ear whenever I could contrive to occupy the chair beside her. She was sinfully attractive.

Meanwhile I had met the man who perhaps influenced my life, for the next several years, more than any other friend of the period. He was Henry Walter Jones, a druggist, and his shop a block or two from my home had become for me the most fascinating place in Chicago. There is a little essay about Jonesy in a slim volume of mine called *Persons from Porlock* that I hope somebody will care to read. It is sentimental, nostalgic, and perhaps a little too wistful, but that is the way I feel about Jonesy. Suffice it now to say that he was a man of middle age when I met him, a plump stocky little man with a sandy moustache and a high white forehead, in whom with rapture I discovered another lover of books. Perhaps it was his extraordinary conversations with his customers that first attracted me to him. He lost no opportunity to illustrate his most ordinary remarks with quotations from the standard poets, all of whom he seemed to know by heart, although Longfellow was his favorite. We were friends from the beginning; and the long hours I spent with Jonesy, I know now, were as well spent as the long earlier hours passed in my grandfather's bookshop.

Jonesy collected autographs and mineral curiosities, but his most delightful possession was a line of scrapbooks that he had been pasting up for heaven knows how many years. Everything I had ever wanted to know, whether of life or letters, seemed to be in Jonesy's scrapbooks. The oldest clippings went back to his boyhood. Otherwise, his library was not notable; it was simply a line of old books in a corner of his back room, among which stood out the "poetical works" of Longfellow, Tennyson, and Oliver Wendell Holmes. There were also obscure prose works by such American humorists as Josh Billings, Artemus Ward, and Petroleum V. Nasby. He was fond of the simpler poets and the school of humor that practiced outlandish misspellings. He was an excellent talker, particularly when he was remembering his boyhood; his stories of juvenile misdemeanor in several small towns of Illinois rivaled the adventures of Tom Sawyer.

But there were other attractions. I had already begun to smoke, surreptitiously of course, and Jonesy encouraged me in the habit and sometimes presented me with cigars out of the front showcase. Sometimes after hours we would sit behind the closed door of his shop, looking out into the night, and smoke our final cigars together. One night I entered to find him sitting in semi-darkness. He put up a hand to interrupt my greeting and, for a few minutes, continued to smoke in silence. Then he deposited his stub in a tray and said: "Starrett, I've just concluded an interesting experiment. No doubt you've wondered how many puffs there are in the average cigar. Well, sir, there are exactly three hundred and eighty-five. I've just counted them." I expressed the satisfaction it gave me to acquire this remarkable piece of information, known to only two men in the world, and thereafter the evening proceeded as usual. But I was fascinated all over again to have encountered a mind capable of inaugurating such a delightful research.

I had been seeing a lot of Jonesy after my return from London, and already we were two book-sodden old cronies. The choir singing was going nicely, Grandfather Starrett was still living, and I was still adding occasional volumes to the shelves in Mother's china cabinet when, one evening along toward dusk, something important happened. I was chatting innocently at Jonesy's cigar counter when the adventure began. A light rain was falling; we could smell the peculiar odor rising from the screen door. Suddenly a small boy loomed up through the mist with a note which Jonesy, accustomed to receiving holograph communications from his customers, accepted automatically. "For you, Starrett," he said. I was surprised, for nobody but Mother was supposed to know where I was, and she would have telephoned. The note, which was anonymous, was even more surprising. "If you are interested," it read, "it would be nice to see you. The boy will tell you where I am. Do come, won't you. Remember, it's the third floor!" The place was only a couple of blocks away.

It was a jolly little mystery, I thought, the more so as I had been reading a lot of Stevenson just then, including his *New Arabian Nights*.

Jonesy grinned like an old satyr. "Looks like a tryst, Starrett," he chuckled.

"It could be a trap," I said cautiously, with my head full of Stevenson; but curiosity impelled me to respond.

Rain was still falling, proverbially good weather for what fol-

The Round Table at Schlogl's on Ben Hecht's Departure for New York

From left standing at back: Richard Schenider, the "literary waiter"; Dwight Haven of the Daily News Advertising Department; Keith Preston, Daily News book columnist; Pascal Covici, our publisher; Ben Hecht (with cigar); Vincent Starrett; Henry Justin Smith (centered against mirror); from left seated: Philip R. Davis, lawyer and poet; Alfred MacArthur, brother of Charles; Ashton Stevens (face concealed); Billy McGee, Covici's partner; Charles Collins, drama critic; Harry Hansen; LeRoy R. Goble, advertising man; John Gunther; "Pete" Hecht, Ben's brother; Dr. Morris Fishbein; J. U. Nicholson, poet; Lloyd Lewis, historian.

Jack London
in 1916, Shortly Before His Death

lowed. The house proved to be an apartment building with many occupants; I struck matches in a dark hallway and read the names under the doorbells; there was none I knew. The long stairflight was dark, too, and my suspicions mounted. But I groped my way to the third floor, found a door on a dark landing, and knocked timorously. Presently there were footsteps beyond the barrier and I was confronted by a bosomy dark woman of formidable appearance. "Hello," she said, and added cordially, "Go right through to the front. She's expecting you."

The episode was getting more and more mysterious; but I preceded the strange woman along the passage to the living room, and there at last was somebody I knew—a woman, just as the boy had said—the adorable Helen, no less, the redhead from the church choir. "Hello," she said. "Are you surprised?" Behind the words lay an amused smile, a glance of almost frightening familiarity. . . . and suddenly I knew that everything was going to be all right.

In such fashion, and a very good fashion it is, I came perhaps to manhood. Somebody has said that adolescence is the period between puberty and adultery, an amusing definition, but it would be inaccurate to say that I left my adolescence behind on that memorable evening. In many ways, I realize, my life has been one long adolescence. But I am not nearly as innocent as once I was, and sometimes I am a little sad about this, and sometimes quite happy. Life is like that, I imagine.

When it was certain that I was through with school forever, I looked around for employment and found it with another publishing house, Houghton Mifflin & Company. There was a Chicago office in connection with its subscription department, and my job was to deliver back-breaking sets of Longfellow, Whittier, Lowell —indeed, most of the New England group of whiskered poets— to wives who, in their husbands' absence, had undertaken to purchase one or more of the bards on the installment plan. Part of my job, also, was to collect the monthly installments.

There were other jobs of a sort, brief and unsatisfactory, and if I learned nothing else I learned a great deal about Chicago. For the first time, I saw all sides of the city, and in those early years of the new century Chicago was an interesting and exciting place. Transportation was beginning to be mechanized, the change had been in progress for some time; but there were still horses in the streets and the automobile was still a novelty. I liked to ride streetcars, and this was just as well for I had a lot of riding to do. On the cultural side, as it were, I enjoyed the advertising cards that formed a continuous panel around the upper walls of the coaches, and was particularly fond of those involving rhymes. There were some memorable rhymes then running in the streetcars, so to speak, for in effect they were serial stories and all the more interesting for their continuity.

My favorite advertisement was a series of rhymes and pictures called *Spotless Town*, a gayly illustrated and sprightly piece of doggerel celebrating the virtues of Sapolio. Some of these have been reprinted for connoisseurs and collectors; the original cards are, I believe, cherished items of Americana. It was a genial bit of cleverness. One got to know all the leading citizens of Spotless Town—the mayor, the doctor, the butcher, the baker, and (notably) the "Maid of Spotless Town," who became, I am sorry to say, the heroine of numerous rhymes that the streetcar-riding public did not get to see. Another series of masterly rhymes involved a certain Phoebe Snow, who used the Lackawanna Railroad in her journeys and so managed to keep her garments clean. Yet another series of deft rhymes celebrated the adventures of Sunny Jim, whose appealing philosophy of life popularized a famous breakfast food. All these and many more formed a colorful panorama that the public loved, and I am sorry they have disappeared from our public service vehicles.

Thus school days ended and another life began. Girls were suddenly important, almost as important as books. Choir practice was on Thursday nights. Several jobs had been shot from under me. Life was real, life was earnest, and life was fun also. Ultimately only two strong ties with boyhood remained. These were Jack

Chandler and Nellie Hamilton, and even Nellie was beginning to get a little tired of my doglike devotion. In little ways she tried to discourage me, kindly enough; and in the end it was she who introduced me to the girl I ultimately married—although that was still some years in the future.

When I first saw Lillian Hartsig she was thumping a piano merrily. She turned long enough to acknowledge the introduction, smiled pleasantly, and went back to her playing. She played admirably. I did not instantly fall in love with her, but not long afterward I was "going with" Lillian Hartsig and, although I did not then suspect it, the first important change in my life was impending.

VIII

AN INTERESTING ESSAY might be written on why young men enter the newspaper business. I have known reporters who, before they became reporters, were post-office clerks, bank tellers, bond salesmen, pugilists, clergymen. For years I worked with one who had been an undertaker's assistant, and with another who had been a tramp. Nowadays many young fellows go directly from their journalism classes into their chosen profession; but I don't remember meeting many such graduates in my time. I think they were suspect. Chicago was a tough city in those days, as it is today, and tough newspapermen were required to cope with the city's reputation. In my own case, I became a journalist after I had failed at nearly everything else.

The story begins on a morning in 1906, a few months before my twentieth birthday. I had set out to find a job in the Chicago newspaper world. But the city editor of the *Daily News* could not use a young man without experience, and harrassed young men at the *Tribune* and the *Record-Herald* said much the same thing in much the same words. There was no job for me at the *Journal* or the *Evening Post*. Even the unimportant *Dispatch* could find no merit in me. At length there was only one newspaper left, the

Inter-Ocean. Shortly I was seated with the city editor, a handsome young man with steel grey hair; his name was Harry Daniel. The business of the day had not begun for Mr. Daniel; he was kind enough to talk with me for some time. His remarks ran somewhat as follows:

"So you'd like to be a newspaper reporter, would you, Starrett? Let me tell you how you've gone about it. You went to the *Tribune* or the *Daily News* first, and they told you they couldn't use you because you had no experience. After that you went to every other newspaper in Chicago except the *Inter-Ocean*, and they all sang you the same song. You came here last because you thought this was the least important newspaper in Chicago. You'd rather work for one of the other papers, but you're willing to start here if you have to." He was grinning cheerfully throughout this recital; I was not offended. "And now," continued Mr. Daniel, "you're a bit discouraged. You wonder how the hell you're ever going to get experience unless somebody gives you a chance. Isn't that about it?"

I nodded uncomfortably.

"Well," he said in friendly fashion, "we've all been through it, Starrett. That's the way we all begin, and I'll tell you what I'll do. I like your looks and I think you may make a newspaperman. I'll give you a chance. I need a couple of young reporters just now and maybe you'll be one of them. I can't pay you very much. My budget doesn't allow it. How would you like to work for me for two weeks for your expenses, until you see how you like it, and I see how good you are? We'll pay you whatever it costs you out of your own pocket, carfare and telephone calls and that sort of thing. At the end of two weeks, if you've made good, I'll give you twelve dollars a week to start. Then if we decide to let you out, you can go back to the other papers and, when they ask you their trick question about previous experience, you can say you were on the *Inter-Ocean*. How about it?"

Even then I knew it was a decent offer from a decent fellow, and I lost no time in closing with it. I have never regretted the step

I took that afternoon and I am still grateful to Harry Daniel, a good newspaperman and an even better human being.

I reported at one o'clock the following afternoon and was put to work at once. The trivial nature of my first assignments surprised me; I had hoped to be asked to understudy the drama critic, at least. Actually, I became a "picture chaser," although occasionally I was permitted to type a few paragraphs to accompany the photographs I had solicited. The other reporters, experienced men, had all started the same way, they said. They were friendly when they had time to be, and some of them were helpful—when they had time to be.

My first assignments, although unimportant, were educational and illuminating. When a citizen was murdered, when a young woman committed suicide, when somebody was injured in an unusual accident, when a high-school girl won a beauty contest, when an old couple celebrated fifty years of wedlock, the cry was for photographs to illustrate these notable events in human history, and I was one of several youngsters whose principal duty it was to visit the homes of such celebrities and ask for pictures. If these could not be obtained by solicitation, it was our duty to obtain them by cunning; that is to say, by whatever stealthy means occurred to us. At the end of a fortnight I became a member of the regular staff, at twelve dollars a week, and I remained with the paper for the next eleven months. By that time I had acquired enough experience to dazzle any editor in the world, for the *Inter-Ocean* was a wonderful proving ground.

Our night city editor was the fabulous Walter Howey who, as the newspaper world knows, went onward and upward in the profession until he became one of the greatest of Hearst's editors. It is common knowledge, too, that he figured largely and profanely, under another name, in Ben Hecht's and Charles MacArthur's newspaper drama, *The Front Page*. When I knew him first he was a slender young man of almost angelic appearance, with blond curls and an ironic blue eye—only one; the other was blind. But he had a chain-lightning mind, I realized quickly, and was not the night editor of a Chicago morning newspaper because of his good looks. It was, I know now, a privilege to begin a career under Walter Howey. It was, in fact, a whole newspaper education. It was he who taught me to write acceptably. At first my style was florid and my stories were over-written. I used to open the morning paper eagerly, hoping to find one of my pyrotechnic accounts of an unimportant fire featured prominently on the front page; but too often I found it hidden away on a back page, so mutilated by the copy desk that it hurt. And it was hard for me to understand the necessity for crowding all the vital facts of a story into the first paragraph. In my philosophy of writing, the facts were relatively unimportant; I liked to lead up to them in leisurely fashion, keeping the reader in suspense about what had happened. Howey was more patient with me than the copy desk. I suspect he had once written that way himself. His approach was kindly and cunning; it was at once benevolent and satirical. "Why, this is wonderful, Starrett!" he would say. "In a novel it would be simply grand. I particularly like your verbs. Your people always 'declare,' or 'vouchsafe,' or 'explode,' or something like that. However, I have a suggestion to make. The strongest verb in any dialogue is the little word *said*. Say 'he said' and 'she said.' That way the half-witted reader isn't so lost in admiration of your prose that he misses the point of your story." And then he would grin like a friendly crocodile and pat my shoulder and tell me I was coming on fine.

Among my colleagues in those memorable first months were Ring Lardner and his brother Rex; Newton Fuessle, later a successful novelist; Oliver Marble Gale, later an unsuccessful novelist; William L. Bliss, a remarkable crime reporter; Oswald Schuette, later a well-known Washington correspondent; and a dozen other sterling characters who attained at least local fame in their profession. Our drama critic was Burns Mantle, who went on to greater celebrity in New York. Our leading cartoonist was long, lean, quizzical, friendly H. T. Webster, whose humorous creations,

76

including "Caspar Milquetoast," in time attained nation-wide popularity.

Lardner and his brother were cubs like myself; we drew the humbler assignments. I can remember only one story that Ring and I covered together, and it was unimportant; but he was a delightful companion. Except that he was younger then, he looked very much as he did years afterward when his photograph appeared frequently in the magazines; he was excessively tall, gangling, and owl-eyed, with a high bald forehead that made him look rather like a schoolmaster or a magician. I think he laughed more often in his *Inter-Ocean* days than later, when even his most humorous conversation was deadpan. But although I knew him well enough, we did not become intimates. A closer companion was Tristram Tupper, a romantic Virginian, a sort of Galahad of the news lanes, whose ambitions were as impossibly literary as my own. I lost touch with him when I left the *Inter-Ocean*, but years afterward I learned that he had published half a dozen romantic novels, all popular in their time. Then one day I saw a dispatch from Europe—it was during World War II—and found in it a line about the meritorious conduct of a Brigadier General Tristram Tupper, who could only be my old friend and companion, Tris Tupper, or so I supposed. I have had no further word of him. Possibly he is a major-general now, and I can think of nobody more admirably suited to the life of a major-general.

It was an interesting newspaper office in which I received my first training, and as I pass the old building today—it is now a motion picture theater, but the old name is still cut in stone over the arch—I like to stop and let the years roll back to the lively days when it housed as exhilarating a collection of characters as any novelist has dared to invent.

It was an interesting city, too, in which I received my first newspaper training. Judge Dunne, a Democrat, was mayor and was trying to be a good one. He had been a reform candidate, and clean-ups of every kind were impending or in progress. The newspapers called them "crusades," and took a lively part in them.

Nevertheless, there was plenty of crime that went uncorrected and unpunished. One read of gambling syndicates, liquor syndicates, and vice lords, much as one reads of them today. Presumably, the lawbreakers were in league with the "higher-ups"—possibly with the city hall and the police. There were plenty of scandals. Undoubtedly, vice and gambling existed on a then almost unparalleled scale and were commercially profitable to all concerned. On the other side were a dozen picturesque reformers, including the women's clubs, important social workers like Jane Addams, and a number of well-known clergymen. Gangs as we came to know them had yet, I think, to arrive; but there were adumbrations of that development. It has been said that they began with the newspaper wars for place and circulation that followed the coming of Hearst in the first years of the century, and possibly there is some truth in the charge. Chicago was then called a "frontier town," an apt enough description; but as I think of its other aspects—cultural, educational and religious—it was a medieval city in which the good and the bad dwelt side by side, cheek by jowl, as in old Rome and Florence.

Into this fascinating maelstrom of vice and virtue, euphemistically called the "melting pot," I plunged with youthful rapture, happy to be on the side of the angels, but almost equally happy to have a front seat for the other side of the show. My greatest pride was my police and fire badge—then issued to all members of the working press—by displaying which I was able to barge my way through fire lines and police cordons and make a nuisance of myself. The feeling of importance it gave me was like nothing I had ever experienced before. Even when it was not actively in use, I wore it under my coat lapel, with one metal point showing. The home boys of our neighborhood were green with envy. It never impressed Mother, but for two cents Dad would have borrowed it every time he heard the fire engines pass the house. He said he had once owned a sheriff's star, himself, but had lost it in a fight with six thugs who sprang at him from the mouth of an alley.

My first police assignment was a murder case somewhere on

the West Side, where a homicidal butcher had used his cleaver to hack off his wife's head. Happily, he was in custody. Another reporter was handling the story; my only task was to obtain photographs of the butcher, his wife, and members of the family circle. The shop occupied the ground floor of a three-story building and the butcher lived on the top level. I rang the downstairs front doorbell for some time, then climbed the long stairway, and thumped on the upstairs door. Apparently, there was nobody in the house, but I strolled around to the back anyway. Again I climbed three flights of stairs and thumped on the back door, and still there was no response. Then I noted that a rear window was open a few inches at the bottom. Obviously it gave on to a back bedroom; but the blind was down—I could not see within. My duty seemed plain enough, but one's first burglary is always a nervous occasion. Cautiously I eased up the window until it was possible to crawl through, pushed the blind aside without releasing it, blundered on all fours into a bed that lay beneath the window, and stepped gingerly to the floor. Then I turned and leaned across the bed to release the blind. Sunlight flooded the room and revealed the bed more clearly. I saw that it had an occupant. *She* was there—the murdered woman herself—clad only in her gore. The severed head and body had been reunited, but there was an appreciable gap between, and the whole spectacle was appalling. . . . Without further ado, I climbed back through my window and fled the neighborhood. I have seen many mutilated bodies since, but never with the same sense of shock.

Not long afterward I entered a cottage in Irving Park one night and experienced another kind of fright. An entire family had been poisoned, nobody knew how, and it was thought one of the dear people themselves might have been responsible. It was the classic situation, indeed: one of the sons was less dangerously ill than the others and was therefore suspect. Several members of the family were dead; the rest were in hospitals. I am not sure that a solution ever was found, but in any case it was not my business to seek a solution. My job, as usual, was to obtain photographs. I entered this time through a front window and found myself in the usual clutter of living room furniture, through which I picked my way with a flashlight. The mantelpiece was alive with photographs and, as I had no idea which was which, I seized them all. A dresser in the front bedroom held another gallery of photographs which I added to the collection. It was at this point, as I stood spraying my small light about the chamber, that I heard alarming sounds from the rear of the cottage. A door closed softly somewhere and light footsteps approached the front of the house. I shut off my light and tiptoed to the bedroom door, intending to make a quick getaway; but now the footsteps were in the dining room, only a few feet away. It was impossible to reach my front window without being caught. Then the footsteps stopped and someone stood in the doorway leading to the living room, breathing lightly. I realized that the intruder had become aware of *me*. Blackness lay all around us; I half expected a shot out of the dark. The silence was suddenly intolerable. Then, two minds functioned brilliantly at the same instant. Two flashlights split the darkness simultaneously; and there we were, almost face to face—the intruder and I. "*My God!*" he said.

He was Billy Black, the crack crime reporter from my own newspaper, seeking clues for a solution.

Not all my adventures were of this sort, however, and after a time I was permitted to write my own stories instead of telephoning them in for a rewrite man to mutilate. One of the most amusing of these assignments took me to the scene of an elopement. A boy and girl of tender years, well under the legal age for marriage, were the principals. The *Inter-Ocean* heard of the project from one of the bride's friends, who thought it would be nice to have a reporter at the wedding. Howey, too, thought it was a good idea. "Help them to elope, Starrett," he ordered, his single eye twinkling roguishly. "Go with them every step of the way until they go to bed. You needn't go to bed with them, but stay as long as possible. I want the best feature story we ever printed. Hop to it, kid!"

I managed to get them married before press time, and years

afterward I used the innocent episode as the basis for a hilarious short story called "Advice to the Lovelorn." In my fiction the bride's father pursued us all over town; in cabs, on streetcars, on merry-go-rounds, in everything but airplanes—and was ultimately slugged by the bridegroom—but the actuality was unaccompanied by pursuit or violence.

One memorable assignment, after I had won my spurs, took me on a tour of the notorious "Red Light District," then centered in and around Twenty-second Street. A conference of state's attorneys from all parts of Illinois was being held in Chicago. After the inevitable banquet Captain McCann, who was in charge of the police district in which the levee was located, took the down-state lawyers through the vice area. It was intended to be a sort of educational tour, I think, and certainly it was educational to me. I had never been inside a house of prostitution before, and to find myself in a dozen of them in the course of a single evening was astonishing and a little terrifying. Reporters from all the newspapers accompanied the party. We visited all the more famous or infamous houses, including the Everleigh Club, which was the most famous and infamous of them all. As all had been warned of our coming, they were on their best behavior.

We reached the Everleigh Club fairly late. Although I had heard much about the splendors of this notorious house of entertainment, it eclipsed all descriptions. It was flagrantly luxurious. The actual business of the place went on upstairs. Most of the first floor seemed to be one vast living room and was, in fact, two living rooms, for the club occupied two adjoining houses that had been knocked into one. Expensive rugs and draperies were everywhere, creating the impression of an extravagant stage setting. There were some good oil paintings on the walls, not all of them nudes. As for the company, it would have been possible to imagine one's self as attending a distinguished social event. The girls looked much like other girls, except that they were prettier and more vivacious; and I suppose they were more sophisticated. They were scantily but attractively gowned and I saw little open vulgarity. We sat around the huge room in little nooks and alcoves, each with a Sadie Thompson for company, and drank the excellent liquor served by the house. On the whole, the entertainment was only a little more startling than might have been witnessed at a musical comedy.

We may have lost a state's attorney or two at the Everleigh Club—I wouldn't be surprised—but, for myself, I found the young woman who sat with me quiet, ladylike, and garrulous on many subjects, all of them in good taste. She was an actress, she told me, stopping at the club until she got another part, which may for all I know have been true. And of course I met the famous Everleigh sisters, Ada and Minna. They greeted us at the front door; but, except that they were tall and gracious, I have forgotten them. All in all, it was a fascinating experience for Mother's eldest son; but a little unnerving, too. Somehow I have never been able to sentimentalize or romanticize prostitutes. On a number of other occasions connected with my work, I visited houses of ill fame, as we called them in print. To tell the truth, though, I was always a little leery of the peccable ladies.

On the whole, my career on the *Inter-Ocean* was not notable but it was instructive. It was hard and fast and constantly exciting. Above all, it was satisfyingly miscellaneous. I interviewed minor celebrities, was at the scene of major disasters, and met most of the criminal lawyers then practicing their arts. I knew hundreds of politicians, policemen, press agents, vaudeville hoofers, bell boys, con men, and simple householders unknown to me previously; and nearly every street and suburb held memories of crime and violence in which, in my own way, I had participated. In short, I thought then as I think now, that it was the only life for me, and I was happy to be part of it. Nevertheless, I liked best the moments of relaxation that followed the larger drama of the day or night; to sit around and listen to the tall tales of the other reporters when the long chores were over. Often the stories they told off the record were better than the same stories told in print. They were racier, more alive, less inhibited; and they reminded the narrators of past triumphs that were as the breath of life to me—reminiscences of a great Arabian Nights' entertainment that would never be written. I longed to write the book myself.

This feeling was stronger when I met the famous reporters of the time (most of them on other newspapers) whose exploits and escapades were legends of the profession. It was a day of great reporters, some of whom I knew and some of whom I worshipped from afar. Among my colleagues of the time who went on to further distinction were Junius Wood of the *Daily News*, Arthur James Pegler of the *American*, Chris Hagerty of the Associated Press, Charles Collins of the *Record-Herald*, and Walter Noble Burns, who was for a time at least on every newspaper in Chicago. Among those who already had achieved a national celebrity were John T. McCutcheon of the *Tribune* and Richard Henry Little of the *Record-Herald*, who seemed to me little less than demigods.

Dick Little, not long returned from the Russo–Japanese War, was a popular figure at the Press Club, which occasionally I visited although I was not a member; and one day, learning of my newest ambition, which was to be a war correspondent, he invited me to lunch with him. He was a friendly giant, six feet four in his socks, with peering eyes behind thick lenses, and he laid himself out to entertain me. It had been a broth of a war, he twinkled, and the Russians had taken care of all his creature needs with remarkable generosity; they had even supplied him with a spot of romance when romance was his fancy. I have no idea whether he invented the tales he told me for my benefit or lived them as related; but it was a stimulating recital that helped to complete my picture of a war correspondent as the most enviable of all reporters. My only fear, I said, was that all the wars would be over before I got a chance to see one. "Oh no," he said, "there'll always be a war going on some place—there always has been, hasn't there? Some day there'll be the damnedest war in Europe the world has ever known. I only hope I'll be around to see it."

More and more, newspaper work pleased me, and more and more I thought I would rather be a foreign correspondent than a drama critic. Dickens had been a court reporter, Henty and David Ker and Rudyard Kipling had been war correspondents. A number of books by Richard Harding Davis, perhaps the greatest war reporter of them all, were on my shelves. I began to build a small library of tales celebrating the romance of newspaper life: *The Street of Adventure*, by Philip Gibbs (Fleet Street, of course); Kipling's *The Light That Failed* (but I liked only the war-correspondent chapters); Davis's *Gallagher and Other Stories; The Stolen Story*, by Jesse Lynch Williams; and that tour de force of reportorial adventure, *The False Gods*, now long forgotten but still worth a dollar secondhand: its author was George Horace Lorimer. Of this muster of titles, Gibbs's *Street of Adventure* is still the best; perhaps it is the best novel about war correspondents ever written, although there are moments when I prefer *Routledge Rides Alone*, by Will Levington Comfort, which came along in 1910.

That first year knocked a lot of the dreaminess out of me; so much so that for a time I almost gave up my long dream of a literary career. I was content to be a newspaperman. Ultimately I thought my salary should be amended upward and made uncertain overtures to my superiors; but twelve dollars seemed to be the limit of Harry Daniel's generosity—some of the stars, he told me, received only twenty-five—and I decided to leave the *Inter-Ocean* for another newspaper. I mentioned my decision to Daniel and he said: "They'll ask you how much money you were making here and try to give you the same amount. Be sure to tell them you were getting nineteen dollars a week."

He was right again, and when the city editor of the *Daily News* asked me what previous experience I had, I replied, "One year on the *Inter-Ocean*."

When he asked me how much I had been getting, I said, "Nineteen dollars a week." "Very well," he said, "we'll give you nineteen to start."

I had picked the *News* because I was tired of the long night watches on a morning newspaper and thought I would like to change for a different set of hours. Lillian Hartsig, who was thinking of marrying me if I ever made enough money, also thought it was a good idea. And nineteen dollars a week looked pretty good, too.

IX

I CERTAINLY got a new set of hours. On the *Daily News* I reported for duty at seven o'clock in the morning instead of one o'clock in the afternoon, as I had done at the *Inter-Ocean*. It was an unholy hour that meant getting up at five-thirty, when the city was still dark, snatching a hasty breakfast at home if there was time (in the Loop if there was not), and making the long journey downtown on the Madison Street surface line. Somehow I was not too happy about the new arrangement. I detested early rising and, until I got used to it, wished heartily I had had sense enough to continue with a morning newspaper.

In those days the *Daily News* Building was in Wells Street near Madison, facing west. The historic old firetrap passed some years ago to make way for a parking lot. I think I shall always miss it, for it was an interesting, even fantastic pile, with an interior economy that its sober outward aspect belied. Its architect must have had a whimsical mind. Wherever one went inside, passing from room to room, there seemed to be either two steps up or two steps down. It was a miracle in such a place, dedicated as it was to hurry, that accidents were not of daily occurrence. To reach the local room, one passed from the street through a revolving door into the business office, strolled past a line of cages (behind the last of which lurked Miss Harriet Dewey, the cashier, who had advanced small sums to Eugene Field in his time), mounted the inevitable two steps to another level, and took the elevator to the fourth floor. I say *the* elevator, not *an* elevator, for there was only one; a leisurely, hesitant old cage operated by an ancient pensioner of the establishment who seemed to pull the car upward by dragging downward on a steel cable. At the fourth floor, which was the top floor, one emerged on an upper level, descended the steps (perhaps three) to a lower level, turned sharply left, and descended two more steps to one's objective. Something like that. It was a curiously roundabout way of reaching one's desk and, for a young man who habitually arrived late and in a hurry, a hazardous one.

The local or city room was a long, somewhat narrow, box overlooking the "El" in Wells Street, although that thoroughfare was then called Fifth Avenue. It was cluttered with desks and tables, most of the desks standing open and displaying battered old typewriters. The city editor and his assistant occupied adjoining desks near the door and thus were admirably placed to catch tardy reporters staggering in half asleep at seven-five or seven-seven o'clock. Just inside the entrance sat an impudent small boy with a time sheet—time clocks were put in later—and just beyond him was a single telephone booth. Incredible as it may seem today, there was only one. There were other telephones, to be sure, but they were scattered here and there on the important desks, the city editor having two. An open telephone on the wall communicated directly with a reporter at police headquarters; it was operated by a handle which one turned, as one turns a coffee mill. Off to one side bristled a curious arrangement of curving pipes or tubes out of which, from time to time, shot metal containers enclosed in leather, rather like large cartridges, carrying copy from the City Press Association, a mile away. During certain hours of the day the rush and thud of these arriving carriers was almost constant, and a dozen copy boys hurried the flimsies to the city desk. These were the hours when all the telephones seemed to ring at once, and all the typewriters clattered a wild dissonance, and the air was filled with staccato voices, and the room was alive with hurrying editors, reporters, copy boys, and printers; all intent on turning out the five o'clock edition at two-fifty-seven. Nothing could be busier than that long untidy room when it was really busy, but in the cold gray dawn of a winter morning, before the activities

Richard Harding Davis

Lieutenant Thomas Kennedy
Newspaperman and Poet, about 1917

of the day had begun, it could be one of the most forbidding rooms imaginable; yet for ten years I spent more waking hours within its walls than I did at home. And after the first few months it was not really forbidding. It was warm and friendly and, to a romantic newcomer, as full of drama and suspense as a detective novel.

Our publisher was the famous Chicagoan, Victor F. Lawson, whom we met occasionally in the corridors and less occasionally in the crowded little elevator, wearing his familiar brown derby with a flat top, and, of course, his familiar brown beard. He never addressed a word to me in ten years and I addressed no word to him. We were not even "ships that pass in the night and hail each other in passing." Almost equally aloof was Charles H. Dennis, later to be managing editor, but then in charge of the editorial page; an amiable gentleman who had been Eugene Field's editor and still dreamed of the good old days, in the almost secret little office in which he was even then meditating his reminiscences of the paper's most famous alumnus. In time these appeared as weekend features in the *Daily News* and subsequently they formed the basis of his well-known book, *Eugene Field's Creative Years*. Our managing editor was Charles M. Faye, familiarly known as "the Old Man." He was supposed to be an ogre, a circumstance known to him and so appealing to his sense of humor that sometimes he acted like one. But his ferocity was just so much window dressing. In point of fact, he was an old softie who looked at children through a mist of tears and made a fuss over puppies. I had a lot of trouble with Mr. Faye before I learned the truth about him; after that he was a pushover.

The great man of the *Daily News* was Henry Justin Smith, although perhaps not everybody then knew it. Henry Smith was news editor when I met him—a few steps above the city editor, a few steps below the managing editor; a sort of liaison officer between the two, with authority over copy and cable desks. A severe looking man, I thought, with whom it was unlikely I should ever feel impelled to fraternize. No adumbrations of our long and friendly relationship reached me as I shook hands with him perfunctorily on my first day; yet, of all the editors under whom I have worked, he was the one who influenced me most, whom I came most to like and admire, and whom I remember with the greatest affection. In appearance he was tall, dark, spectacled, and thin, with a neat black moustache and a prodigious Roman nose; a martinet and a fanatic, one would have said, and one would have been partly right. But he contrived also at times to look like Sargent's full-length, striding portrait of Robert Louis Stevenson, the one with Fanny lurking in the background. Perhaps it was his angularity and his eyes that created the resemblance. I once mentioned this to him and his response was one of his blasting grunts which might mean anything; but I think he was pleased. It was a liberty, however, and one didn't take liberties with Smith without carefully weighing his mood.

He was just as crusty as he looked, but his brusque exterior concealed a sensitive nature; it was the protective armor of an understanding and sympathetic human being. He was a stern man, with a scathing tongue, when sternness was in order; but although his reserve was tremendous, amounting almost to shyness, he occasionally let down the bars and one caught a fleeting glimpse of the kindliness and humor of the man within. Reporters said that he "worked hard to keep people from knowing what a good fellow he was." Also, I have heard him called "an essayist gone wrong," and possibly he *was* a man destined for higher effort than daily journalism; but he was a brilliant journalist, and he went on to enough literary celebrity, I think, to satisfy that facet of his ambition. In the first chapter of his *Deadlines* (a remarkably vivid account of one day in the old *Daily News* office I knew) he characterized himself very well, sometimes as news editor, sometimes in certain aspects of the reporter called Josslyn.

I got to know him best during the long afternoons I sometimes spent with him on the "dog watch"—after three o'clock, when the five-o'clock edition was off his mind and most of the staff had gone home. At such times, with old Clarence Bradley to read any emergency copy that might require reading, we held the fort together and I began to learn things about Smith. His sympathy for decent people was enormous and his contempt for the sort of citizens who made sensational headlines was beyond words—although frequently he found words with which to characterize them. Sometimes he staggered me with some revelation of his secret thought, and one day I learned his private opinion of the sort of journalism he despised. We were alone in the big local room, and perhaps I was looking a bit too pleased with myself. In any case, I think he liked me and wanted to correct any false heroics I might be harboring about the profession we both served. Lifting one sardonic eyebrow, he said: "Charlie, you've been in newspaper work long enough now to have an opinion. Suppose you were a respectable citizen and one night a young man rang your doorbell, saying he was a reporter for the Chicago *Daily News* come to interview you on a matter you believed to be none of his business—what would you do?"

Eager to give him the right answer, the answer he expected, I fumbled the ball. I replied, "Golly, H. J., I don't know. I suppose I'd invite him in, give him a drink, and tell him what he wanted to know, wouldn't you?"

"No," said Henry Justin Smith, with a strange smile. "I'd throw the-son-of-a-bitch out on his ear."

This was about the strongest language I ever heard Smith use, and I thought then, as I think now, that it was his considered opinion of certain aspects of the profession he adorned. But much as he deplored the shabbier aspects of journalism, which he called a "filthy trade," he was incorrigibly romantic about his craft, as readers of his several books are aware. He loved good writing, practiced it himself, and encouraged his reporters to practice it. His words of praise for a good job of writing were characteristically brief; sometimes they were mere grunts of commendation; but his young men worked hard for them and were sufficiently rewarded by his guarded admission that stories written with one's life blood were "not bad, not bad at all, kid!"

But I am ahead of my story. My colleagues on the reportorial staff included a number of young men who later came to prominence, notably Harry Hansen, Junius Wood, and Paul Scott Mowrer. A little later, as reporters came and went, there were Wallace Smith and Ben Hecht, while the rank and file at all times included so many good newspapermen that I should like to fill a page with their names. With particular affection I think of Bob Buck, Milton Fuessle, Charley Huff, Grover Sexton, Sam Lederer, Tony Czarnecki, Stanley Faye, Gene Morgan, Jimmy Butts, Jake Workman, Con Rourke, Russell Palmer, George Sheldon, Kent Sykes, George Briggs, and a dozen more. It was a good staff but some of its more picturesque members were yet to arrive. Carl Sandburg, Keith Preston, John Gunther, Robert J. Casey, and Howard Vincent O'Brien, with whom my name is sometimes mentioned when *Daily News* writers are discussed, were a little after my time, although I came to know them all as the years went on. Downstairs in the art room, which occasionally I visited, were three comic artists destined for later fame: Gaar Williams, Dan Fitzpatrick, and Ted Brown, then youngsters getting their start under Luther Bradley, one of the greatest cartoonists of the day. These are the names and figures that come most quickly to mind when I recall my years on the *Daily News*. These and Amy Leslie. For I have been unable to verify the rumor that one of the freckle-faced copy boys who responded to my call was named Westbrook Pegler.

Junius Wood, when I first knew him, was city hall reporter, a grouchy, companionable fellow with a quizzical eye, a sort of cat-that-swallowed-the-canary look which I came in time to understand. Nine times out of ten, it meant that he really had swallowed the canary. He went on to international celebrity as a foreign correspondent, an almost fabulous figure of newspaperdom, whose adventures (if he could have been persuaded to write them) would have been the most entertaining chronicle of our time. Six years my senior in years and experience, he was my friend from the beginning and looked after me, with sardonic good humor, until

90

the day we started for Mexico together in 1914. After that, to my regret, our daily paths crossed less often.

Harry Hansen came to the *News* a little after I did. It is his memory that I was the first person to greet him when he asked for a job. He had been having some difficulty reaching the city editor and I was able to tell him how to waylay the great man on his way to lunch. Hansen, too, went on to great days and deeds in World War I, and subsequently in the hectic 1920's became a noted figure in the Chicago "literary renascence." His book, *Midwest Portraits,* is one of the source books of that period. It was he, if anybody, who founded the famous Round Table at Schlogl's Restaurant, still celebrated in Chicago legend.

Milton Fuessle, whose desk for some years was next to mine, was a younger brother of Newton Fuessle, who had been a colleague on the *Inter-Ocean.* He was a good reporter and a sprightly stylist. Although he possessed all his brother's literary ambition, he had not, I think, his brother's talent. In after years he became a successful advertising executive, and it was he who created and popularized the word *halitosis* for the Listerine people.[1] Possibly this in itself is enough to make him immortal. His crony, Wallace Smith, came along a few years later and made a name for himself as reporter and draftsman, for in addition to his very considerable writing ability, he had a notable talent for fantastic illustration. He was a picturesque fellow who sometimes appeared in the local room in full riding regalia when he expected to go horsebacking later in the day. He died young, leaving a handful of vivid stories and sketches behind him. His book, *The Little Tigress,* is an admirable miscellany filled with the fire and dust of Mexico.

Of Ben Hecht it will be more convenient to speak in another chapter. He came to the *News* in 1914, seven years after I did, and remained after I had departed. When I first met him he was working for the *Journal* and courting Marie Armstrong, the *Journal*'s girl reporter, whom he subsequently married. It is not apt at this time to discuss the part he played in the literary renascence of the

---

1 He was the author of the famous line, "Often a bridesmaid, never a bride."

1920's; but it is not too much to say that there could have been no renascence without him. With his arrival on the *News*, that "incubator of Chicago authors," as Meyer Levin was later to call it, our front page took on a note of color that it had conspicuously lacked, and there was no doubt in anybody's mind that a genius dwelt among us. He sparked the entire staff to such feats of rhetoric that, for years, the columns of the *Daily News* contained some of the best-written stories in America.

I have spoken of Amy Leslie as a colleague, and so indeed she was, although I saw little of her at any time. Occasionally she visited the local room, floating in like an escaped circus tent, to borrow a typewriter for half an hour; and it was an epochal event to watch her pound out one of her flamboyant reviews. As dean of drama critics, her influence was enormous; she may easily have been the most famous woman in Chicago, always excepting Jane Addams. Although small of stature, with tiny hands and feet, she was almost preposterously fat. It was difficult to believe that she once had been a slim and alluring dancer on the New York stage and a key figure in the life of Stephen Crane; but such was the case, and for me it was part of her curious attraction. She was, perhaps, the most generous drama critic in America. She knew and liked everybody in the profession and wrote reams of florid copy about her favorites every week, piling up her weird adjectives and adverbs like an elephant piling logs. The reporters made fun of her turgid columns and overwhelming style, but the truth is that she attained some extraordinary effects, and may even have been a literary influence around the office. We all stood a little in awe of her; she had a sharp tongue when she cared to use it, and could polish off a brash youngster with the roughness of a drill sergeant. I scarcely knew her myself, but once when she borrowed my pencil to correct a page of her copy, I was almost swept out to sea by the intimacy and enormously flattered that the great legend known as Amy Leslie had condescended to speak with me.

That was my first speech with Miss Leslie. My second and last occurred some years afterward when I had left the *News* and was writing a monograph on Stephen Crane. Recalling her early association with Crane, the full story of which I did not then know, I ventured to ask her on the street one day whether she had preserved any letters from Stephen that she would allow me to read and use. She almost bit my head off as she turned me down. "Certainly not!" she snapped. Then she turned her back on me and sailed away like a ship under canvas, leaving me standing in Wells Street a little dazed. At that I came off better than Ashton Stevens, to whom (as a friend of all parties) I subsequently bequeathed the research. He made the mistake of bringing up the matter of Crane's letters in a private dining room somewhere, and was threatened with a wine bottle, he told me, for daring to mention the subject. It became clear to me at last that Miss Leslie had no intention of releasing Stephen's early letters, which undoubtedly she had, and about that time I dropped the inquiry for keeps. Probably I never shall know what secrets they contained, for I am confident that she destroyed them before she died.

As to the Eugene Field tradition in the office, it would be easy to make too much of it. Nobody in the local room remembered the poet (who had then been dead for twelve years) and reporters do not talk much about a paper's traditions, whatever they may think. To satisfy my private hero-worship, since I was not precisely intimate with Mr. Dennis, it was necessary to go to the composing room, where a few old printers held Field's memory in affection and even preserved fragments of his copy. Each, indeed, insisted that he possessed the last bit of copy Gene had written. They were glad to bring the precious relics down for my inspection, and one— Bill Butts—even scissored off two lines of the poet's "last manuscript" and made me a present of them. Miss Dewey, too, when she learned that I was interested in Field, gave me a note he once had written her, asking for a modest advance on his salary. I rapidly discovered, however, that not many *Daily News* men of 1907 were as romantic about Eugene Field as I who had just come to work there. George Ade and John McCutcheon were closer to them in spirit and had the advantage of being successful living celebrities, albeit neither had been connected with the *News* for many years.

It is increasingly difficult for me to recall the Chicago I knew in those early newspaper days. A great city changes too imperceptibly for one to be acutely conscious of its growth. Old buildings come down and new ones rise to take their places, but superficially the city is the same. There is no sharp line of division between the old order and the new that is marked at the moment of occurrence. Only in retrospect can one hope to establish the significant instant that closed one era forever and marked the beginning of another. And retrospect, I think, reveals an unsuspected truth—that change is not just a matter of taller buildings and longer boulevards, but a matter also of altered lives, and altered habits, and altered points of view, with which external aspects may have nothing in the world to do. Looking back, I have failed completely to isolate a single moment of change. On the external side, however, as far back as I can remember, Chicago has been in process of being torn down and built up; just possibly the old buildings I now miss as I stroll about the Loop are still there in some dimension I cannot hope to penetrate. Or possibly memory is a dimension.

For me, at any rate, the Masonic Temple still rears its twenty stories at State and Randolph streets, and it is still the tallest office building in the world. And the old Board of Trade building still stands at the head of LaSalle Street. And the old Grand Pacific Hotel still opens its genial doors at Clark and Jackson. And the old Ashland Block, and the old Monadnock building—but no, the old Monadnock still stands; I walked through its lower corridors only the other day. As I did so, an old whimsy of mine suddenly came back to me. It still seemed good. The building had seemed so big once, so filled with every possible convenience for its tenants —restaurants, clothing establishments, barber shops, tobacconists —that I used to imagine myself a fugitive from justice there, occupying a single small suite somewhere high up, sought far and

94

wide by the police but never venturing into the light of day where I might be apprehended. I had it all figured out. The cleaners and scrub women would be a hazard, of course, and some ingenuity would be required to avoid them at night; but I thought it could be done. It was one of my first story plots: a criminal living out the years of his life in such a city within walls.[2]

How the restaurants remain in memory! King's, in Fifth Avenue, now Wells Street, is the first that comes to mind. It stood almost directly across the street from the *Daily News* building and not too far from the *Record-Herald* office. It was a favorite rendezvous of newspapermen. Among the journalists who once frequented it were George Ade, Finley Peter Dunne, James O'Donnell Bennett, Bert Leston Taylor, Henry Barrett Chamberlin, and Henry Justin Smith; scores of others also patronized the famous establishment operated by Mrs. King. The fame of the place for good food at moderate prices was considerable, and Mrs. King's seven daughters were no less an attraction to the young men of the press. Legend has it that the midnight surprise at King's was a blend of chicken and sundry unknowns in a tasty cream sauce. "What's the name of this?" a benzine-perfumed printer is said to have asked one night. "Chicken à la King," wisecracked a visiting reporter; and there it was for all time. The price then was a quarter. That, I say, is the legend. I realize that other cities and other days claim chicken à la king for their own. However that may be, business flourished night and day at King's until the restaurant occupied two store-fronts. And all Mrs. King's seven daughters married newspapermen.

Up the street a little from the office, in the same block, was Schlogl's, that "ancient tavern," as Harry Hansen calls it in *Midwest Portraits*, which was to become so famous during the literary renascence of the twenties. It had been there since the great fire of 1871, a little German barroom and restaurant with a notable cuisine and a friendly clientele. Its first customers, I suppose, were the numerous Germans who flocked there, attracted by

2 I have since written the story.

its cooking. When I came to know it, in the early years of the century, it was a favorite haunt of politicians and lawyers, many of them from the city hall and county building, a few squares away. Newspapermen dropped in also, and gradually the wider celebrity of Schlogl's was established. As it was less than a hundred yards from the *Daily News* building, certain of the *News* men began to find it as attractive as it was convenient. But the place was popular with dozens of journalists of the neighborhood for years before it became the daily rendezvous of the *News* crowd and the weekly meeting place of half the literati of Chicago. Its national fame was still some years away, however, for the Round Table cannot be said to have been established until Harry Hansen became literary editor of the *News* and Keith Preston became its book columnist.

Another place where newspapermen went to drink was the Press Club, a huge upstairs room in Madison Street, where a tremendous poker game was always in progress. It was headquarters for afternoon newspaper reporters who were through for the day and morning newspaper reporters who had not yet reported for duty; and, of course, there was a bar attached. There was also a library that nobody ever used and a nest of couches that everybody used at some time or another. Oldsters of the profession, many of them retired, sometimes dropped in for a nap before dinner. I have seen Opie Read's giant frame stretched out there, and the slighter frame of Colonel William Lightfoot Visscher, the ex-pony express rider, who looked like a pint-size Buffalo Bill. Other celebrities one might meet at the Press Club were Stanley Waterloo, the novelist who wrote *The Story of Ab*, and the newspaper poets, Wilbur Nesbit and S. E. Kiser.

But the great man of the Press Club was Opie Read, and I am happy to have known him. In my opinion, he is one of the best of our second-line American novelists. My appreciation of him in a book called *Buried Cæsars* is possibly a little over-ardent, but it asserts many things I still believe about him. He was a regional novelist, before the phrase was invented, and a good one. Such books as *The Jucklins, Len Gansett, A Kentucky Colonel, My*

Young Master, The Wives of the Prophet, are important titles in the cavalcade of the American novel. Some day Read will be "discovered" and hailed as a significant figure in our literature. William Marion Reedy called him "the greatest 'almoster' this country ever had." He was a big, jovial man, over six feet in height, and with a coonskin cap would have looked like Daniel Boone. One of my finest memories is of "listening in" at a Press Club bull session while Opie regaled his cronies with tales of the Old South racier and better than any he ever wrote.

No less celebrities for me than these, however, were some of the working reporters I used to meet on assignments. Let me call the roll as I like to remember it: There was Walter Noble Burns, a remarkable crime reporter and a fine writer, who later wrote a number of popular books about the Old West. He was a handsome fellow who, inspired by the cup that cheers, could act and sound like Sherlock Holmes playing Hamlet—a thought that occurred to me one afternoon when I saw him pluck a decapitated head from a murdered body and apostrophize it as if it were the skull of Yorick. The police used to read his daily stories to get their clues. There was Charles MacArthur, who became famous as a playwright, and Hilding Johnson, his principal creation; for "Hildy Johnson" in Hecht and MacArthur's great newspaper comedy, *The Front Page*, was almost as much MacArthur's creation as God's. Citizens who believe that play to be exaggerated know nothing about the newspaper world of which I am writing, especially the Hearst newspaper world. Possibly it is the best newspaper drama ever written, and actually it is not greatly overdrawn. Poor Hildy! He died a few years after its great success and it was said that he had killed himself trying to live up to his stage reputation. I last saw him, laughing his head off, at the first night performance in Chicago. MacArthur was there, too, but keeping out of sight. He wore an old blue shirt and looked more like the fireman assigned to the house than one of the authors of the play.

There was Bob Casey of the *Journal*, later a noted war correspondent; but when I first knew him he was writing mystery stories for the pulps at a cent a word. And George Bernard Donlin of the *Record-Herald,* who doubled in book and drama criticism and went on to become editor of the *Dial.* I met him occasionally on highbrow assignments where his black ribboned prince-nez and his cane, to say nothing of his troublesome deafness, made him an outstanding figure. And Ben Atwell, the *Journal's* city editor, "the man God sent," as his more sentimental reporters used to call him when he was not listening. And good-natured Mary Synon, who in a few years was to write *The Good Red Bricks,* that fine saga of Chicago's West Side. And Carl Pratt and Larry Malm, the Gold Dust Twins of police headquarters, neither of whom ever wrote a line. They were "leg men" who poured their tales of crime and violence into a telephone, to be rewritten by somebody in the office. Their value to their newspapers was considerable, however, for the detectives at headquarters liked them and kept them informed about police activities. Pratt was a particular favorite because of his peculiar talents as an entertainer; he was an amazing clog dancer and an acceptable performer on the banjo. Sometimes he exercised both talents at once while an admiring circle of the city's finest clapped in unison, and the prisoners in the lockup downstairs wondered what the hell was going on.

And there was Arthur Pegler—Arthur James Pegler—male parent of the renowned Westbrook, who was unique in my experience. Readers of his hilarious short story, "That Hahnheimer Affair," know all they need to know about a Hearst newspaper office of the period. Pegler, who was born in England, was one of the great reporters of my time. I used to meet him in courtrooms and police stations, wherever life was to be seen at its damndest, and always he was the center of a group of admiring cubs listening avidly to his colorful conversation. To youngsters like myself, he was the beau ideal of a great newspaper reporter, for he wore a red carnation in his buttonhole, carried a cane, and was otherwise conspicuous. He was at his best, perhaps, after a jury had retired and a dozen of us were lounging in a deserted courtroom waiting for a verdict. Then he would yarn for hours on end, in his inimitable fashion, inventing as he went along, and I don't think I ever heard him repeat himself. His profanity, too, was notable without being malicious. He swore entirely for humorous effect. Pegler, for example, never was simply hungry; he was always "hungry as a bitch wolf," or something similarly arresting. His experiences ranged from big game hunting in Africa to garden parties at Windsor Castle. He was an exciting companion on assignment.

Three reporters whom I came to know at this time were hoping, like myself, to make literature their career. They were Tom Kennedy of the *Journal*, LeRoy Hennessy of the *American*, and Frank Honeywell of the City Press Association, whom I met frequently on assignments. Kennedy and Hennessy were both poets of promise, as I hoped I was, and it was our practice to read our latest stanzas to one another when we met. Their criticism of my verse was sharp but friendly, and I have much to thank them for.

These, then, were some of the men I knew and liked, and with whom I worked, in my first days on the *Daily News*. I could produce a longer list of men I knew and did *not* like; but why go into that?

X

M Y CITY EDITOR was Herbert Durand, who was called "Babe" by his intimates and "that bastard" by other members of the staff. Not all of them, perhaps, but enough of them to suggest a division of opinion about the man. Of course city editors are queer birds at best. Some of them are city editors because they were good reporters in their time; but a good reporter does not necessarily make a good city editor. It is not just a matter of experience; it is in large part a matter of temperament. Most good reporters that I have known preferred to remain reporters. When, as occasionally happened, they were kicked upstairs, they regretted the promotion and began to think wistfully of escape. Durand was not of that kind. He liked giving orders. He was friendly and affable when he happened to feel like it, and he was bitter and satirical when it was his mood to be disagreeable. When all this has been said, the fact remains that he got out a good newspaper. I got along with him after I came to understand that what he demanded was implicit obedience, and that he could be flattered if the flattery was not too flagrant. But Harry Smith saved my job a number of times in the first months of my association with the "Babe."

My first assignments on the *Daily News* were similar to my *Inter-Ocean* assignments. The drama of American life does not change. Its tragedies and its comedies were much the same fifty years ago as they are today. Generally speaking, headlines are for sinners, not for saints. Some people attract publicity; others shun it. There are thousands of good citizens of both sexes whose names never get into the papers, except occasionally in the obscure corners devoted to bowling scores and suburban marriages. I am as good a practicing cynic about the damned human race as the next man, but my hat is off to the innocent majority who live their lives so quietly that no whisper of their activities reaches editorial ears, or would command editorial attention if it did. Newspapers thrive on sensations and maudlin sentiment. News editors are not interested in the dull chronicles of blameless daily lives. Yet, by a curious paradox, it is for this blameless majority that the scandals are written. Sensitive newspapermen are aware of these ironies and resent the tawdry aspects of the profession they love.

For a time I was stationed at police headquarters and accompanied the police to scenes of crime and disaster. Presently, with my background of sensational reading to help out, I developed a detective-story mind and sometimes ventured to play detective on my own. I discovered clues that were discounted by the police, but which made readable copy for a day or two. It pleased me to trace the course of bullets fired by homicidal citizens at their wives or mistresses, and deduce that a murderer must have been firing from the bathtub or the top of a piano; that sort of thing. Competition among the crime reporters of the day was fierce and sometimes unscrupulous. If it occurred to us that a janitor's missing mother-in-

100

law might have been lured into the janitor's furnace, and the clues did not fit that attractive hypothesis, we helped the story to head-lines by discovering incinerated bones that somehow the police had missed. Until checked in the police laboratory, our mutton bones supplied those imperative thrills that good citizens look for over the breakfast coffee. As one never could tell what such reporters as Harry Friend and Al Baenziger of the Hearst papers might be inspired to discover at the scene of a murder, it was simple self-protection either to anticipate their discoveries or agree with them in advance on what was to be discovered. And it was not only reporters who faked clues; police and lawyers were almost equally resourceful. Nevertheless, a lot of the crime news that even then made Chicago outstanding was indubitably true. We had some astounding crimes and, for the most part, they were ably reported. We simply made them a little more entertaining between the event and its solution.

In time I was permitted to report the trials of some of our better murderers, and came to know the great criminal lawyers of the day, including the celebrated Clarence Darrow and the noto-rious Charles Erbstein; but my stories are well lost in the old files and may so remain for all of me. As a result of many courtroom experiences, however, years later I wrote a short story that has been widely praised as a satirically realistic picture of a murder trial: "The Eleventh Juror," indeed, has been called a "crime classic," and possibly it is my best short story. I have been told that the gimmick upon which the plot turns—the presence in a jury box of the actual murderer—is implausible, but I do not agree. It has happened once, to my knowledge, and may well have happened oftener.

I had much still to learn, also, about the simple mechanics of reporting, so to call them. Much of this primer aspect of my edu-cation came from Bob Buck, one of our bright and shining stars, whose methods were forthright and ingenious: I suppose no better police reporter ever gave Chicago's police department nervous in-digestion. My earliest memory of him as mentor involves a

101

gambling crusade which had been inaugurated by the newspapers, and was being supported by the police with no particular enthusiasm. In an old office building in LaSalle Street, rumor had it, a local gambler was operating a fabulous clip joint. It existed somewhere behind a false front, it was said, and it was Bob's duty and mine to find it. For some time we sleuthed about the corridors of the old firetrap, opening doors and closing them quickly, apologizing and explaining, listening for suspicious sounds. Then Buck said, "Let's get out of this," and we descended to the street. "You wait here," he ordered, and I saw him vanish into a corner drugstore.

In a few minutes he was back, greatly pleased with himself, and in ten minutes there was an uproar in the neighboring thoroughfares as the nearest fire engine house discharged its apparatus into the crowds. An engine, a hook-and-ladder truck, and a hose cart debouched into LaSalle Street; and, on the heels of three companies of instructed firemen, we two ranged through that dingy building in search of a fire that did not exist. Neither did the gambling joint; but that was not Buck's fault or that of his friend, the chief of the fire department.

In such fashion, or quite like it, I continued my career with the *Daily News* and, in time, began to see my name in print. Sometimes it was Charles V. E. Starrett and sometimes, more enigmatically, C. V. E. Starrett. Either way, it dazed and shook me so that I could scarcely read the masterpiece that followed the by-line. Somehow I did always manage to read it, however, and to find without difficulty—later, almost at a glance—the outrageous liberties taken with it by the copy readers. For, in spite of Howey's lyric satire, I still clung to the florid or melodramatic phrase and strove for sentence balance. Sentences like "The prisoner writhed in an ecstasy of fear" always came out. They used to give the copy readers a mild form of apoplexy.

One of my earliest assignments taught me something that all newspapermen know and appreciate but dare not count on—the

102

curious operations of chance that sometimes simplify a difficult task. Events that would seem too fortuitous in fiction, and would be rejected as implausible by a writer, occur so frequently in newspaper work that they have at times the appearance of divine intervention. A good reporter has been called a reporter who somehow contrives always to be at the right place at the right time; but the miracle, whatever it is, occurs for quite ordinary fellows, too. Sometimes it operates for cubs who don't know which way to turn, and blunder into successes without even taking thought. I can't date the episode I have in mind but the season must have been spring, for, as usual, a number of rivers in the Middle West had overflowed their banks and inundated a number of villages and towns. Even such largish cities as Logansport, Indiana, were partly under water; and first reports of the floods were sensational. As many as two hundred people were said to have lost their lives in Logansport, although later information cut down that figure. The story was being covered adequately enough by the Associated Press, but there was a special reason why a *Daily News* reporter had to be sent to the spot. As it happened, the wife of our telegraph editor was visiting in Logansport and had been trapped there by the flood. Sig Gruenstein, the editor in question, had heard nothing from his wife for several days and was so anxious, to put it mildly, as the hours passed and more and more alarming reports poured in from the flooded area, that he was unable to concentrate on his work. It was all Smith could do to keep Sig from starting off at once to find his wife.

To ease the situation, I was dispatched to the scene with only one instruction—to find Mrs. Gruenstein. I was to disregard every other aspect of the flood and to devote myself exclusively to her rescue. Gruenstein gave me all the information he could about his wife's conceivable whereabouts, and I hurried off on a mission which I regarded as all but hopeless. Finding one woman in a place the size of Logansport, while it was partly under water, seemed to me rather like seeking Dr. Livingstone in Africa. All wires were down and no trains were running. It was almost impossible to reach the Indiana city. I was told, however, that the Chicago *Tribune* was sending a special train of flat cars to Logansport, carrying a detachment of naval reservists and a flotilla of lifeboats; and that possibly I might be given a lift. So it turned out. When I found the *Tribune* special in the railroad yards and explained my mission, I was invited to accompany the expedition.

In time we reached the outskirts of Logansport, at which point the tracks were under water, and learned from citizens who watched us arrive that the whole business section of the city was flooded to a depth that made passage of small boats possible. With some difficulty our own boats were launched from the flatcars and I accompanied the first rescue party as far as the main street of the city, where I was disembarked on a point of high land not yet reached by the water. Small boats of every description were cruising through the district, bringing parties of refugees from the inundated sections to the higher areas; there was a suggestion of Venice in the lively scene. It was a puzzling situation for me. I never had been in Logansport before and didn't know one street from another. But I had to start some place and so, for a few moments, I stood quietly on my temporary platform—a stretch of sidewalk that was being used as a landing place—watching the arrival of refugees and considering my predicament. I had noted at once that a large flatboat was coming up the main street and heading for our landing. As it nosed in to the platform, a competent looking citizen sprang out and turned to assist a lady from the boat. When he had finished, I said to him courteously: "I'm Starrett of the Chicago *Daily News*. I'm sorry to be a nuisance at this time, but I don't know anything about your city. I was sent down here to find a Mrs. Sigmund Gruenstein and I don't know where to start. I wonder if you . . ."

I don't know what I was going to ask him. There was no reason to suppose he ever had heard of Mrs. Gruenstein; but then and there the miracle happened. He said, "Why, *this* is Mrs. Gruenstein," and indicated the woman who had just stepped upon the platform.

That is precisely what happened. Within a few minutes of my arrival in a strange city, on a mission that might have lasted for days, I had accomplished my task and was in touch with the missing woman. She told me she was all right, was with friends, and would communicate with her husband as soon as possible. With that, I left her. Presently I hired a small boat to take me back to the waiting special, and ultimately I reached a suburban railroad station and a telegraph office. I was of two minds about the development: whether to wait an hour or two before sending my tidings, or to announce success at once. It occurred to me that I would get more credit for the rescue if I waited a bit. In the end, though, my better nature triumphed and I sent my message that the lost had been found. Sig Gruenstein made more of the episode than it deserved. Harry Smith, too, professed to think that I had been very clever; but there was nothing clever about it. I found the lady by sheer accident or perhaps, as I have suggested, by some sort of miracle. I recall the episode because it is the most extraordinary example of beginner's luck in my experience.

While I am on the subject of floods, I am reminded that on another occasion I was sent to Cairo, Illinois, where several rivers were threatening their levees, and there met a handsome young lieutenant of infantry in charge of relief work. I can still see him striding the streets of the city, turning the heads of all the girls that passed. As he was friendly and helpful, I too admired him. When the emergency was over, however, I thought no more about him. Then, during one of the deadliest months of World War II, I read that Lieut. Gen. Simon Bolivar Buckner had died in action at Okinawa, and suddenly I remembered where I first had heard his name.

As soon as Smith came to see that I was a better feature writer than a reporter of spot news, he thought up some picturesque assignments for me. It was at his suggestion that I went driving through the North Shore townships with a popcorn and peanut vender. I discovered obscure cousins of Abraham Lincoln in obscure sections of the state, none of whom ever had seen their distinguished kinsman. I interviewed toy manufacturers and proprietors of bird hospitals; and innumerable arriving and departing explorers, opera stars, band leaders, Irish poets, and such-like celebrities.

One of my most successful features, which attained the front page, had an interesting sequel and made me the unwitting collaborator of an eminent woman of letters. For no good reason, except that babies are always popular, I was dispatched one morning to a small maternity hospital in North Clark Street to look into the statistics of adoption. The superintendent was away, but his son made me welcome and, in the course of our conversation, revealed an aspect of baby farming that seemed to me sensational. Quite casually he told me that every year maternity hospitals turned over hundreds of babies to women who palmed them off on their husbands as their own. These were women who were unable to bear children themselves, or who did not care to bear them, but were unwilling to confess the truth to their husbands. The infants were acquired, usually, while the husbands were out of town, I was told. I don't know how true this story is, or was, but it was a good story, and the young man permitted me to quote the hospital. Returning to the office, I wrote a story calculated to stir the press and pulpit of the nation. It began: "All over the city of Chicago, husbands are dandling babies on their knees believing them to be their own, but they were never more mistaken in their lives." Something like that. Then I plunged into the startling statistics and the reasons for the deception.

The story made the front page, in spite of stiff competition, and caused a lot of comment. It was picked up by other newspapers and went out over the country through the news services, for I had said that the situation was similar in other cities. On all sides there were denials and affirmations. Educators, clergymen, social workers, and others were interviewed on the subject, and letters poured into the office. After a time the uproar died away and I forgot the episode until one day, a number of years afterward, as I sat at luncheon in a fly-blown little restaurant in a small town in

106

southern Illinois. Looking around for something to read while I ate, I came upon an old number of the *Green Book*, a popular theatrical magazine, in which with mounting astonishment I read an article by the playwright, Margaret Mayo, about her successful comedy, *Baby Mine*, and the circumstances in which it had been written. It had been inspired, she said, by a newspaper article she had read in some eastern journal; then she quoted the first two paragraphs of my *Daily News* story verbatim.

My immediate reaction was one of pride; then I thought of all the money Miss Mayo had been making out of *Baby Mine*, and I began to be annoyed with her. Ultimately, a few weeks later, I wrote her a letter in which I told her that I was the author of the news story she had quoted and that I was delighted to think I had had a finger in her famous play. She replied with a charming letter that I still possess, thanking me tardily for my assistance. She said she never would forget the thrill that swept over her as she read my "wonderful lie"—that was what she called it—and that in the future she always would secretly regard me as her co-author. At this point, perhaps frightened by her reckless admission, she warned me that of course if I ever attempted to collect anything on the strength of my contribution, she would have to resist and possibly even take my claim to law. It was a clear warning not to take her letter too seriously; but it was a friendly letter, too, and I think she was genuinely grateful. As I had neither seen nor read the play, I obtained a copy from a secondhand shop and kept it for a number of years. It was unique in one respect. Under the words "By Margaret Mayo" I had written in ink "and Vincent Starrett."

Somewhere in this early period the First Ward Ball was held at the Coliseum for the last time in Chicago underworld history, and I was one of the many reporters on the scene. It would be difficult to describe adequately this fantastic carnival, which brought out, I suppose, every denizen of the levee who was not dead or dying. Every girl in the vice district, every madam, every pimp, every brothel keeper, every saloon keeper, was on hand for this most famous and most infamous event in the social life of the district.

107

Politicians were on hand in hundreds, including the two First Ward aldermen; the guests were as numerous as the underworld citizens. It was an annual event against which Chicago's reformers and clergymen had preached for years without avail, a device of Aldermen Coughlin ("Bathhouse John") and Kenna ("Hinky Dink") for enriching their campaign funds by about fifty thousand dollars at the Christmas season. The "Bath" had it one year and "Hinky Dink" the next. For years the peccable ladies of the levee had been forced to buy tickets at fifty cents each, and their masters to take large blocks. The orgy itself was like nothing so much as a "witches' Sabbath" scaled to the imaginative level of politicians and prostitutes. Champagne and other liquors flowed like tap water. In the gilded boxes sat notorious women of the underworld and renowned political figures of the municipality watching a floor show of unparalleled tawdriness. Hordes of dancers in bizarre costumes, drunk and sober, ebbed and flowed on the world's largest dance floor. They were overdressed and they were underdressed. As the evening advanced, the party grew wilder, and it was daylight before the cabs and coaches delivered the last of their fares to the houses from which they had emanated. It was the underworld's last grand fling, and I am glad to have seen it. In a way, it was a historic event.[1]

Not all that a newspaperman sees and hears gets into print, not immediately anyway. Really good stories sometimes are suppressed for anywhere from eight to eighty excellent reasons. But a good story is a good story whenever it is told. As I think back over my two decades of active newspaper work, I note with interest that it is the amusing side of my experience that I remember. I remember, for example, an excessively hot morning in the month of July, 1909, when it was my task to cover a meeting of the International Council of Women.

"Mrs. Grannis," I said to the first delegate I met, a sweet little old lady with no trace of humor in her alert little mind, "I have

[1] Apparently this was at Christmas, 1908.

108

heard it said that the Roman Catholics are somewhat reticent on this question of suffrage for women. Why do you suppose that is?" She nodded understandingly and her blue eyes lighted with an inner fire. She leaned toward me so that no one else would hear her reply. Her answer came in a sinister whisper. "The Vatican," she breathed fiercely, "the Vatican is behind it all." Then, leaning nearer still, in the deepest of confidential murmurs she added, "The Vatican, you know, is *terribly Roman Catholic!*"

Quaint little old lady! I think I ought to save her name for posterity. She was Mrs. Elizabeth B. Grannis of New York, and she was then eighty-three years of age. It is reasonable to suppose that she is no longer living. The accuracy of her final assertion is beyond challenge, I suppose. Thanks to Mrs. Grannis, I shall never forget the religion of the Vatican.

Possibly my greatest disappointment, poignant enough at the time, occurred in that hectic week when Theodore Roosevelt was hospitalized in Chicago. He was shot and wounded by a crank in Milwaukee on the night of October 14, 1912, and brought to Chicago's Mercy Hospital, where public attention was focussed on him as it had not been for years. Hourly bulletins on his condition were released by his physicians, but no one was allowed to see the patient. Of course every paper in town wanted a personal interview with the former president. Even a wan smile from him or a glimpse of him in his hospital bed would have been good for a headline. But the doctors were adamant and, indeed, there was a considerable police guard around the hospital to prevent journalistic (or other) intrusion. The number of reporters who surrounded the hospital also was large—possibly there were fifty. It was the big story of the month.

On the third day of the Colonel's incarceration, two boy scouts in the uniform of their benevolent order showed up at the office of the *Daily News*, clutching a roll of paper. They ran into me in the corridor and asked the way to the editor's office. I questioned them and it developed that their troop had passed resolutions of sympathy for Colonel Roosevelt and that they had a copy of the resolutions for the paper. They had also a second copy, possibly for another newspaper.

I had a sudden brain wave. "Wait a minute," I said, and hurried in to the city desk, where I talked earnestly to Durand for several minutes. Then I returned to the boys. "Boys," I said, "we're going out to the hospital to give these resolutions to Colonel Roosevelt, himself. Won't that be fine?"

They thought it would be great, so we piled into a taxicab and drove first to a costumer's where I rented a uniform as nearly like that of a scoutmaster as possible, put it on in the costumer's back room, and returned to the taxi. We drove rapidly to the hospital and disembarked at the main entrance. A dozen reporters from other newspapers were lounging on the hospital steps, and all of them recognized me at once. Their eyes popped. For a moment I wondered if I was about to be betrayed, but envious as they were of my enterprise, they were sporting about it. With my two boys beside me, and clutching the precious scroll in my hand, I ascended the steps through the writhing ranks of my colleagues and vanished from their view inside the building.

In point of fact, we actually reached the Colonel's floor and were starting for his room before we were caught and turned back. The dazed guards in the lower lobby had listened to my story about the resolutions and allowed us to pass. However, within a hundred feet of the sick room, we were apprehended and refused admittance, although the resolutions were accepted and taken in to the patient.

Somewhere in this Arabian Nights' existence occurred an amusing episode that I like to remember. One of my colleagues— I shall call him Chuck—is the central figure of the incident. A versatile fellow, he was not only a remarkable writer but a remarkable drunkard, as were too many of the brilliant newspapermen I have known. He was a clergyman's son, I believe, and so no doubt an excellent man to cover the Chicago advent of a world-famous evangelist. Anyway, he was assigned to the story and did very well with it. Then the city editor had an idea. *A prayer a day!* A neat little one-minute prayer especially composed by the evangelist for the Chicago *Daily News*, to be featured in a neat little box on the front page. Chuck was asked to arrange it, and arrange it he did. It was good publicity for the evangelist, who was not averse to publicity. In a little time, though, the good man tired of it, and Chuck had increasing difficulty getting his daily prayer in time for the main edition. At length Chuck suggested that he himself write the prayers as long as the campaign for souls lasted. The evangelist agreed, but stipulated that Chuck must bring him the copy for approval before it appeared in print. This arrangement lasted for another week, and Chuck wrote some really inspiring one-minute prayers which duly appeared on the front page under the evangelist's signature.

But one afternoon—it could have been predicted—Chuck couldn't find the keys of his typewriter. He reeled over to my desk. "Lemme dictate this damn thing, will ya?" he pleaded.

"All right," I said, "go ahead," and wheeled a sheet of paper into my typewriter. "What's the text?" I asked, bouncing my thumb on the space bar.

Chuck was leaning over me, pale and heaving. "Hope!" he gulped. "H-hope!"

Obediently I wrote down "Hope!" and looked up. Chuck was clinging to the desk with both hands. "I've gotta get out of this," he said, and reeled out of the local room, leaving his problem in my hands.

That ended the one-minute prayers. I did my best for Chuck. I wrote the prayer on "Hope!" myself, and it even appeared in the paper. But, for some reason, the series was discontinued the next day.

Not all the tales and anecdotes in this chapter are memories of my first year on the *Daily News*. I have jumped around a bit, looking forward and backward at the same time, seeking to bring together in one group certain experiences on the lighter side without reference to chronology. They are typical of the sort of life I lived for some years and serve to introduce some of my colleagues, and to reproduce somewhat of the atmosphere of that grand old rag in the early days of the century.

It will have been noted that I have said little about crime. I might have written much; but too much already has been written about crime in Chicago, and usually as if it were uniquely a Chicago phenomenon. This is not to say that Chicago's reputation is undeserved; it is richly deserved. There has always been crime in Chicago, as in all big cities, but for the most part it exists in a sort of fourth dimension as far as decent citizens are concerned. You can find it if you go looking for it, of course—you can find it fast. But mostly you read about it in the newspapers. Often enough during my reportorial days I crossed its trail, so to speak, but always after the fact. After more than sixty years' experience in the "wickedest city in the world," I never have seen a murder. This is my answer to those foreign friends who never fail to look me over humorously for bullet holes as soon as I disclose my residence. The gangsters one reads about exist, all right; they kill exactly as reported. But unless you visit places frequented by gangsters, usually you don't meet gangsters. Even lesser crimes are inconspicuously committed. Sometimes, reading late in my book room, I catch rumors of the city's perpetual crime wave: revolver shots in the distance or cars racing wildly through the night to an accompaniment of such fusillades; and then I know that for a moment I have been close to the phenomenon itself. But for the most part, even that is only a sort of game played by the police and minor hoodlums to keep their hand in. I suspect they enjoy it equally.

To resume the chronological narrative, after a fashion, when I had worked at my new job for about a year at the stipulated salary of nineteen dollars a week, I began to wonder if I would ever get a raise. I have never been much good at asking for more money but, as it happened, I had no occasion to do so at this time. A little after three o'clock, one afternoon, as I loitered at my typewriter, heavy footsteps approached and I looked up to see the managing editor himself bearing down on me. Quick panic swept over me. My first thought was that I had erred unforgivably and was about to be fired. My nineteen dollars began to look more attractive.

The Old Man stopped beside me and began to stutter in his usual unnerving way. It seemed a full minute before his shattering revelation came out: "How m-m-m-much m-m-m-money are we p-p-p-paying you now, Mr. Starrett?"

I said quickly, "Nineteen dollars a week, Mr. Faye," and was prepared, if necessary, to take a cut. He said, "Hereafter it will b-b-b-be twenty-five dollars, Mr. Starrett," and strode off without waiting to hear my stumbling thanks.

I think this was the only time I ever received a raise in salary without having to battle for it. But it was enough, just barely enough, for me to marry on. I resumed my campaign against the red-haired piano player, which never had seriously lagged, and at length persuaded her that we could make a go of it. Even so, it was the hot summer of 1909 before Lillian Hartsig and I were married. Although the ceremony was at night, Durand good-naturedly gave me the whole day off to get ready. My colleagues also took the tidings without shock, but warned me that I would live to regret my rash action.

"You won't have a dime left over for books, of course," said Harry Hansen judicially.

"Poor old Charlie!" said Dick Hebb, the assistant city editor. "He'll never again lie diagonally in bed."

"If she plays the piano," said Smith, a musician himself, "she'll be just what the doctor ordered."

XI

DURING MY TEN YEARS with the *Daily News* inevitably I witnessed several major events in human history and hundreds of minor events, and wrote copiously about them all. That first writing must have acted as catharsis, for I find that my recollection of them is a bit nebulous; even the clearest memories are beginning to fade out like pictures on a screen. On the whole I was not a particularly good reporter, for the comic element of American life interested me more than the sober facts I was sent to obtain. On the other hand, the fact remains that I lasted for ten years on an important newspaper, so I may have been as good as the average. Not all my days were passed as hilariously as the previous chapter might suggest. Serious matters also engaged me from time to time, some memorable and terrible, some as dull and uninspiring as the trips I made perhaps once a month to Springfield, when the legislature was in session. Or as dull as the campaign trips I sometimes was called on to make with political barnstormers. These last were, perhaps, the assignments I detested most, for I loathed politics and politicians with an instinctive hatred that, I am happy to report, still flourishes.

Election-night vigils were boring, too, I thought. Those were the times when everybody on the paper worked late. My clearest memory is of that night in 1916, when we all went to bed believing Charles Evans Hughes had been elected president of the United States, and woke in the morning to find that we had been mistaken. All the newspapers had made plans to announce the successful candidate by means of whistles, searchlights, and other extra-curricular devices. The *Daily News* had installed a searchlight on a tall building somewhere in the Loop, which was to swing its beam horizontally across the city if Hughes was elected and project it up and down vertically, like an animated weather chart, if Wilson was the victor. The Hearst newspapers announced similar plans that called for just the opposite procedure; and one or two of the other newspapers worked out ingenious code messages to be delivered by screaming sirens. These, too, were in conflict; so that, when the big moment arrived, all the whistles and searchlights went into action at once, each telling a different story. Bewildered citizens resorted to the telephone and, until well into the morning hours of November 8, I assured callers that Mr. Hughes had been elected.

Memories of the pioneer flyers are numerous. The first aviator I ever knew was Walter Brookins, a daredevil who visited Chicago

114

with a crate-like biplane about 1909. He was a genial lad with something of Tom Sawyer about him. Later I covered the first air meets at the old Hawthorne Race Track and talked with three great figures of American aviation, Wilbur and Orville Wright and Glenn Curtiss. Those were the days when it was unbelievable for a flyer to take his plane a few feet into the air and fly a few times around a circular track. After such a display, hordes of people who had paid their way into the grounds would go home satisfied that they had witnessed a miracle. And I helped to cover the first important air meet in Chicago (at Grant Park) in 1911, where at least two of the early flyers—Bill Badger and St. Croix Johnston— were killed. One of my assignments at that time was to persuade one of the aviators to take me up with him. Lincoln Beachey, the most colorful and reckless of them all, was suggested and, if Beachey had been willing, I suppose I would have made the flight. Happily for me—I was scared stiff—he flatly refused to take me, and that was that.

I was also one of the army of reporters who helped to cover the *Eastland* disaster. The now famous excursion liner turned over at her dock at the Clark Street bridge on the morning of July 24, 1915, and drowned eight hundred and twelve men, women, and children as they were about to depart for a holiday on the lake. It was a major catastrophe, and probably every reporter on the *News* helped with the story before the long day was over. As it happened, our librarian, McCausland, was an eye witness of the event. Coming down to the office on the "El," he happened to look out of the window as his train crossed the river, at the moment the overloaded liner turned over on her side. Instead of leaving the train and hurrying to the scene, as many newspapermen might have done, Mac very sensibly continued to the Madison Street station and burst into our office with the first news of the disaster.

Throughout most of the morning I was kept at the office, writing accounts of the tragedy as they were telephoned in by reporters on the scene; in the early afternoon I too was dispatched to the spot, and for a time watched the grisly work of rescue. It was an

115

appalling spectacle. By the time I reached the bridge, a hole had been cut or burned through the vessel's exposed side, and the bodies of victims were being hoisted through the aperture. Rows of drowned bodies lay along the dock below the bridge, and there were other rows along the sidewalk at bridge level. I suppose a hundred were on view when I reached the scene. As new bodies were removed from the interior of the capsized steamer, they were hurried up the steps to street level and examined by physicians, a corps of whom stood at the head of the steps, for signs of life. I remember the methodical competence of these men as their fore-fingers pushed up the closed eyelids. A glance appeared to be all they needed to say whether a spark of life remained. Some few of the victims were turned over to other rescue workers or hurried away in waiting ambulances. But, for the most part, the report of the examining doctors was a monotonous repetition—"Gone," "Gone," "Gone!" It was the most gruesome event in my newspaper career.

Much as I disliked politics, I was nevertheless pleased to be one of the *News* men selected to cover the Republican National Convention of 1912, which was held in Chicago. That was the convention that nominated William Howard Taft, and which I "bolted" with Theodore Roosevelt, without instructions from the office. The Colonel was one of my personal gods just then, as he was one of the personal gods of Harry Hansen, and we both accompanied him when he shook the dust of the Coliseum from his feet and called his own convention to order in Orchestra Hall. This, as history records, was the beginning (as it was also perhaps the end) of the Bull Moose party. All but forgetting our duties, in our enthusiasm for our hero, Hansen and I grabbed seats in the front row and cheered as wildly as any of the delegates. The Colonel read his acceptance speech from a manuscript in his usual belligerent fashion, and threw it away, a page at a time, until the platform was littered with little squares of paper. There must have been some avid collectors in his audience, for long before the historic event was at end, that is, while the Colonel was still reading, a dozen souvenir hunters were scrambling about the speaker's legs for the sudden windfall. He didn't seem to mind, however, and when he reached the words, "I accept the nomination," the demonstration must have been heard for miles.

Incidentally, it was at the Republican convention (before I deserted it) that I first met Richard Harding Davis, who also had long been a hero of mine. I recognized him at once from his portraits, as he stood near me on the convention floor close to the platform. We were both watching the antics of Laurence Y. Sherman, one of the delegates, later a senator from Illinois, who was shouting at the chairman in an effort to gain attention. "Funny old boy, isn't he?" smiled R. H. D. at last; and with a start I realized that my idol was speaking to me. I was so proud of the attention that for hours I went around in a daze. I was to meet him again in 1914, and to become his friend, but the memory of that first meeting has remained with me. Davis had that effect on people who admired him and whom he chose to like.

Another of my heroes about this time was Dr. Frederick A. Cook, around whom still rages the North Pole controversy inaugurated by his claim of discovery. I met and interviewed him when he came to Chicago after the publication of his book, *My Attainment of the Pole*, and I never met a more satisfying celebrity in my life, or one who bore himself with greater dignity in humiliating circumstances. I have never wavered in my belief that he reached the Pole before Admiral Peary; at least that he thought he had done so.

For the rest, I have visited all the great cities of America where crime and disaster and human error or folly have made newspaper headlines. I have seen men go to pieces on the witness stand and women weep as they were led away to prison. Sometimes I think I have seen everything and seen it too often. It is pleasanter to remember the friends I made in the daily round. Two men come quickly to mind—Clarence Darrow and Kenesaw Mountain Landis. The details of their courtroom dramas may be found in

117

other books; I have only personal impressions to report. But of this I am certain: two more dramatic characters never existed together in the same city, for the entertainment and delight of newspapermen.

Judge Landis was already on the federal bench when I came to know him, and already a favorite with the headline hunters; for was he not the man who had fined John D. Rockefeller twenty-nine million dollars within recent memory? He was made to order for the newspapers, a dependable source of copy at any moment of the day or night. By the common people, so to call them, he was idolized long before he became high commissioner of baseball. They went to him with their problems as, in more intimate matters, they might have gone to their doctor or their priest. His advice was sought by simple people on simple matters because for thousands of newspaper readers he had become a shining symbol of honesty and justice. For this, in large part, the newspapers were responsible; and for this and other reasons he was friendly to newspapermen.

I remember him best in his unbuttoned moments, in the intervals of a long trial or after the day's grind was over, when he foregathered with the reporters for an exchange of banter. At such times the tales he told were usually off the record. His stories were excellent and his manner of telling them was a delight, for he was a profane man in private converse and his profanity was picturesque and humorous. One memorable and circumstantial narrative had to do with a woman who had given birth to a child in his courtroom. He pretended to think she had done it solely to worry *him*, and described her offense in lurid terms, although it was clear that he had helped notably in the accouchement. Swearing was almost second nature with him; I think he often swore without realizing it. Once I saw him emerging from the old Grand Opera House in Clark Street with his wife, as the theater was discharging its audience. It was raining hard and the eminent jurist was trying to get a taxi. Ultimately, he got one; but as Mrs. Landis dashed for the curb she skidded on the wet pavement and almost fell. Happily, I was near enough to hear his words. "Be careful,

118

my dear," he said with tender anxiety as he steadied her, "or you'll
break your God-damned neck!"

In court it was his jovial practice to liven up a dull trial for the
benefit of the reporters by taking over the cross-examination of a
witness himself—a practice that frightened attorneys on both sides
of the case almost equally.

He was a terror to witnesses who had something to conceal. I
have seen lawbreakers cringe from his ferocious grin of mock
camaraderie as he probed for whatever it was he wanted to elicit
from them. Once he interrupted a solemn session of court in a
case I have forgotten to call me up to the bench. I wondered what
misdemeanor I had been guilty of to warrant this public exposure;
but he was only bored by the proceedings, for when I stood beside
him, he leaned over and whispered that his brother Fred was in
town. "That's the one that writes books, you know," he added.
"You appear to be as sick of this trial as I am. Why don't you look
him up? His favorite bar is the Auditorium and his favorite author
is Conan Doyle." It was by such drolleries, so to call them, that he
endeared himself to reporters.

It was pleasant, also, to be on easy terms with Clarence Darrow, the most celebrated criminal lawyer of his day. He, too, was
a magnificent storyteller. He was also a tremendous reader and
our conversations, when we met in a courtroom, were likely to be
about the books we had been reading. His literary taste was sound
but a little on the gloomy side, I thought. His favorite twentieth-
century novels were Maugham's *Of Human Bondage* and Butler's
The Way of All Flesh. It was once my unnecessary task to introduce him to a Chicago audience when he lectured on books, but I
did not stand long between Clarence Darrow and his admirers,
who filled the old Studebaker Theater.

I remember our last meeting. A few years before his death I
bumped into him in the Hotel Sherman and heard his fine voice
for the last time. We both happened to step into the same elevator,
which was already crowded, and as it shot upward he suddenly
recognized me. His booming voice filled the narrow compartment.

119

"Well! Hello, Starrett! Nice to see you." And then, quizzically, while the little audience of strangers pricked up its ears, "Still writing detective stories?"

Faintly embarrassed, I answered: "Still at it, Mr. Darrow. You don't mean to say you haven't read my latest!"

"Never read a detective story in my life," he trumpeted. "I'd read yours if I read anybody's, Starrett."

"Why not?" I asked, and the big voice boomed: "They don't tell the truth. I never met a detective who was honest, did you?"

I think I replied that his experience of detectives had been greater than mine, or something of the sort, and then one or the other of us left the elevator. I never saw him again.

Other names occur and crowd one another for position. I think of James Hamilton Lewis, lawyer, soldier, United States senator from Illinois, and possessor of the most luxuriant sunburst of carefully trimmed pink whiskers in the country; of Carter H. Harrison, the younger, five-term mayor of Chicago, a scholar and a gentleman and withal one of the ablest politicians of his day; of Harold F. McCormick, who brought grand opera to Chicago and made up the deficits from his own pocket; of Jane Addams of Hull House, first lady of Chicago's underprivileged millions; and Mrs. Potter Palmer, first lady of Chicago's four hundred; of Charles A. Comiskey and his Hitless Wonders, the Chicago White Sox; of George Wellington Streeter, old Cap Streeter, the belligerent squatter who owned the Chicago lake front but couldn't prove it. Clearly, it was a good day to be alive, in Chicago, when these paladins, these paragons, these paradoxes, these almost legendary figures were performing their appointed tasks and filling the columns of the newspapers: when Frederick Stock was conducting the Chicago Symphony, when Frank Lloyd Wright and Daniel H. Burnham were planning and building the "Chicago Beautiful," and Mrs. Starrett's School for Girls was embarrassing your reporter with unfounded rumors of a split personality. Dear old lady, we tried one day to figure out a possible relationship and failed; but with what affection do I remember her. Nowadays when women of a certain age approach me with moist eyes and murmur, "Oh, Mr. Starrett, I knew your dear mother!" I always know what they mean and am sorry to have to disappoint them.

Of visiting celebrities whom it was my pleasure or my duty to meet, there were so many that I could fill a page with their names. Somewhere in the files of the *Daily News* are the words I wrote about them half a century ago; and there they may remain. I remember only that Victor Herbert was short and stout; that William J. Locke was tall and thin; that Gilbert Parker was dignified, bearded and amiable; that Alfred Noyes was reserved and cautious; that Hopkinson Smith was dull and pompous; that William Watson was shy and apprehensive; that Lord Kitchener looked precisely like his portrait; that once I accepted one of Gertrude Atherton's cigarettes. Once upon a time I met these famous men and women, reported something they said to me, and then forgot them. It is discouraging not to be able to recall a single epigram but, as most of them were writers, I can only suppose they saved their epigrams for their books. Authors do not recklessly toss about their best lines just to amuse newspaper reporters. The case of Mrs. Atherton remains in memory because she was the first woman I ever had seen smoking a cigarette. When she lit up, I instantly suspected her of every other sin in the calendar. It was a letdown when her cigarettes turned out to be cubebs.

Most conspicuous of the many writers I met and interviewed in those early years, I suppose, was Arnold Bennett. This diffident, rather suspicious man came to Chicago with his publisher, George H. Doran, and I met them at the LaSalle Street Station. I had read little by Bennett at this time, but was familiar with the legend of his meticulous attention to detail in his novels. Immediately I saw that he was inquisitive about the details of life, too. As he came down the central stairway from the train shed, his heavy-lidded eyes were everywhere at once. Nothing escaped the attention of that restless gaze. He even paused halfway down the flight to pick up a cigarette box that somebody had discarded because it was empty. When he had confirmed this circumstance, the novelist tossed it away, in his turn, and passed out of the station into the arms of his enemies, the American reporters. Later I met him again at the Press Club—or perhaps the Cliff Dwellers—where a luncheon had been arranged in his honor. He had accepted the invitation only on the condition that he would not be asked to speak, but even so he seemed completely bored by the whole performance. He ate stolidly, answered an occasional question from those who sat on either side of him, and smiled a hard smile in which there was no mirth when the chairman announced that Mr. Somebody would deliver the address Mr. Bennett would have delivered if Mr. Bennett would have delivered an address. There were three such speeches, in point of fact, by three different members of the club who believed themselves to be wits; but Bennett was not amused. It was a distinguished gathering, however; I suppose every living member of the club was on hand to greet the famous author, and there was a score of important guests. Some of them had brought books to be signed, among them Karl Edwin Harriman and myself. I had brought only one, but Harriman had brought close to a dozen. With the others, we sent our books down the long table with our cards in them, and for a time the English novelist toiled grimly. At length he paused for a sharper look at one of the cards. His eye brightened, an authentic smile twisted his lips under his ragged moustache, and he wrote: "For Karl Edwin Harriman, who is getting to be an old friend."

It was in 1913, I think, that the Immortals came to town; I mean the members of the National Institute of Arts and Letters. A series of talks had been arranged, and half a dozen of the visitors spoke to a packed house in Fullerton Hall, at the Art Institute. In anticipation of this event, I had been dispatched to an outlying station to meet the incoming gods. There was only one I really cared greatly to meet and finally I met him. Adventuring through the coaches, I peered in at the open door of a compartment and there he sat, his perfect Sherlockian profile etched against the windowpane. He was looking thoughtfully out of the window, but

122

turned his head when I spoke. "Good morning, Mr. Gillette," I said; and added cleverly, for I was young and clever, "A penny for your thoughts."

His eyes lighted and his face crinkled. "You would like to know my thoughts, young man?" said William Gillette. "I was thinking what a delightful paradox it would be if this train were to roll down the embankment and all the Immortals were to be killed!"

It was my first meeting with William Gillette but not, I am happy to remember, my last. Although his comment on the Immortals is the best story I have to tell about Gillette, we talked for some time as the train roared toward Chicago, for I had many questions to ask about his famous play, *Sherlock Holmes*, which I had seen as a boy and from which I never quite recovered. One of the questions was about the cigar episode in the Stepney gas chamber. Old inhabitants will remember the incident: Sherlock Holmes, trapped in the underground chamber by Moriarty's hoodlums, calmly lights a cigar, taunts his captors with their ineptitude, then suddenly smashes the lamp and plunges the stage into darkness—darkness unrelieved except for the single spot of light from the detective's cigar. "Follow the cigar!" shout the hoodlums (or words to that effect), and then they charge down upon the spot of stationary light only to find the cigar on a window ledge, where the wily detective had placed it before effecting his departure.

This charming bit of melodrama had pleased me a great deal, but I had often wondered what would happen to the play if the cigar should happen to go out. I asked Gillette about this and he said, "I'm always careful to puff it up into a fine red glow—perhaps you've noticed that—and I can't recall that it ever did go out. However, the possibility has not escaped me. There's always a stagehand close by in the wings, puffing like mad at a second cigar." Years later, when I recalled this conversation to my favorite actor, he added a postscript: "We've improved on that business since then. I still light and smoke a cigar at the proper moment; but it is a small flashlight that I leave on the window ledge."

Particularly do I recall with pleasure now, in sadder cultural days, meetings with the singing stars of Chicago's first grand opera company. The arrival of each new foreign songbird—I am thinking only of the women—was good for a sparkling feature story. I remember Mary Garden best, possibly because I once helped to remove (or put on, I have forgotten which) her blue velvet spats. I have no sprightly anecdotes to tell about her; but there must be many who, like myself, remember her Dance of the Seven Veils in Strauss's *Salomé* almost as if it were a personal adventure. That was a sensational event, for it was supposed to be a daring presentation and certainly it was a topic of conversation for weeks after the fact. It stirred up the old controversy about morality and art as perhaps no cultural innovation has done before or has done since. Advance publicity had been so thorough and so comprehensive that the chief of police, then Colonel Leroy T. Steward, attended the first performance and branded Miss Garden's symbolic dance as disgusting. She "wallowed around like a cat in a bed of catnip," he said. "If the same show were produced on Halsted Street, it would be called cheap," said the Colonel, "but over at the Auditorium it's called art."

Some of the critics felt that way about it, too, although their comment was less forthright. Clergymen thundered their most sulphurous clichés, and the head of the Chicago Law and Order League demanded the suppression of the opera. He wished Miss Garden would come to see him, he said, that he might try to reform her. Miss Garden, no timid artist, responded with proper spirit, and the row stole the headlines for days. All this uproar centered about the star's remarkable dance, which was certainly as unrestrained as Oscar Wilde himself could have wished.

I managed to be present at that notorious first performance on November 25, 1910, and decided that, when an attractive woman dances that kind of dance, it is *always* Art. Is it too farfetched to think of this joyous episode as the first note of revolt in Chicago's cultural awakening that flowered a few years later in the literary "renaissance" of the 1920's?

124

As I look back on my *Daily News* days, however, it is not these moments of association with celebrities that I sometimes wish I might live over again. Interesting as they were, they were less interesting than the leisurely afternoons I spent in the office after the main edition of the day had reached the news stands. By three o'clock most of the staff had departed, the domesticated reporters to their homes, the more turbulent spirits to their favorite barrooms, and the quietly competent Smith had taken over the "dog watch" with a couple of copy readers and a brace of reporters for possible emergencies. It was extraordinary how the atmosphere of the place changed about that hour. Thereafter, until five-thirty, we who remained were more or less free to pass the time as we wished. Then the veteran Clarence Bradley, chief of the copy desk and a scholar of sorts, might lose himself in a French novel (which he read in the original) while Smith and Fred Chappell, the make-up man, discussed the latest three-hundred-page pamphlet by H. G. Wells. Then the reporters thus kept in after school might read or write as they pleased. It pleased some of us to read Stephen Crane and Arthur Machen—that was I—and others to toil at literary masterpieces aimed at the *Saturday Evening Post*, which then cost only a nickel and paid its contributors five cents a word.

With the coming of Ben Hecht, in 1914, I acquired a colleague after my own heart, and it is fair to say that for a time we influenced each other's thinking not a little. Hecht, too, preferred the quiet afternoons to the busy mornings, for he was just then beginning to write the poems and short stories that were soon to mark the appearance of a new and exciting talent. Not to disparage his later novels and stories, those that followed *Erik Dorn*, some of his finest work was produced at this time. He was a prodigious worker and the clatter of his typewriter in a remote corner of the local room was almost as constant as a telegraph key. Sometimes, tiring of manual labor, he wrote his stories (his poems always) on yellow copy paper with a thick black pencil; and once, at least, possibly to build the legend of Ben Hecht, he brought down a gorgeous sofa pillow and sat on the floor in his private corner to write his colorful lines and stanzas in, as it were, a proper milieu.

Smith, too, was meditating his books at this time and possibly had begun to write them. When I learned that he had been commissioned to write a series of articles for a national magazine, my awe of him increased. He was unfailingly sympathetic to our ambitions, Hecht's and mine, and sometimes paused beside us to ask what we were writing. Our conversations at such times were literary as all get-out; and the genial side of Harry Smith was never more delightful than at such moments. I recall a brief but typical bit of dialogue. Said Hecht recklessly: "Nothing like it has ever been written before!" He was speaking of something of his own.

"Published," corrected Smith, with a grim chuckle. "You mean nothing like it has ever been published before. Who can say what has been *written*, with Charlie Starrett and me pounding away all these years?"

But it was on the subject of other people's books that we argued most heatedly; we seldom agreed completely about an author's merits. Each had his own stable of favorites. Burton Rascoe, in *A Bookman's Daybook*, asserts that at this time I "educated the whole prolific local room" of the *Daily News*, which, although a flattering assertion, is recklessly inaccurate. I know what he means, however. At that time I did introduce a number of the reporters—those who were able to read—to books and authors they never had heard of, and so possibly broadened their horizons for a time at least; and undoubtedly I started some very unlikely fellows *collecting* books in the bibliophilic sense. My desk was usually islanded with little heaps of exciting new discoveries, and, when asked about them, I probably became enthusiastic. There was a time, I think, when I had half the staff reading Arthur Symons and James Huneker, and even George Moore. But to suggest that I educated such men as Smith and Hecht was just Burton's way of being complimentary to one old friend at the expense of other old friends. I did introduce Hecht to Arthur Machen, Stephen Crane,

126

Ambrose Bierce, and certain other personal enthusiasms. He retaliated by introducing me to such writers as Huysmans, Baudelaire, Remy de Gourmont—indeed a whole school of French decadents—and some of the grimmer Russians. I tried to make a first edition collector of Ben but I never really succeeded, for he never fell as completely victim to bibliomania as I did. Quite properly, he thought the contents of a book more important than the words *First Edition* on the verso of a title page. In point of fact, I agree with him; but at that time I was beginning to build my first library of collector's items, and liked to talk about it. In those days, too, I suffered from a sort of 1890's hangover, which accounted for my devotion to Symons and Huneker, whose works I proselyted earnestly.

My grand passion, however, was Arthur Machen, whom I had discovered in a chance copy of *The Three Imposters*, and I preached Machen at Smith and Hecht, week in and week out, with mounting enthusiasm. Then Hecht read *The Three Imposters*, and Machen's style swept *him* overboard, too.

Ben's "masters" just then were notably decadent, as were mine, when they were not starkly realistic, and they all contributed to the phenomenon called Ben Hecht who became one of the most colorful writing personalities of his time. Perhaps because I saw them being written and listened to many of them in manuscript, I still prefer his early poems and short stories to his novels and other writings, always excepting *The Front Page*, an indubitable masterpiece. Some of the best writing he ever did went into the little tales and sketches he published in early numbers of Margaret Anderson's *Little Review*, and those he contributed to the *Daily News*, subsequently published as *1001 Afternoons in Chicago*.

As I was saying, Hecht never became a complete convert to "collecting," but he used to accompany me on book-hunting expeditions, to which his lively companionship and imagination lent a piquant sense of adventure. Once he fell under the spell of Ouija and brought a board to the office, which we manipulated after working hours just for the hell of it. I think Ben almost fell for the fraud. At any rate, we got in touch with a deceased gentleman named Wilson who gave us a great deal of astonishing information.

"What's the most valuable book in the world?" Hecht asked me suddenly, one afternoon. He had been in a brown study for several minutes, and I had supposed him to be composing a sonnet to his lady's eyebrows.

"*Tamerlane*, in its first edition," I said immediately, although of course it wasn't and isn't. Still, it was rare enough, for in those days only half a dozen copies were known to be in existence.

"Let's ask Mr. Wilson where there's a copy of it," said Ben.

We played with the board for fifteen or twenty minutes before it consented to give us a clue. Then, painstakingly, it gave us three letters: J A N.

Hecht was in ecstasy. "Do you know anybody named Jan?" he asked.

I said there was a small bookseller on Adams Street whose name was Jansky.

"That's him!" cried Ben ungrammatically, and we went back to Mr. Wilson. "Do you mean Jansky, the bookseller?" we asked; and Mr. Wilson said *Yes*.

By this time I was as excited as Hecht. We asked Mr. Wilson precisely where in Jansky's shop the rare item reposed, and after a bit of coaching Mr. Wilson indicated (by an imperfect jumble of letters) that the volume was in a ten-cent bin outside Jansky's door.

It was nearly quitting time anyway. Ben said, "Come on!" and grabbed his hat; and in some haste we proceeded to Jansky's.

Thereafter for perhaps an hour, sometimes on hands and knees, we feverishly explored a dusty barrow in quest of a tiny pamphlet that did not in the end materialize.

I think we both lost faith in Mr. Wilson that afternoon, although Hecht later accepted his guidance in an assignment involving a missing body.

By such innocent divertissements did Ben Hecht and I enliven

128

our afternoons in the early weeks of the fateful year 1914, before the end of which an event occurred that put an end to literary activities for many months.

XII

ALONG ABOUT THE MIDDLE OF APRIL one of my dreams came true. Henry Justin Smith, who knew my ambitions almost as well as I knew them myself, suddenly asked me how I would like to go to Mexico, and I said I would like it very much. Trouble with Mexico had been brewing for some time as a result of what historians call the "Tampico incident," and war was now imminent. A day or two later I was summoned to Mr. Dennis's office, and he said:

"Mr. Starrett, we've decided to send you and Junius Wood to Mexico. You will be leaving almost at once. I won't tell you how to proceed. Covering a war is like covering anything else. All we want is the news and you and Wood are good newspapermen. We want you to represent the *Daily News* well and the *Daily News* will be behind you in everything. You may have anything you need in the way of funds, within reason. I mean that," he added with a charming smile, "but I'll just tell you a little story. During the War with Spain, in 1898, we sent a talented young man like yourself to Cuba. His ambition, like yours, was to be a war correspondent. On his arrival he purchased a horse, a couple of revolvers, a handsome pair of binoculars, several service uniforms, and I'm not sure that he didn't also acquire a cavalry sabre. I'm sure that he looked splendid; but in the first engagement he was privileged to see, as he sat dramatically in the saddle of his expensive charger, he was shot and killed, and none of the items he had purchased were of the slightest use to the *Daily News* thereafter. So, be reasonable, Mr. Starrett. Your expense account will not be challenged. We want you to have everything you feel you may need; but remember that what we are principally interested in is your continued existence and your dispatches from the front. We shall all be happy to see you again at the close of the campaign.

"That's all," concluded Charles H. Dennis jovially, as he shook hands with me. "Good luck to you, my boy! Mr. Smith will give you your instructions."

Next day I was on my way to Galveston, Texas, where American forces were gathering for the imminent conflict. Junius Wood had been sent east to join the navy, while I had been assigned to the Fifth Brigade of the army, Brigadier-General Frederick Funston commanding, which was waiting to embark at Galveston.

My brothers Stanley and Harold had luncheon with me that day and accompanied me to the train, a little nervous about my first foreign assignment, a little envious of my good fortune; and Dad showed up at the station, slightly oiled, and tried to tell me how proud he was.

And, indeed, no more innocent Alice ever adventured through the looking glass of coming events than I in my first war assignment. However, I had good friends and competent colleagues to help me over my early difficulties. Two of my literary heroes, Jack London and Richard Harding Davis, already were registered at the Hotel Galvez when I checked in, and I lost no time in introducing myself to them. They were immensely kind and London introduced me to his wife, assuring me that she would look after me as conscientiously as she looked after him. Somehow this reassured me—I was a bit dazed and walking on air—and indeed it all worked out very much as London had said it would. I liked the famous pair, Jack and Charmian, at once and was grateful for their kindness, although their habit of addressing each other as "Mate" and "Mate Woman" always made me want to creep away someplace and be quietly sick.

Davis was even more friendly, for it was he who arranged for me to sail on the transport *Kilpatrick*, the General's flagship, as one of the five correspondents assigned to that unit. Late in the afternoon of April 23 I found a scrawled note from the senior correspondent shoved half under the door of my hotel room. "My dear Mr. Starrett: I'm asked by General Funston to tell you that you are authorized to go on one of the transports and to be at the wharf at nine. Congratulations. Richard Harding Davis."

It was a way he had. I was new at the war game and it was his duty, as he saw it, and also his privilege, to help me. I have not forgotten it. I have not forgotten Davis.

Actually we sailed at five in the afternoon, but it was the next evening before I had an opportunity to thank Davis for his courtesy. He was the most picturesque figure on the transport, of course. He wore the broad-brimmed grey felt (with cummerbund) familiar to readers of his books and riding togs that resembled a service uniform. And he had a trick of inhaling sharply, then blowing out his cheeks, that was curiously effective. I had noticed it before in the few minutes I spent in his company at the Republican Convention of 1912. At that time, also, although in civilian garb, he had looked like a war correspondent, but indeed Davis always managed to look like a man going to war. He was an excellent actor, the sort of player whose brooding eye keeps the spectators' glance upon him when he is doing nothing at all. In general, it is true, he liked to be alone but he was not unamiable and never discourteous. Perhaps he was a bit of a prima donna but he had earned the right to be. I liked him enormously.

I found him in a deck chair far forward on the upper deck, smoking a cigar and looking out into the windy darkness. "Pull up a chair," he said; and then, "I've just had my first thrill of the campaign. Some green lights swam by over there in the dark just before you came up. Probably one of our gunboats, but all I saw were green lights against the dark. They reminded me of Cuba and '98. I think we're in for a lively time in Mexico."

When I thanked him for his assistance he stopped me with a gesture. Thereafter we sat and smoked for an hour while he told me stories of previous campaigns and answered my eager questions about his books. My enthusiasm for his work was as sincere as it was ingenuous and he was obviously pleased. We spoke of

131

Soldiers of Fortune, which was my favorite among his books, and he told me of its origin and background. All in all, it was a notable occasion for me; but I don't suppose we had another dozen words together before we landed on Mexican soil. Once, indeed, he turned to me as I sat beside him on deck, earnestly turning out copy for Mr. Dennis, and asked me what I found to write about. I said, "Maybe I see things you fellows don't," by which I meant that what was old to them was new and exciting to me. London and he both guyed me a bit about my excessive industry but I didn't mind. I was having the time of my life in the best company in the world, and to be joshed by Richard Harding Davis and Jack London was an important event in my existence.

The other correspondents on board were Frederick Palmer, a distinguished veteran, and Joseph Medill Patterson of the Chicago *Tribune*, of whom more later. A fifth, unaccredited to the expedition, was George Addison Hughes of the Los Angeles *Times*, who somehow managed to enlist himself among the stewards and thus work his passage. I met Hughes rather by accident when a slim, white-coated youth brushed against me in the semi-darkness one evening and whispered, "*Ps-st*, London! Don't give me away. I'm a newspaperman too. I'd like to talk with you sometime." Then he disappeared along a gloomy passage before I had time to correct his error.

Yet another picturesque figure was the dashing commander of the expedition, General Funston, a stout, gnome-like little man with a brown beard, who strolled the upper deck of the transport with clinking spurs. It was no secret on board the flagship that he was planning a dash to Mexico City that would make the laurels of General Winfield Scott look a bit faded. But while we were still a day from Vera Cruz the wireless brought us the dismal tidings of armistice, and when the Fifth Brigade arrived it was to find the Marines and Bluejackets in control of the city.

The defenders of the port had fled. Ragged holes in the walls of waterside buildings testified to the markmanship of navy gunners, and heaps of smoking debris still littered many of the streets.

Business had been resumed, however, the inhabitants had come out of hiding, and the *cantinas* were doing a rousing business. There was only one complaint from friend and foe alike. The first shot fired by the cruiser *Chester* had ruined the only ice factory in Vera Cruz—surely, as Bill Shepherd observed, the "most unfortunate shot ever fired in battle." Because of it we drank warm beer in the *cantinas* for weeks.

But I am getting ahead of my story. We tramped into the city a dozen strong, to greet the more fortunate correspondents who had been earlier upon the scene and to try to find accommodations in the overcrowded hotels. Ultimately Patterson and I got a room together at the Hotel Diligencias that we occupied fraternally for several weeks. This famous hotel was literally bursting with correspondents, some of them sleeping three to a bed; but indeed the whole city was overrun with correspondents before many days had passed. Ultimately, I believe, there were no less than sixty. They kept arriving on every ship, some for short visits and others for the duration. Among those I came to know best were John T. McCutcheon, Charles Michelson, William G. Shepherd, Robert Dunn, Jimmy Hare (dean of war photographers), and the English journalist Oliver Madox Hueffer, who represented one of the great London dailies. Other notable figures on the spot were Edwin Emerson, Jr., Medill McCormick, Arthur Ruhl, James B. Connolly, and the illustrators Henry Reuterdahl and R. F. Zogbaum. My cronies, however, were two local correspondents long resident in Mexico, Napoleon A. Jennings and "Doc" Crossman, whose first name I never learned. Jennings, who represented the New York *Herald*, turned out to be the author of that scarce volume *A Texas Ranger*, one of the rarities of southwestern literature. When he learned that I owned a copy of his famous and elusive book he was so pleased that he all but adopted me.

About this time also I came to know two technicolor military heroes, one of whom went on to considerable distinction. The first was Tracy Richardson, a blue-eyed young man from Lamar, Missouri, a soldier of fortune who might have been the prototype of Robert Clay in Davis's *Soldiers of Fortune*, so well did he fulfill the role of romantic adventurer. When we met in Vera Cruz this mild-mannered, personable young man, whose eyes could pierce one like a knife-thrust, already had fought in half a dozen Latin-American revolutions, sometimes on one side and sometimes on the other. He was then serving for the first time under the flag of his own country. His precise connection with the army I never found out, but I believe he made dangerous trips into the interior and brought back information valuable to the General. I don't know what happened to Tracy ultimately, and I should like to know. When he came through Chicago, a few years after the Mexican fiasco, he had seen service in World War I, first with the Princess Pats and later with the American Expeditionary Force. He was then recovering from a number of wounds and itching to get back into the biggest war he had ever seen.

The other military hero I met only casually. He was a captain of Infantry, I think, and he too was engaged in some sort of intelligence work ahead of the army. At any rate, he was in and out of Vera Cruz on unpublicized missions. He was a tall, good-looking fellow with the most disreputable army hat I had ever seen, whose fancy it was to smoke an old-fashioned corncob pipe. His name was Douglas MacArthur.

But I am ahead of my story again. Although the fighting had ceased officially, there was still considerable sniping in the early morning hours, when efforts were made to knock off some of our sentries; and outlying Marine detachments constantly were threatened by marauding bands of guerillas, although nothing of headline proportions ever came of this. Any kind of rumor was good for a dispatch, however, and some extraordinary dispatches based entirely on rumor were permitted to cross the censor's desk. Spot news—cable news—was hard to come by and ultimately we were reduced to writing essays on the early history of Mexico. To all of us it looked as if the war had ended before it had begun.

Life in the tropical seaport was colorful, however. In the afternoon a military band played in the *plaza*, and after dark it was

134

pleasant to stroll down to the Malecon and look at the lights of our battleships in the outer harbor. Most of the inhabitants, and probably all visitors, ate outdoors under the awnings of the numerous restaurants, whose tables blocked the sidewalks and made strolling difficult. At one of these I played a game of dominoes with Nap Jennings and Doc Crossman that never really ended. We began it one afternoon shortly after my arrival and continued it day after day for several months without losing a *peso* apiece. I think if I wanted to live a completely peaceful and happy life, untroubled by war or wife or conscience, or even by literature, I would choose to live it under the *portales* of a good restaurant in a subtropical foreign city, playing dominoes with Crossman and Jennings.

Sometimes I went shopping with Charmian London, who always needed someone to help carry the bales of loot she purchased in the curio and lace shops. She looted Vera Cruz, I should think, about as thoroughly as ever it had been done before. At one time and another, when Jack was otherwise occupied, we must have visited every pawn shop in the port. If there were any bookshops in Vera Cruz we didn't find them. Once in our absence a small item of news emanated from the General's headquarters, but Jack put it on the cable for me and remembered to sign my name to it. As he neglected to mention the circumstance to me, I was surprised when I received a congratulatory wire from my managing editor complimenting me on a news beat.

My memories of Jack London are slighter than they should be, considering my opportunities, but I came to know him very well. We took our typhoid innoculations together shortly after our arrival and the incident led to the first of our many discussions about books. There was a book under his arm as we sat together in the military hospital waiting our turn. "I always take a book with me to a hospital," he said reminiscently. "I almost welcome a major operation because it gives me a chance to catch up on my reading." A little later we attended our first bullfight together, shortly before bullfights were abolished by the General. It was miserable sport, however. Apparently the principal murderer had been told that Jack was a person of importance, for after his kill he tossed his cap into our box and Jack put some money in it and tossed it down again.

When John McCutcheon and Medill McCormick arrived the Chicago contingent was a strong one. By this time Junius Wood had come down on a battleship and was joining us in our daily revels. The whole occasion had become a glorious holiday for everybody, a carnival, a regatta, a gymkhana, a harlequinade, almost a Mardi Gras.

One afternoon I went treasure hunting. The scene was the Isla de los Sacrificios, a few miles from Vera Cruz, where a Spanish explorer, who touched there in 1518, had found traces of human sacrifice in one of the temples. With Davis and London I took off in a motorboat on the world-old quest, and for something under three hours we trod the stealthy sands looking for likely caches before we called it a day. That evening I had dinner with the General. To my surprise he had heard about our expedition. "Find anything, Starrett?" he asked kindly, with a twinkle in his eye.

"Nothing," I had to say sadly.

"Never admit it," he said. "I've half a dozen old Spanish coins a man gave me the other day. I'll give you one of them and you can say you found it. I gave Davis one not twenty minutes ago."

Of the events of May 2, 1914, I shall speak in some detail for it was an adventure that may have come close to costing me my life. Indeed, for a few minutes on that day it appeared that half a dozen of us would be liquidated together in a notable massacre of American correspondents.

After the capture of the port the Mexican forces had fallen back into the interior, and some three dozen newsmen were impatiently waiting the first rumor of renewed hostilities. It came on May 2 with the report that an enemy force had descended on El Tejar, site of the city's water works, and demanded the surrender of the Marine garrison at that point.

136

Seven war reporters thought the report worth investigating and departed for the front in horse-drawn victorias, the only means of transportation available. In high spirits we raced one another to Los Cocos, a suburban rail point, hoping to catch a military train that would take us the rest of the distance. But there was no train, the carriage road had ended abruptly, and our *cocheros* called a strike, refusing to risk their ancient animals on the railroad tracks. With Tejar still nine miles away, we pushed forward on foot through savage heat and dust, discarding unnecessary garments at every milestone. All but Joseph Medill Patterson, who had unaccountably disappeared. Half an hour later he passed us with a whoop and a hurrah, mounted on one of the ricketiest ponies ever offered for hire—rented from a truck farmer at an exorbitant fee. We insulted him as he rode past, suggesting that he carry the pony a while, and his spirited retorts floated back to us on the dust of his passage. In a little time he was out of sight around a bend in the tracks.

The road led past tangled groves of palm and prairies of knee-high tropical grasses; past native huts and sluggish evil-smelling streams; past native men and women toiling in the fields and naked native children with flies around their eyes. It was hot in Mexico that day. Only two men managed to look distinguished. They were the veterans Richard Harding Davis and Frederick Palmer, who in all circumstances contrived to seem a little picturesque and legendary. But at the seventh kilometer even Davis dipped his valuable head into a dirty stream of water.

At the eighth kilometer a miracle happened. Four Mexican laborers appeared in our path trundling a handcar along the narrow-gauge track. Of course we took over at once. We rented the Mexicans for four pesos and the car for five, and were pushed to the eleventh kilometer in something like style. Then the road forked and gave us another problem. Our laborers appeared to think we should turn to the right, so to the right we turned—which was wrong—and that was how we happened to meet Patterson again. He came riding toward us on his hired pony, his long legs scraping the ground, accompanied by a squad of men in khaki driving a heavily-burdened mule. He began to shout at us from a distance of about a hundred yards. "Mexicans!' he yelled. "Mexicans ahead!" Then they all came up slowly and we saw that the men in khaki were four members of an American medical unit. Patterson had overtaken them on their way to Tejar with supplies, and they had all turned back to warn our party that men with rifles and bandoliers were lurking in the brush.

Only Davis and Bobby Dunn had pistols; the medicos and the rest of the newspaper crowd were without weapons. But as it began to look as if we would all have to turn back, another interruption occurred. There was a shout behind us, and around the bend from Vera Cruz came striding two more Americans in uniform, both adequately armed. They turned out to be Lieutenant Shelby and Corporal Niffen of the Fourth Infantry; and to this day I don't know what they were doing there at that minute. The Lieutenant pondered our composite story and reached a soldier's decision. "Well," he said reflectively, "they need these stores at the station, so I guess we'll have to take them. Let's go!" And we all reversed ourselves again, like people in a game, and started back along the right hand road—which was still the wrong one, for we had hardly gone a mile when we walked bang into an outpost of Mexican federals.

For a few moments it was touch and go, with the prospects of an American massacre excellent. I could already see my name in the headlines. An alarming number of swarthy ruffians in rags and patches stood about and fingered their rifles nervously, while the Lieutenant strained his high-school Spanish to explain our non-combatant status. Would El Capitan be so good as to tell him whether there were American troops ahead, asked the Lieutenant. We were a hospital train and we had lost our way; and what a hot day it was—wasn't it?—and would anybody like a cigarette?

The little officer in charge of the outpost was surly and suspicious but he accepted the cigarette. Then Patterson had a turn at him in what may have been Spanish—it wasn't English—and Davis came through with a dulcet little speech that was half Spanish and half baby talk, and somebody remembered a line or two of Latin that bothered El Capitan enormously. A number of times he looked as if he was about to give the order that would make heroes of us all.

Possibly it was Palmer and Jimmy Hare who turned the trick, although the cigarettes may have helped. In the midst of the negotiations they lined up the whole commando for a photograph, urging them gently into place with the jovial insistence of newspaper photographers at a Lutheran picnic. Suddenly everybody was smiling at Hare, and Jimmy was taking pictures like mad, or pretending to take them—I never found out which. That ended the adventure. When the orgy of photographing was over the Mexican officer, all shrugs and smiles, conducted us back to the left hand road, pointed the way to Tejar, and wished us bon voyage. We reached the camp about nightfall, without further mishap, and surprised the Marines considerably. The surrender demand had been only a bluff. There had been no battle. Nothing at all had happened.

"We've learned one thing anyway," said Patterson in retrospect. "When a man points a gun at you, take his picture. He is so pleased that he forgets he was going to shoot you."

Life in Vera Cruz bored considerably after the affair at Tejar. Boxing matches between rival regimental champions helped to beguile the monotony of "watchful waiting," and for a time the favorite pastime of the correspondents was roulette. Dick Davis, who was lucky, claimed to have a "system," but although I followed it in every particular I was never able to duplicate his good fortune.

For some time, however, some of the high-salaried reporters had been meditating a dash through the Mexican lines to the capital, a reckless undertaking probably inspired by Davis, and I was invited to accompany them but declined. In the end Davis and Medill McCormick tried it together and were lost to us for some weeks. Somewhere along the line they were arrested and jailed, but ultimately they reached Mexico City. Ultimately, too, they came back to the port with such a thrilling tale of adventure that I have since kicked myself for the sudden access of caution that had held me back.

An amusing incident occurred just after their return that is worth recording. One of the first to congratulate Davis was Oliver Madox Hueffer, the brilliant British correspondent. It had been some weeks since the two men had seen each other, of course, but it is unbelievable that Davis had forgotten Hueffer, as he pretended. The American could be a bit lordly at times, and perhaps this was one of the times. The meeting occurred at a street corner; it was my historic privilege to witness it.

Hueffer advanced smiling with outstretched hand. "Glad to see you back again," he said heartily. "What a grand time you must have had!"

"Ha—Oh yes, of course," said Davis. He accepted the clasp meagerly and added, "Do you know, old boy, I do believe I've forgotten you."

Hueffer's smile became heartier, his hand clasp became stronger. "That's all right, old man," he said generously. "You may have forgotten me but I shall never forget *you*—Mr. London!"

Thus the days and weeks and months went by with dinners under the *portales* and concerts in the *plaza* and "smokers" on the battleships in the harbor, and all the other routine of peaceful occupation, until that fateful August of 1914, when Hell erupted in Europe and correspondents were scattered from Brussels to Petrograd. The last I saw of Davis was shortly after his return to Vera Cruz. He had given me the use of his room—a cooler one than mine—during his absence and was now waiting the arrival of the ship that was to take him home. "Good luck," he said as we shook hands, "you'll be following me soon, I imagine. We'll all be on the other side before many months. See you in Paris!"

I never saw him again.

Not long after the main body of correspondents had departed, Junius Wood and I went up to the city, train service having been resumed after a fashion. On the way up we met a historical personage. He was on his way to Vera Cruz and our paths crossed at a small station, the name of which I have forgotten. At that point the *up* train and the *down* train happened to synchronize, and passengers of both trains mingled amicably before the two trains moved on. One of the passengers on the down train was a handsome bearded gentleman in civilian garb who was known to Wood. The two shook hands and chatted briefly, then I was introduced to Admiral Cradock, the commander of the British cruiser squadron at Vera Cruz. At the moment the name meant little to me; but it was not long before it was in the headlines of the world, for Cradock and his entire fleet went down in the great sea battle off the Falkland Islands within a few days of our encounter.

Wood, better versed in the diplomatic intrigue of the moment, asked the Admiral some pertinent questions. Aware that the British were supporting President Huerta while Washington was demanding his abdication, my companion suddenly asked, "Were you in Mexico City telling Huerta to resign, Admiral?"

"I told him we were withdrawing from the controversy and leaving it to the United States," was the frank reply. "The old man took it pretty hard. He wanted a night to think it over, and he went to the Zoo to meditate with an old lion that he admired. Weird, isn't it! Next morning he told me he would leave."

A State Department secretary would have said less in more words. And it was the truth. Huerta bypassed the American forces in Vera Cruz and sailed into exile from Puerto Mexico. The British cruisers steamed out of Vera Cruz at daybreak, a few hours after our meeting with the British Admiral. When they could get up steam the Kaiser's ships followed, and Cradock went down with his men in the engagement that ensued.

If only I had taken the Spanish course in high school instead of Latin, I might have had a thoroughly good time in Mexico City; but at least I was in a cultured metropolis again and could spend my afternoons in the bookshops and my evenings at the theater. The bookshops were fascinating. Even so, it was a dull stretch of

141

weeks as far as news was concerned. The big news was now in Europe and correspondents kept dropping out of sight as they were called to the larger scene. At length only three of us were left. Daily we played billiards at the American Club and waited for something to happen.

Then one afternoon a rumor reached us of fighting in the hills beyond the city. *Fighting!* We had been inventing dispatches about guerilla warfare in the hills for so long that the real thing seemed an answer to prayer. The village of Xochimilco, some eighteen kilometers from the heart of the city and the source of the city's water supply, had been captured by the Zapatistas. So ran the exhilarating report.

Thus once again I departed for the front in an open carriage, an absurd situation rather like driving to hounds in a hansom cab. The Mexican officer in command at the pumping station was glad to see us. Life had been boring for him also. He twirled his handsome mustachios and made us welcome. So we had come all the way from the city to see a battle! Well, now that we were there, perhaps we had better see the colonel. Perhaps the colonel would have news for us.

We found the colonel with the farthest outpost of the federal forces, a nondescript outfit reclining at ease on a wooded hill, and climbed the green hillside gratefully, glad to get away from the sun. Behind impromptu breastworks of earth and stones the ragged troops were smoking peacefully and chatting with their women. Except for the well-cleaned rifles of American manufacture, the outpost might have been a gypsy encampment resting in the heat of the day. Again our hopes and disappointments were made known, and the colonel was sympathetic. He seemed to feel that in some way he was to blame. His voice was poignant with regret. If only we had come yesterday! If only we had waited till tomorrow! We gathered that we had selected the wrong afternoon; presumably battles were fought on Tuesdays and Thursdays.

Suddenly he reached a decision. Pointing fiercely to a neighboring hilltop, he ordered the women to a place of safety, and went

142

into conference with his lieutenant. De Prida, our interpreter, was called into the conference. "The colonel is going to fight a battle for you," he explained hurriedly. "You must be surprised. And you must take a picture of the colonel."

The colonel was pointing at a distant hilltop, his officers grouped around him. One of my companions unstrapped his kodak. Shrill orders were sounding through the camp; the men were running to arms. Suddenly the colonel snatched a rifle from one of his men and discharged it at the imaginary enemy. When he had concluded this performance, he said, "Ah!" An order was given and the ragged soldiery, lying behind its parapet of stone, poured a volley across the shimmering valley, aiming at the crest of the distant hill. Now the colonel was looking earnestly through his binoculars. He screamed a command, and a second volley shook the treetops. The *soldaderas*, huddled behind their protective boulders, screamed with pleasure.

Then something happened that was not on the program. Out of a tree clump on the enemy hilltop sprang a little puff of smoke. It was followed by another, and a bullet zinged into the federal outpost and imbedded itself in a tree. On its heels sped another—and another—and another. A series of little white puffs blossomed against the green distance, gracefully—like piano notes—and the faint sound of the volley reached us with the shower of lead. A grimacing little sergeant at the colonel's elbow coughed suddenly and sat down on the stones that covered the floor of the hill. Then he turned over and stretched himself out as if to sleep, his face pillowed in the crook of his arm. A ragged soldier with long lank hair and protruding teeth died more spectacularly beside him a moment later. These were our only casualties, for in less time than it takes to tell it every man of us was flat on his face among the stones.

We had flushed a covey of Zapatistas on the other hilltop. From my position behind a big stone on the safer side of the hill I looked cautiously about me for the colonel. He was down among his men, hugging the earth, perhaps wondering at the idiocy that had impelled him to furnish copy for a newspaper. Not far away and in similar predicament were my two companions, one of whom caught my eye and made an eloquent and obscene gesture.

The episode had now lasted about a quarter of an hour, but it was another fifteen minutes before the exchange of courtesies was over and the firing ceased. It ceased as suddenly as it had begun and we crept cautiously from our concealment, and ran for the hillside. It was at this instant, when apparently everything was over, that a single last shot was fired by one of the Zapatistas. I had turned for an instant to look back, and a moment later found myself on my hands and knees, struggling to rise. De Prida saw me collapse and hurried to my assistance. When he had got me to my feet with some difficulty, I saw that my leg was bleeding through my trousers and my first thought was, "My God! I've been shot. What a story for the paper!" I had been shot in the right thigh by a spent ball, at almost the precise spot where Ray Henderson had once gouged out a piece of my flesh with a cavalry saber.

And that is the true story of my inglorious wound about which I still occasionally brag. I received it while endeavoring to escape from a situation I had myself helped to bring about. It laid me up for a few days but has not troubled me since. Somehow my companions got me down the hill and the colonel sent us back to the city in his red car. Before we left we thanked him for his co-operation, apologized for the trouble we had caused, and assured him that the photographs were quite safe—although they were not.

Such was the battle of Xochimilco, which does not figure in Mexican chronicles. Our dispatches were sensational, of course; but we did not then raise the question that has since occurred to me. As I look back on the affair with the philosophy of more than fifty years, I wonder to what extent we three interlopers were responsible for the death of the grimacing little sergeant and the ragged Indian with the protruding teeth, not to mention any of the Zapatistas who may have been killed. It is the duty of a good newspaperman, when there is no news, to go out and get it, and getting

144

it sometimes means making it. But I still am a little dubious about the whole affair.

XIII

SHORTLY AFTER my inglorious retreat from Xochimilco I was ordered back to Chicago. I made strenuous efforts to get myself sent to Europe, where World War I was booming along nicely, but my editors courteously refused to send me. Harry Hansen, I was told, already had been sent to Germany, and I could not really blame the office. Hansen, who spoke fluent German, had been on hand and had departed at a moment's notice. So I returned to the United States on a navy transport and sometime in September found myself back on local assignments.

However, I was not kept long at home. Later that autumn I was loaned to the Washington staff for a few weeks while Leroy Vernon took a vacation; and shortly I was established in a dismal room in a Washington boarding house with Lillian. It was a sort of belated honeymoon for her, and for me an opportunity to visit the Washington bookshops. So, at any rate, I think of it in retrospect. There was nobody in Washington I really wanted to see except Ambrose Bierce and Walter Johnson, the great pitcher of the Washington Senators, and I missed them both. Nevertheless, I was able to crowd a few memorable encounters into the brief experience.

Washington, in the latter months of 1914, was actively preparing for war, or actively trying to keep out of it, depending on how you read history; and, either way, it was a hotbed of diplomatic intrigue. Nearly three years were to elapse before American soldiers were sent to France, but I suppose few people doubted that, sooner or later, we would be at war with Germany. If anybody really tried hard to keep us out of it, I should say it was Count von Bernstorff, the German ambassador, not Woodrow Wilson; but I have nothing significant to contribute to the history of that period.

My duties were not onerous for most of Vernon's work was being done by an assistant. I was little more than a "leg man" or bellhop. My beat was the State, War, and Navy departments, however, and in the course of events I naturally met a lot of famous Americans, some of them admirable citizens and some of them stuffed shirts. Occasionally I got in on a presidential interview, and daily I visited the offices of the secretary of state, then William Jennings Bryan, whom I did not like. He was a forbidding fanatic, with approximately the culture and intelligence of a Tennessee snake-handler, as he was later to demonstrate. His position and sense of importance had gone to his head, and he wore a chip on his shoulder as one might wear an epaulet. One had almost to salaam to the great man and kiss his hand to be decently treated. Questions which he considered indiscreet or impertinent only got the questioner a scolding. My first impression of him was that he looked precisely like the cartoons of him printed in the newspapers. In his youth he had been a handsome man, no doubt, for he had fine, even noble features which, over the years, had become gross. His egotism was almost beyond endurance. It was well known, of course, that he never touched liquor; the correspondents thought he would have been a better human being if he had. Already he had begun the practice of serving grape juice at diplomatic dinners instead of the customary wines, and this had not helped to make him popular either. Newsmen who were not friendly to him—and these were numerous—called him disrespectfully "the Juicer."

My first run-in with the Juicer occurred early in my Washington experience. I had been introduced to him by Harry Gause only the day before and had made the mistake of calling him "Mr. Bryan." I saw a frown cross his brow, and Gause told me later that I should have called him "Mr. Secretary." It was the sort of innocent mistake that annoyed him most. I think he never liked me afterward. At any rate, I met him again the following day, waited politely until the other reporters had asked their questions, then quietly put one of my own that did not admit of a direct answer; it

146

contained a large "if." Apparently he thought I was trying to put him on the spot and promptly bawled me out—rudely, I thought. "You don't come here to ask me honest questions," he thundered, "but to try to get a headline." I stammered some sort of apology and that was that; but my colleagues chuckled when we had left the holy of holies and said, "Well, Chicago got it today!" It appeared that somebody "got it" nearly every day. I had to interview this eminent fathead daily for weeks, and I never got any other impression of him than one of portentous ignorance, egotism, and vulgarity.

One of the correspondents' favorite victims in their constant quest for news was a young man named Franklin Delano Roosevelt, then assistant secretary of the navy. Young Mr. Roosevelt was tall, slender, handsome in a shrewd-looking way, and exceedingly affable. It was a pleasure to drop in at his office and it is interesting now to remember that I used to sit on a corner of his desk and help myself to his cigarettes. He was then active, even athletic, in his movements; the disability that later crippled him was still some years in the future. I learned that he was a stamp collector and, after a fashion, a book collector, and sometimes we chatted about our hobbies, as collectors sometimes do. His specialty was books about the sea and naval warfare, but he thought my passion for detective stories not unadmirable. "Sherlock Holmes?" he questioned tentatively, when I had revealed my secret vice. "I think I have read all the Holmes adventures ever written. I hope there'll be more some day. They don't come any better."

I agreed with enthusiasm, and he added, "What was that story about the red-headed man who got a job copying the Encyclopaedia by hand?"

"*The Red-Headed League*," I said. "It's the one nearly everybody remembers first."

"But I'm not sure the snake story wasn't a better yarn," he said reminiscently.

"It's Conan Doyle's own favorite," I agreed.

"I see we have a lot in common," said Franklin D. Roosevelt. "Drop in when you care to. When the cigarettes aren't on the desk, they're in the left-hand top drawer."

Years later we made Franklin D. Roosevelt an honorary member of the Baker Street Irregulars; but at the time of which I am writing that aggregation of Holmes fanatics had not come into existence.

President Wilson was a detective-story reader, too. He was a man who seldom relaxed with newspapermen and, when he did, it always seemed to be somewhat of an effort. He found it difficult to be genial, I think, although one felt that he would have liked to be genial. Our relations, such as they were, were those of master and pupil on the few occasions that I conversed with him outside the official news conference. I made one or two train journeys with him, however, as one of the posse in the press coach, and it was on one of these that he confessed his pleasure in the *roman policier* and even unbent enough to venture on a joke—rather an old joke, I'm afraid.

I entered the presidential coach with the other newsmen, carrying a book under my arm, and as he greeted me his frosty eye took in the book, which was an English edition of *Max Carrados*, by Ernest Bramah, the first appearance in the world of that admirable detective. With his wintry little smile, the President of the United States plucked the volume from under my arm to see what manner of thing I was reading. He glanced at the spine and read the title aloud. "A good yarn?" he questioned.

"First rate," I replied. "Detective short stories, Mr. President, about a blind detective."

"Really?" he said. "With super-sensory powers, I suppose? An interesting idea. Do you read many detective stories?"

"Too many," I admitted. "All the good ones I can get hold of—and quite a lot of bad ones."

"I'm afraid Anna Katherine Green is still my standard of excellence," he said, "but I suppose she's out of fashion now. Well, they're all good relaxation in times like these. I always try to have one on hand for a bad night."

That was three or four years before he made the reputation of J. S. Fletcher, in America, by his praise of *The Middle Temple Murder*, and I would like to think it was I who turned his mind in that direction. But of course it wasn't. Few people ever turned Woodrow Wilson's mind in any direction except Woodrow Wilson.

"I have also read *Division and Reunion*," I grinned, naming the first of his own books I could think of.

"Have you, indeed?" he retorted dryly. "I daresay you found it less entertaining than Sherlock Holmes."

"Would you care to have that book, Mr. President?" I asked, indicating my *Max Carrados* still in his hand. "I would be glad to . . ."

"Thank you," he said, returning the volume quickly. "It looks very interesting. But, as the old saying goes, I *have* a book!"

No doubt it was a well-intentioned piece of geniality; but somehow I felt reproved.

It was on that journey that a hick correspondent from one of the smaller cities was tossed bodily from the train, under my astonished eyes, by three husky Washington correspondents, and left at a way station to get back to Washington as best he might. The affair was conducted gravely, almost as if it were a rite, and no words were spoken except by the banished correspondent, who protested as he was hustled down the aisle and out onto the platform. "Take it easy, boys," he kept repeating. "What's the matter, anyway? What have I done?" What he had done, it developed later, was to speak lightly of the President of the United States and a lady with whom the President's name had been linked by gossip. I have no idea what the three Washington correspondents thought about the whisper; they hurled the scandalmonger off the train simply because they believed it was not a matter for leering discussion. They didn't like the young man from the sticks or the nature of his remarks. They explained briefly what his offense had been, then the subject was dropped. The incident gave me a high opinion of the press corps in Washington.

Of the several foreign ambassadors whom I met and interviewed, I remember Bernstorff best. He was a tall blond German with a small fair moustache and cold blue eyes; a handsome man and a popular one, I think, with nearly everybody. His position in Washington before we entered the war was a difficult one, and it seemed to me that he met the difficulties admirably. Nobody more deeply regretted the break between Germany and the United States than Bernstorff, who had married an American wife and had long been a distinguished figure in Washington society. He was unfailingly cordial with newspapermen and the least evasive of all the foreign ministers I met.

Always a good source of news, when they happened to be in Washington, were the two senators from Illinois: James Hamilton Lewis and Lawrence Y. Sherman. I had known Lewis very well as a lawyer in Chicago. His pink whiskers and gorgeous waistcoat were part of the Chicago spectacle. I had heard him many times in court, where he was traditionally half lawyer and half actor and very good in both roles. It was axiomatic, indeed, that when Lewis had been engaged for the defense the prosecution was in a bad way unless it could come up with a better actor than J. Ham. As part of the Washington spectacle, Lewis's eloquence and sartorial splendor were in nowise dimmed; he added lustre to the scene. His speeches in the Senate were masterpieces of windy rhetoric, sparkling with quotations from Shakespeare and an occasional Latin poet. Merely as specimens of virtuosity they were worth listening to—*once*.

Sherman, too, I had known for some years. I met him first in Springfield, Illinois, in my early days as a reporter and found him congenial. From first to last, his greatest asset was his startling resemblance to Lincoln, the young clean-shaven Lincoln of the early photographs. It was a resemblance he did not have to cultivate and, with proper press-agentry, it might have taken him to the highest office in the land. Will Colvin, a Springfield newspaperman,

150

Ben Hecht

Charles MacArthur

who became his secretary in the days when Sherman was being groomed for the Senate, had precisely that in mind but was unable to bring it off; I don't know why. "I can see him in the presidential chair," Colvin used to say, with a drink or two under his belt, "and that is where I am going to put him!" However, Sherman never got beyond the Senate, which was just as well, for his physical resemblance to Lincoln was all he could have brought to the presidency. I think he tried to cultivate the Lincoln manner; at any rate, he exhibited a Lincolnian sense of humor at times and usually had a good story to tell newsmen.

It was Senator Sherman who told me why male dogs sometimes stand on three legs and raise the fourth at a significant angle. "It's really an atavistic gesture," he said one day, as we stood together and watched a little animal baptize a tree. "The *first* dog, when he relieved himself against a building, forgot to put his foot against it and the building fell on him. Since then every dog has been careful to avoid that fate."

Such are my recollections of the distinguished Junior Senator from Illinois. I'm afraid they may not do him justice. He was a jovial companion and a delightful raconteur, and I'm afraid I listened with more pleasure to his racy stories than to whatever political philosophy he had to offer.

One of the first things I did in Washington, when I had a free evening, was to call upon Ambrose Bierce. That was the intention anyway; but when I established a connection it was not with Bierce that I spoke. Major Bierce, said his secretary, was not in Washington. It was a disappointment. For years I had been looking forward to a meeting with the author of *Tales of Soldiers and Civilians*, with whom a few years before I had exchanged letters. He was one of the highest peaks in my whole mountain range of literary idols, and the prospect of meeting him in Washington had helped to make my assignment exciting. Something about my breathless inquiry and my obvious disappointment must have touched the secretary, for she invited me to call. I went at once to the hotel and learned to my dismay that Ambrose Bierce had vanished in Mexico nearly a year before. The circumstance had not been publicized by the family, still hoping to hear from him; and the information came out slowly, for Miss Carrie Christiansen was aware that I was a newspaper reporter. She was immensely kind, however, and sensing my admiration told me the story as far as she knew it.

Nearing his seventy-first birthday and afflicted with asthma, the remarkable old man had suddenly decided to visit Mexico during the winter of 1913, hoping to meet the revolutionary leader Francisco Villa, whom he admired. Several letters had been received from him en route and a final letter had been received by his daughter Helen shortly after his arrival in the southern republic. It appeared that he had joined a division of Villa's army, and mention was made of a prospective advance on Ojinaga. And that was all; the rest was silence. That had been his last word to any member of his immediate circle, and it is still the last direct word from the man himself. His daughter and his secretary were hoping desperately that there would be another communication, and fearing the tidings it might contain. Quiet efforts had been made to trace the writer's movements in Mexico. American agents in that country had been alerted by the State Department, and the War Department also had taken a hand in the search. It was thought that he might have been taken prisoner and might still be held captive in some stinking Mexican jail. All this Miss Christiansen told me in confidence; then suddenly she relented and permitted me to make the story public.

To me it seemed a more important matter than the war in Europe and I lost no time in putting it on the wire. My short dispatch, which appeared on the first page of the *Daily News* next day, was a clean news beat, but it did not allay the disappointment I felt at missing Ambrose Bierce. Thereafter I saw Miss Christiansen a number of times, and we corresponded almost to the day of her death. I have no reason to believe she knew any more about the writer's disappearance than she told me at our first meeting, although the publicity my revelation developed gave rise to several

152

romantic legends. One story reported Bierce's execution by a Villista firing squad. Another told of his death from illness, or fatigue, tenderly watched over by Villa's soldiers. A bold reporter asserted that Helen Bierce knew her father to be alive and well in England, a member of Lord Kitchener's staff. Still another report placed Bierce in a mental institution in California. All this was just falsehood and yellow journalism, or so I believe. I think the great American short-story writer died in Mexico shortly after writing the last letter received by his daughter, but in what circumstances I have no idea. Probably his fate never will be known, and possibly it is better that way. There is something curiously appropriate about the manner of his passing. His celebrity will always be the higher—so curiously are we constituted—because of the obscurity that masks his death.

For the rest of my stay in Washington, needless to say, I bothered the departments of War and State almost daily for tidings of Bierce, thus keeping the search for him alive as far as possible; but nothing came of it except new rumors, new falsehoods, and new disappointments.

Fortunately, there were several good bookshops in Washington, so the weeks I spent there were not a total loss. My favorite was a dark little hole in the wall far up Pennsylvania Avenue, on the way to the Capitol, operated by Daniel Schiller, a bearded old Hebrew who looked more like Moses than Moses himself. It was a chaotic old-book depository through which one almost had to pick one's way with a candle. I doubt that Schiller knew what he had in the shop, but he was an amiable gentleman who gave even chance customers the run of the place. I was told that the shop was frequented by senators, congressmen, and even diplomats. Once I encountered Franklin D. Roosevelt browsing through old volumes of naval lore, and we chatted briefly about Herman Melville. He had been looking up the author of *Moby-Dick* in naval records, not long before, and told me something I had not previously known— that Melville had been for a time an ordinary seaman in the United States Navy.

"By the way," he said suddenly, "why aren't you working this afternoon?"

"I'm playing hooky," I said.

"So am I," said Franklin D. Roosevelt, and we grinned at each other sympathetically.

My only other clear memory of Washington days is a visit to Keith's Theater, where I heard and met the famous old minstrel James Thornton and his wife Bonnie. The rest of the bill was a bust as far as I was concerned, but the opportunity to meet the man who had written "When You Were Sweet Sixteen"—to say nothing of "My Sweetheart's the Man in the Moon" and "The Irish Jubilee"—was too good to miss. The "sweet sixteen" ballad had been one of the songs our street corner quartet had roared with approval when I was myself sixteen; while "The Irish Jubilee" was just about the only song Dad knew; I had heard all its interminable verses many times. So, on Dad's behalf and my own, I took Lillian backstage after the Thorntons had removed themselves and congratulated them on their performance, which was more than anybody else did, for their popularity was then waning. Both were pleased as Punch, and Jimmy was able to straighten out for me a number of the lines of "Jubilee" that Dad had garbled. I wouldn't have missed them for worlds. But I was sorry to have missed an encounter, a few weeks earlier, between Jimmy and Colonel William F. Cody. The theater manager told me about it with great glee. Cody also had been eager to meet an old favorite, and Jimmy had been brought around to his box. The manager made the introductions. "Jimmy," he said, "I want you to meet the famous Buffalo Bill, who is an admirer of yours." "Glad to know you, Mr. Bill," said Jimmy, shaking hands solemnly. "What part of Buffalo do you come from?"

Early in 1915 I was recalled to Chicago and hurried off to Mexico for the second time. General Carranza was then more or less firmly seated in the presidential chair; but the bandit Villa was harassing the Texas border and, what with one thing and another, our relations with our neighbor to the south were seriously threatened again. My stay was brief, however, and unexciting. I interviewed the old General in Vera Cruz and he assured me that everything was going splendidly, although there was every reason to believe the contrary. The place had degenerated notably, I observed, since the departure of the Americans; but Jennings and Crossman were still there and for a few weeks we resumed our endless game of dominoes.

Then I was back on local assignments in Chicago, realizing that I hated them and would always hate them. Suddenly I was eager to end the chapter for keeps, to shake the dust of journalism from my shoes and sink or swim as a free lance. All I needed to make the break was some encouragement from the magazines; but even after I had reached my decision encouragement was slow in coming, and another year was to elapse before I severed relations with the paper.

All this time I had been writing short stories, as opportunity permitted, and the long afternoons on dog watch had produced a horde of them. Occasionally I sold one, but not often enough to convince me that I could make a living writing fiction. My earliest successes, so to call them, had been with pious little Sunday School journals that paid about six dollars a story. Then, with mounting sophistication, I had begun to shoot at broader targets. Now I was bombarding such pseudo-sophisticated magazines as *Snappy Stories, Saucy Stories*, and *The Parisienne*, with adolescent tales and sketches, and occasionally seeing one in print. These brought larger figures, sometimes as much as twenty dollars, but the average was nearer twelve dollars. Now and then I was able to sell a bit of verse or persiflage to *The Smart Set*, then the goal of every writer with a talent for smart-alexander; but at no time before 1916 had there been reason to suppose my future might lie outside a newspaper office.

Then one day something happened. I had written a story of mystery and adventure, with a reporter in the leading role, and sent it to *Collier's Weekly*, where a divine creature named Viola

Roseboro was fiction editor. And one day Miss Roseboro accepted my story. How well I remember that day! It had been a dull one before her letter arrived, but suddenly it was a day of gilt and glory, of bombs bursting in air, for the letter was accompanied by a beautiful check for seventy-five dollars. Have I said that my weekly wage was then forty-five dollars? Yes, it had crawled up to that figure, and was likely to stay there.

My first impulse was to throw up my job at once. Before doing so, I rushed over to Ben Hecht, my story-writing colleague, and shoved the letter into his face. He read it with just a trace of envy, I thought, but his words were warm and comforting. "Nice going, Charlie," he said. "That's the first break. It ought to be easy now."

"Good Lord!" I said. "I can write a story as good as that every week."

He agreed, but pointed out the flaw in my reasoning. "They can't print one every week," he said. "They have to use *some* stories by other writers."

So I did not at once sever connections with the *Daily News*. However, the episode strengthened my determination to be a magazine writer, and thereafter I pounded my typewriter more furiously than ever. My more ambitious stories, aimed at the *Smart Set*, came back with depressing regularity, and it was some time before I landed one in those Olympian pages. But if the checks sent me by Henry L. Mencken and George Jean Nathan were few and far between—and ridiculously inadequate—their letters of rejection were friendly and helpful. For the most part, my dealings were with Mencken; I have a nice little collection of his inspiring letters of rejection. Sometimes, to soften the blow, he would lay the blame on his associate. "I'm really very sorry about this," he would write. "Blame it on Nathan, a rank Presbyterian." Or perhaps: "I have made several attempts to convince Nathan that we ought to have this, but he can't see it that way." Or he might say, "I confess that Nathan's absurd objections to this admirable story begin to make an impression on me. Try us with something else." One note read:

156

"I am sorry that this leaves me flat, but such is the fact. We want rather more robustious stuff. . . . If you ever think of any violent epigrams against leading dignitaries, let me see them by all means." Another said: "Thanks for the chance to see this. Unluckily, I can't take any fiction at the moment. We have enough in type to last until the Second Coming." That sort of spirit among editors goes a long way toward healing a wounded heart.

My dossier on a story called "The Truth About Delbridge" appears to be incomplete, but two letters out of a possible five or six have been saved. They are so typical of the editorial Mencken that I reproduce them in their entirety:

June 12, 1917

DEAR MR. STARRETT: Since I last wrote to you Nathan has gone through "The Truth About Delbridge" very carefully. He agrees with me that it is a very fine piece of work but he raises an objection that I confess begins to make an impression on me—that is, the objection that a story dealing with such an abnormality would probably prove very offensive to a great many readers and perhaps bring down upon us the strong arm of certain moral gentlemen who constantly stand by waiting their opportunity. I am not entirely in accord with this idea but his arguments shake me up to some extent. And so I hesitate definitely to take the story. If you see any way to change the ending so that the man need not dress himself up in women's clothes, I would be inclined to grab the manuscript at once. It has been suggested in the office that it might be possible to get around the matter by making the man hang himself with a doll in his arm but without his present paraphernalia of silk stockings. I incline to believe that this would solve the problem. Please give it your thought and let me hear from you.

Nathan joins me in assuring you that it would delight us very much to have you in the magazine regularly. You know how to write in the way that we like to see writing done. I surely hope that something else will reach us very shortly and that you will be able to overcome our qualms in the present case.

157

I trust that the two books of piety that I sent to you the other day are giving you the spiritual consolation that all of us need in these hard times.

Sincerely yours,
H. L. Mencken

I don't remember what protest I made to this proposition, but a little later I received another letter:

Dear Mr. Starrett: I agree with you that this is well done, but I am in so much doubt that the Smart Set is the place for it that I hesitate to take it. It simply will not fit into our scheme of things.

The objection to the silk stockings and other female trappings is that they make the sexual abnormality of the fellow too palpable. Nathan wants the story, as I do, but these things make him buck. Hence his suggestion that the use of a doll might cover up the thing a bit better. After all, what does it matter to the story? You are for the silk stockings simply because you know that the real suicide wore them. If you had imagined the whole thing you might have hit upon overshoes or a tin vest. The facts be damned.

Let me have your future mss. as above. I spend most of my time here (Baltimore). I can't work in New York.

Sincerely yours,
H. L. Mencken

But to get back to my *Collier's* story, I was particularly arrogant all that day and told off my superiors pretty sharply when they ventured to suggest that I rewrite some little trifle from the City Press Association for the *Daily News*. I was pretty well disliked before the long day ended. Then I went home and told Lillian about it. She, too, was dazzled by the great sum that suddenly had been added to our resources, and of course she believed with me that my future was secure. I have been trying to remember what we did with that check. I think I gave her half of it—say thirty-five dollars—for a new suit. As for my own half, I spent it riotously at

Walter Hill's for some English first editions I had been yearning to possess.

I wrote and sold other stories that year, most of them written on *Daily News* time, and Hecht and I meditated a number of works in collaboration, none of which came to fruition; although one had possibilities, I think. For some reason I had been reading up on those interesting little medieval mechanisms called chastity belts. They fascinated Ben, too, and it occurred to us that a charming story might be written about a crusader's wife who had been locked into one of the things on her lord's departure for the Holy Land. The plot was to turn on the death of the crusader and the discovery of his key by a stranger who was to return to Europe in quest of the lovely lady it would unlock. I don't know whose idea this was; probably Hecht's. At any rate, he wrote the first chapter in an explosion of enthusiasm one night and brought it to the office for my approval. As I recall it, his idea was for the key to be found by a handsome young Saracen; but about that time the whole inspiration went glimmering, and we never did finish the story. Years later I was interested to read Eric Linklater's amusing novelette, *The Crusader's Key*, and note how closely he had approximated our idea; but of course it is an idea that must often have occurred to robust males itching to write an erotic romance. In such delightful fashion, at any rate, did Hecht and I spend long hours in the old *Daily News* office planning the stories that were to make us famous and wealthy.

We wrote a great many stories during the afternoons we spent together, and I am bound to say Hecht had more luck with his than I did with mine. As early as 1915 he was publishing symbolic little tales and sketches in the *Little Review*, and I am reminded that it was I who introduced him to Margaret Anderson, its editor. I don't know what was wrong with my early stories unless it was that they were *too young*. They were too derivative, also, I imagine, for I was influenced by every new writer I encountered whose work I admired. For years my fiction was a medley of many styles and philosophies; I was trying to write sophisticated stories before I was myself sophisticated. Reading over some of my early manuscripts not long ago—just before tearing them up—I found that I no longer knew what they were about. I never have taken a story course in my life, or any other kind of course, and I learned to write acceptably (if I *have* learned to write acceptably) by the grand old system of trial and error, plus the good old system of imitating my betters. It was long before I achieved a style that could honestly be called my own, and I don't blame the editors who rejected my early stuff, although I cursed them heartily enough at the time. In general, my best stories then were sensational stories— as, indeed, they are today. I am a melodramatist by instinct and by preference; but before I could write detective stories for a living I had to get over the notion that I was another Arthur Machen, another Stephen Crane, another Ambrose Bierce, another Robert Louis Stevenson.

All this time also I had been collecting books. It is surprising now to remember that there was a time when I never had heard the magic words "first edition." I have developed this thought else- where along other lines, but I am wondering now just where and when I first began to realize that books of the same title, looking precisely alike, might actually be subtly different. Probably it hap- pened after I had become acquainted with Powner's Bookstore in the old Methodist Church block at Clark and Washington. My passion for books had taken me to the shop, between assignments, and for a time I bought books without caring whether they were first or thirty-first editions. It was meeting the collectors who fre- quented Powner's and listening to their talk, I think, that made me aware of first editions as such. I can't recall that anybody ever ex- plained the mystery to me; I acquired my understanding of it by a form of osmosis. But I was an easy and immediate convert as soon as I realized what it was all about. And let me say at once that I have had more genuine happiness collecting books than in any other single transaction in life. I have always been more interested in other men's books than my own; if it had been otherwise, I might conceivably have done more and better creative work of my own.

There were more distinguished antiquarian bookshops in Chicago than Powner's, but none so convenient and none more fascinatingly miscellaneous. Old Mr. Powner—Charles T. Powner —was a gentleman of the old school who himself collected the editions of Mark Twain. His shop was the noon-hour Mecca of all the impecunious collectors of Chicago and many interesting "finds" were made there. His stock was so extensive and chaotic that one felt anything might turn up in it; and the atmosphere was right, too. His books were displayed in a sort of ordered confusion on tables scattered like islands along the length of the shop, and on the shelves that occupied every wall in the place except for the space neces- sarily given over to doors and windows. The windows, too, were crowded with books and outside the front door there was always a bin brimming with sad looking volumes marked low for quick disposal. I loved the old shop and I still miss it. Wright Howes, later a well-known Chicago bookseller on his own, was one of Powner's clerks just then, and a frequent visitor was J. Christian Bay, Librarian of the John Crerar Library, a notable collector. From these men I acquired some of my early acquaintance with the science of bibliography. But the shop was popular among bookmen of every sort, including the working newspapermen, some of whom I had the pleasure of introducing to the fanatic joys of collecting.

Carl Sandburg was not one of these. Although a prodigious reader and accumulator of books, he cared not a "hoot in hell," he told me, for first editions as such. He frequented Powner's, how- ever, and might be found on pleasant afternoons burrowing in the outdoor bin. "Old Carl," as we already called him more than fifty years ago, was then a reporter on the *Day Book*, a Socialist daily. I can see him now as I saw him then, his gaunt frame bowed over the ten-cent bin, his grey forelock falling into his eyes, as seriously engaged as if he were seeking diamonds in a dust heap, as indeed he was. Once I stood behind him until he had made his selection: a single volume that seemed to please him greatly, for he pounced on it with satisfaction. As he started to enter the shop I barred his progress and snaked the treasure from under his arm. It was Volume IV of Bourrienne's *Memoirs of Napoleon Bonaparte*— only Volume IV. He grinned a little sheepishly and said defensively in his slow drawl, "Well, who wants to know about Napoleon's early life?"

Another time I remember meeting him in Laurence Payne's shop, farther up the street, and seeing him destroy a book under the eyes of an appalled sales clerk. "Old Carl" was in a hurry that evening, for he had a train to catch and wanted something to read on the journey. I have forgotten what the book was, but he decided on it quickly and without hesitation ripped out the first thirty pages of text. I was horrified—and a clerk standing beside us almost fainted. But Sandburg produced the price of the entire volume and gave it to the swooning salesman, together with the larger fragment of the book. "Wrap this up and put my name on it," said the poet easily, slipping the smaller fragment into his pocket. "This will be enough for tonight. If I like it, I'll stop in some time and pick up the rest."

Later I was told that there were book fragments all over town awaiting his call; but on the evening in question I said, "For gosh sakes, Carl, it's a good thing that wasn't a valuable book, or somebody might have exterminated you!" He answered seriously, "Oh, I wouldn't destroy a *valuable* book. I buy these things to read on the train and thirty pages is just about right. A lot of them aren't worth a hoot, anyway."

As I say, it was at Powner's I first began to hear about first editions and began in a small way to acquire them. It was some time before I graduated to the greater antiquarian bookshops— to Walter Hill's and Frank Morris's—high up in the Marshall Field office building. On the whole, I preferred the little hole-in-the-wall places that might hold rarities unknown to the proprietor. One such, Goldman's, in Dearborn Street, featured an outdoor bin; and one morning on assignment I saw that it was piled high with paperbacks, all shiny and new. I paused just long enough to note that they were all books of the eighteen-eighties, in perfect condition, the publications of a deceased book pirate named M. J. Ivers. Obviously, Goldman had found an unsold remainder in some old warehouse. Then memory functioned and I remembered several titles in the series that were important to collectors—pirated editions of English titles that had appeared in this country a little in advance of their London publication. Of these the most desirable was *The Misadventures of John Nicholson,* by Robert Louis Stevenson, a rare book.

I turned over the huge heap as rapidly as possible, concealing my eagerness, and quickly found a pristine copy of the Stevenson opus. As luck would have it, I was due at the office in a few minutes, so I picked out two other titles at random and dashed into the shop. When the Stevenson was safely mine, I questioned the proprietor gently so as not to alarm him, and learned that he had purchased several thousand of the old volumes from a warehouse in Ohio. There was another great heap of them under a staircase at the back of the shop, he said. Clearly there was no time to be wasted; any minute some sharpshooter as alert as I might enter the shop on a similar errand. I hurried back to the office, wrote my story in haste, then begged the afternoon off, and fairly ran back to Goldman's, where I removed my coat and attacked the mountain of paperbacks under the stairs. In some two thousand volumes I found just five other copies of *John Nicholson,* all of which I purchased at ten cents a copy.

I now had six copies of the rare Stevenson item in my possession, and a day or two later I took one of them to Walter Hill, the leading antiquarian bookseller of Chicago. He looked it over carefully and admitted that it was a beautiful copy. "What do you want for it?" he asked.

"I will leave that to you," I said; and he thought twenty-five dollars would be a fair price, so I assumed that he would try to get twice that on the strength of the book's immaculate condition.

I took my twenty-five dollars and went away considerably pleased with myself. About a week later I took him a second copy, saying, "Look, Mr. Hill, I've found another of those beautiful *Nicholsons*. Do you want this one, too?"

He was a little startled, but he said, "Yes, I guess I can use another," and wrote another check for twenty-five dollars.

I waited two weeks before taking him a third copy, and when I tossed it down on his desk he almost bounded out of his chair. Of course he smelled a rat. He said, "I suppose you've found a nest of these someplace. How many more have you?" I said I had three more, but wanted to keep one for my own collection. He grumbled a bit and finally said, "Well, I've got to buy the others to protect my original investment, but it may take me years to work these off. All right, keep one, if you like; and how about twenty dollars apiece for the other two?"

I said that would suit me fine; and thus it came about that Walter Hill had five brilliant copies of *John Nicholson* in the rare Ivers edition, and I had one. I thought I had done very well, and Hill too was satisfied; but within a few months of my discovery a copy of *Nicholson* turned up down east in an edition pirated by George Munro's Sons a few weeks earlier than the Ivers production. The Munro edition was therefore a little more *first*, so to speak, than the Ivers, and it made our Ivers editions only interesting curiosities. However, Hill made no complaint. He had already sold three or four of his five at a profit sufficient to take care of the situation. But for months he looked at me with a lopsided smile when I entered his shop, and asked me how many more *John Nicholsons* I had found. I can't recall that I ever found anything else of the slightest value at Goldman's, although I haunted the place for months; and of course I never told Goldman the story I have just related. It would have distressed him.

I missed some good books, too, I remember with a pang; for example, Herman Melville's copy of Shakespeare, with Melville's name and address in his own hand on the flyleaf. I passed it up one afternoon in Tom Knight's shabby little shop in South State Street, because I did not at the moment have seventy-five cents in my pocket. I was afraid to call Knight's attention to the book by asking him to hold it for me. Next day, when I hurried back for it, of course it was gone. A retrospect of life teems with lost opportunities, it has been said, and this is painfully true in the case of collectors who are buying books with their lunch money. But that sort of thing did not happen very often, I am glad to remember. As a rule, when I had to decide quickly between my luncheon and a book, there was little hesitation. I bought the book.

In my early enthusiasm for first editions, I was carried past all my own danger signals—if, indeed, I ever erected any danger signals. For a time I was collecting along twenty-six lines at once, a situation that kept me perennially broke; even so, I felt that I had begun my book collecting in Chicago too late. Every collector feels that the period just before his own was a "golden age" when he listens to the stories told by older collectors of their miraculous finds a generation before. In Eugene Field's time in Chicago, for example, which preceded my own by a quarter of a century, American first editions could be picked up very inexpensively, for the vogue for "esteemed American authors" which ended with the bank crash of 1929 (it has since come back) had not then begun. Gene and his cronies had a fine field in Chicago. Listening to the stories told about them, I always envied them; and Frank Morris, who had been Field's favorite bookseller, was full of such stories.

The sole survivor of the collectors of that day, I believe, was my old friend, the late William J. Douglass, who also was garrulous about the great days of his youth, and who also helped to make a collector of me. He, too, was one of the grey, bespectacled, bird-like prowlers I used to meet at Powner's, where his ability to spot a rare item of belles-lettres or Americana across the full width of a room was uncanny. He had known everybody, it seemed, who ever had collected books in Chicago—the Field brothers, Roswell and Eugene; DeWitt Miller, the bibliotaph; Francis Wilson, the bibliophilic actor; Leon H. Vincent, the writer about books; and the bibliomaniac clergymen, Bishop Frank Bristol and Frank Gunsaulus, among many others. It is possible that Douglass's influence on me was greater than that of any other individual, although our fields of interest did not notably overlap. He taught me never to scorn an early pamphlet, whatever its subject, and never to quit a bin until the last shabby item had been examined. It is regrettable that he did not write the story of his own bookly adventures; it would have been a fascinating volume. But it was enough for him to possess his books and to live with them.

Will Douglass was a great bookman whose life was at once joyous and tragic, and I am very proud to have known him. He loved books with a pure but reckless passion and, with enough money, would have been the greatest collector of his time. As it happened, he was just a man on a salary with a family to support; but of all the bookmen I have known he is to me the most memorable. Just now one anecdote is sufficient. Approaching his home one Sunday afternoon, near the end of his life, I encountered one of his grandchildren on the doorstep and asked, "Is your grandfather at home?" The youngster, who was perhaps five, replied seriously, "Oh yes, he's upstairs playing with his books."

What an epitaph!

At this time, my last year on the *Daily News*, the staff had changed considerably. Wallace Smith was now one of the star reporters, Russell Palmer was a valued newcomer, and Margery Currey was the paper's capable sob sister. Durand had departed on sick leave, and was shortly to die. Dick Hebb was city editor, with Brooks Beitler as his assistant. Dates are not important, but the year was 1916 and, as I have suggested, I was beginning to tire of it all. Nothing greatly interested me except the books I was collecting and the magazine stories I was trying to write. The glamor of newspaper work had vanished. I know now that I had stayed in the profession too long; five years would have been enough and (except for the Mexican adventure) would have given me all the experience I needed for a background.

When one is just beginning, perhaps for a few years afterward, there is a certain glory about journalism akin to patriotism. One yearns to sacrifice one's life—at least a few meals and a night's

Christopher Morley
1933

Sir Arthur Conan Doyle
1923

sleep—for the dear old paper. One is always on the qui vive for a story. Long hours mean nothing. One will work half the night on a big fire, or awaiting a verdict after a sensational trial, and go home actually refreshed, eager to begin all over again next morning. One goes to the theater almost hoping a fire will break out on the stage, so one may be the first to break the news. One investigates street corner brawls, after hours, on the chance that a murder may develop. One's police card invests one with a mysterious importance in the eyes of a crowd, which is gratifying to one's vanity. One loves to be Starrett of the *Daily News,* and to push one's arrogant nose into other people's business. But there comes a time when all that is just eyewash, when the most attractive assignment is just a pain in the neck. More and more I thought of the satisfying rewards of what I called Literature and wished to try my hand at it professionally.

In an explosion of bitterness and independence one morning, I walked out of the office and did not come back. Nobody called me up and urged me to return. My reportorial days were over. Next morning I sat down before my own typewriter, with Lillian's piano bench for a desk, and began my first detective story.

> *Fog had shut down upon Chicago and a steady drizzle of rain had set in. Michigan Boulevard, hours deserted, glistened wetly under its double row of lights. . . . Rain, fog and midnight had combined to create a gaunt loneliness in the busy avenue. Suddenly . . .*

XIV

M EANWHILE the "Chicago Literary Renascence" had begun. I am informed that, having lived through it from first to last, I ought to know just how and when and where it began. But one of the paradoxes of living in a historic period—a period later designated as historic—is that one doesn't realize its historic quality until afterward, when historians (and other interviewers) begin to

167

ask for reminiscences. Perhaps it is an advantage not to know that one's day is historic; the knowledge might make one self-conscious and so spoil one's feeling for it as a daily adventure. But it is a disadvantage, too, because, when the interviewers get around to asking their questions, too often one has forgotten the answers.

Possibly the Chicago Literary Renascence, or the flutter of literary self-consciousness so designated by the critics, began with the appearance of the first white settler on the shore of Lake Michigan near what is now the mouth of the Chicago River; but to follow the threadlike development of that hypothesis down the years would take too long. It will be convenient to begin in one's own lifetime and preferably with a plausible event still fresh in memory. As suggested in an earlier chapter, the first flicker of the movement may well have been Mary Garden's first bawdy abdominal tremor on the night of November 25, 1910, as stirring a note of revolt as the history of aesthetics can offer; but there will be those who will ask what this had to do with literature or even culture. Happily, other and more relevant dates are available.

Too much has been written about that old article by H. L. Mencken proclaiming Chicago to be the "literary capital of the United States." Nevertheless, it is probably the most conspicuous date (1919) associated with the movement. Mencken's recognition of the phenomenon was the city's first assurance that a literary renascence was in progress; without it, we might never have known that our epidemic of books and writers was anything more than a normal development. It was Mencken who in effect named it and gave it significance. Yet for a decade at least the renascence had been flourishing. Perhaps it began with the appearance of the *Friday Literary Review* of the Chicago *Evening Post* in March, 1909. Certainly, this four-page newspaper supplement (the number of its pages increased with the years) made an instant appeal to the city's younger intellectuals, and to the end of the chapter it continued to stand in the forefront of the city's cultural life. Its first editor was the witty and authoritative Irish critic Francis

Hackett, whose lively comment on current books and current thought added a new and piquant note to the cacaphony of Chicago.

If a less journalistic and more dedicated instance is desirable, the honor of beginning the renascence might be awarded to Harriet Monroe who in October, 1912, began to publish *Poetry: A Magazine of Verse.* As *Poetry* was still flourishing (or failing to flourish) when the renascence ended—perhaps it was the one constant factor in the movement—it might be argued that this famous little magazine constituted in itself the whole literary renascence. It is certain that nearly everybody connected with the movement contributed to its pages at one time and another. Yet Harriet Monroe was herself a hang-over from an earlier Chicago movement, a circumstance that suggests the continuity of such phenomena and the difficulty of dating them. My own choice, if a beginning date is imperative (and if the renascence was *sui generis*), would be the day in 1913 on which *The Little Review* was born. Thus my personal candidate for the honor is the lovely Margaret Anderson. In her magnificently arrogant slogan, "No compromise with the public taste," Miss Anderson struck a note of revolt that thrilled the youngest newspaper reporter to giddy dreams of art for its own sake, and the conviction that starvation in a garret was the proper end of genius.

"A literary movement," said the witty George Russell (AE), "consists of five or six authors who live in the same town and hate each other cordially." That appears to define a literary "movement" with a certain accuracy, but in what does a literary "capital" consist? It is not just a matter of authors, five or six or a dozen, who live in the same town. It is also a matter of publishers, and bookshops, and literary magazines, and book supplements. It is a fortuitous conjunction of all these, plus an enthusiasm growing out of the situation itself—a hubbub that incites established writers to competition, draws new writers into its orbit, and infects the public with a lively awareness of its own importance in the cultural

169

scheme of things. In this state of affairs all the other arts, of course, will flourish similarly. And all these factors are constants, not "sometime" things.

Twice Chicago has had such a setup—almost—but neither time overwhelmingly enough to oust New York, the publishing center, from its favored position as the nation's principal literary Mecca. In the 1890's half a dozen publishers and a score of good writers occasioned a flurry in these parts and gave the city considerable literary prestige. In the first and second decades of the new century half a dozen writers of importance, plus *The Little Review* and *Poetry: A Magazine of Verse*, again brought the literary pot to a boil; but, as before, the excitement failed to last. Both these movements or revivals, or whatever they are to be called, declined for the same reason: the principals, or most of them, ultimately went somewhere else. Always Chicago has been a stopover point for ambitious young writers on their way to New York. When enough of them happen along about the same time, and find conditions favorable, they join forces with the local talent that has been trying to lift the city out of its immoral apathy, and we have a "Chicago movement." There may be a time rhythm in the phenomenon; and it needs two or three colorful key figures to spark it. But eventually nearly everybody feels the actor's call of Broadway. The smaller souls go away hating the provincial scene and thereafter devote their novels and plays to getting even with the people they didn't like in Chicago or Keokuk or Milwaukee. It's a neurosis or something.

So much has been written about the second flowering, so to call it, and there has been so much creasing of brows about its precise dating, that a little past history may not be out of place. There were good writers in Chicago before the second renascence, at any rate before it was called a renascence or renaissance, and some contributed to it and others did not, although they continued to live and write in Chicago. I have mentioned some of the survivors of the first Chicago movement who were to be found at the Press Club—e.g., Opie Read and Stanley Waterloo—but not all the survivors of the nineties were newspapermen. More important than Read or Waterloo, as bridging the gap between the two developments, were Henry B. Fuller, Hamlin Garland, and William Vaughn Moody. At the University of Chicago, before and after the second renascence began, were such men as Robert Herrick and Robert Morss Lovett, the novelists; and other writers of the time who still lived and wrote in Chicago were Henry Kitchell Webster, Emerson Hough, George Barr McCutcheon, I. K. Friedman, Edith Wyatt, Edna Kenton, Alice Gerstenberg, Clara E. Burnham, Maude Radford Warren, Elia W. Peattie, Clara Louise Laughlin, and Wallace Rice. Only Fuller, perhaps, had recognized stature, but it was an interesting school of scribblers and it was not a negligible factor in the city's culture. Of this group Fuller and Miss Wyatt—and of course Harriet Monroe—were figures in both movements; indeed, Fuller and Miss Monroe may be said to have been pivotal in both. The history of the two movements might be written around them. For although Fuller had published his most esteemed novels when the second renascence dawned on the Windy City, and appeared to have finished his task—he was furtively (almost secretly) writing book reviews and editorials for the *Evening Post*—the new movement inspired him to further accomplishments that gave him a respected position among the writers then taking over.

It is no secret to bibliophiles that other writers also inhabited Chicago in the early days of the new century. As a bibliographer, perhaps I may be permitted to remark that the pre-Sandburg period produced a number of books by Chicago authors of such resounding notoriety and such enduring popularity that conceivably they may be read when more relevant books of the time are forgotten. In first edition copies, *The Wonderful Wizard of Oz*, by L. Frank Baum (1900), and *Tarzan of the Apes*, by Edgar Rice Burroughs (1914), are rare and expensive, but both books are still in print and thousands of readers still appear to hold them in high esteem, while *Graustark*, by George Barr McCutcheon (1901), still holds its own among the romantic best-sellers of the past. Chicago publishers brought out these books and many others now avidly sought by collectors. I venture the thought that sometimes it is the collectors who determine the life span of a book—rather more often perhaps than the critics. Who knows what gives a book longevity? If survival is the test of merit we have a problem on our hands more difficult than establishing the calendrical span of the "Chicago Literary Renascence"—and by your leave I shall skip it.

I have purposely omitted one name from the foregoing roster of Chicago's literary workers. By the autumn of the year 1910 there had arrived in the city from Wisconsin a young woman destined to become one of the nation's best loved novelists, a Jewish girl of talent approaching genius who was to bring Chicago its first Pulitzer award. Too diligent and too shy to be a party-goer, and temperamentally unfitted to be an aesthete, she had little time or patience for literary movements. One couldn't march in a parade and see it too, she said. Chicago writers talked too much about the Russians, she thought. Their philosophy was too pessimistic; too—although the phrase had not then been invented— too un-American. Her America was a better place than theirs, she believed; she wanted to write American books, in the American language. Under a modest exterior lay a large self-confidence, a profound belief in the importance of the work she had to do. Her first book, published in 1911, was quite unimportant, however, as were several others; but with *The Girls*, published in 1921, she began to show what was in her, and with *So Big* (1924) she took her place among the better novelists of America, a position she has not yet relinquished. Why Edna Ferber is consistently neglected when the literary history of Chicago is recited I don't know. Her residences outside the city prior to the publication of *So Big* were only temporary. Until 1924 Chicago was her headquarters; the final draft of *So Big* was written at the old Windermere Hotel in the summer of 1923. In my opinion, Edna Ferber is the most interesting figure in the Chicago story, excepting only the major poets of the second renascence. Unfortunately, her solid merits as a social critic have been obscured for the highbrow reviewers by her facile potboilers and the appalling popularity of such technicolor melodramas as *Show Boat*. Not that I have any fault to find with *Show Boat* myself! I like it very much. Only the more precious critics and Miss Ferber find fault with it.

But for me, as I was saying, the fireworks began with a meeting in a Jackson Park studio at which *The Little Review* was born, some time during the summer months of 1913. That, my dears, was an occasion! How anything concrete emerged from the aesthetic uproar is still a mystery to me; but out of the confusion came a little rebel magazine that lived a useful life before it died. There were several meetings, in point of fact, but I remember only the first two, which it was my historic privilege to attend. The studio, fronting on Stony Island Avenue, was the home of Margery Currey, who had recently separated from Floyd Dell and was going it alone. Dell, then literary editor of the *Evening Post*, in succession to Francis Hackett, was in residence in another studio nearby and friendly relations existed between the two establishments. He was the very "portrait of an aesthete" with his black stock, yellow gloves, and airy stick—a slight young man with black sideburns and a scarcely visible moustache.

The neighborhood was a diminutive Latin Quarter populated for the most part by artists, antique dealers, and assorted bohemians; had been so, indeed, since the Chicago World's Fair of 1893. The studios were old shops left over from the earlier excitement, made habitable by the individual whim of their tenants, the display windows hung with rugs and draperies to insure a degree of privacy. As converted by the aesthetes of the second renascence, they were picturesque and attractive; and they were cheap. I should imagine Margery's was the most attractive of them all, although it was congested with unpremeditated hazards. You entered the front door breezily, knocked over a tryptich screen that concealed the immediate interior, and hit your knee against a table just beyond the screen, which set a statuette by Stanley Szukalski to teetering on the table, and by the time you had caught the statuette to keep it from crashing your self-confidence was irrevocably gone and you were ready for tea.

I was still covering murder trials and interviewing opera stars for the *Daily News* and Margery Currey was my colleague. Although I had published little at the time, she was aware of my literary curiosity and had even read my poems in manuscript. When the kind little creature invited me to her party, she added, "We want you to help name a new magazine." As nearly as I can remember, that was the first time I heard Margaret Anderson and her project mentioned; but it struck me as the right kind of party and, when I heard that Theodore Dreiser was to be present, I determined to be there too. Ben Hecht also was invited but for some reason was unable to attend. In anticipation of the event, I thought up several good names for a new magazine, none of which, as it turned out, were quite what Miss Anderson wanted. My fancy ran to such names as *The Unicorn* and *The Eagle's Feather*, and for a few minutes I almost battled myself to prominence when I suggested *Pen and Ink*. Any number of other names were suggested and lively debates followed each suggestion. Arthur Davison Ficke, the poet, who had come from Iowa to be present, suggested *The March Review*, I don't know why, and Miss Anderson at one time seemed to think *The Sea Gull* would be nice. As the evening wore on, however, it became apparent that her first and last choice was *The Little Review*. Her earlier suggestions had been only so much window dressing, I think, to entice us into the game. Fairly early in the proceedings she began to proselyte for *The Little Review* and continued to urge the merits of that title at intervals throughout the evening; that is to say, in the intervals of comparative silence that followed the babble about other titles. I gathered that she had come prepared to call her magazine *The Little Review* and would tolerate no other name. She was very deft about it and very charming, as well as being very pretty, so it did not greatly surprise me when I learned from Margery some days afterward that the name selected for the new journal was *The Little Review*.

174

It was a notable party, however, and I am happy to have been present. The most notable figure of them all, I suppose, was Theodore Dreiser, who was the lion of the evening. It was my first and last view of the author of *Sister Carrie* and I looked at him with interest. Presumably I met him, and I assume that a few words passed between us, but certainly we did not converse at any length. He was a busy man that evening trying to talk to twenty or thirty persons at once. What I saw was a huge hulk of a man standing more than six feet in height, stoop-shouldered, gaunt, and homely as a potato. He had friendly eyes, however, and an earnest manner, and his appearance was made all the more memorable by a wide bandage that swathed his throat and neck to the ears, covering a boil or carbuncle on the back of the neck, or so I was told. It gave his head and shoulders a stiff and massive look. Others present were Sherwood Anderson and his brother Karl, the illustrator, Edna Kenton, Professor George Burman Foster, Floyd Dell, Ernestine Evans, Hi Simons, Llewellyn Jones and his wife (Susan Wilbur), Jerome Blum, the painter, and I think Susan Glaspell and her husband, George Cram Cook. Later in the evening DeWitt C. Wing came in and I met *The Little Review's* first angel, called only *Dick* in Miss Anderson's book, *My Thirty Years' War*, but one of her closest friends. It was a bewildering array of celebrities for a hero-worshipping reporter to meet, and as I was somewhat overwhelmed by the company I was keeping, I stayed close beside the friendly Margery Currey most of the time.

My only other clear memory of a meeting with the decorative Miss Anderson is of an afternoon some months after the events just narrated, when I took Ben Hecht to her editorial studio in the Fine Arts Building and introduced him. I remember Hecht's conversation on the way back to the office. He began a recital of something he was already planning to write for the *Review* and asked, "What do you think I ought to call it?" The article was a typical Hechtic blast at the typical American family, so I said helpfully, "Why not call it 'Blah Blah Blah'?" Hecht laughed and I forgot the incident at once, but to my surprise that was precisely the title his satirical essay carried when it appeared in *The Little Review*. (This was, let me confess at once, my only contribution to the famous little journal, although I would gladly have had something in every issue.) Thereafter I met Miss Anderson perhaps half a dozen times at literary tea parties or at performances of Maurice Browne's Little Theater productions, and although we never saw eye to eye on the merits of my just-then-sentimental verse, I never ceased to admire her. She was, of course, much too beautiful to be an editor. It was almost impossible to believe she was the editor of such a journal as *The Little Review*, but of course that was not her fault. She is clearly of record as being dismayed by her resemblance to magazine cover cuties. However, it is no more than justice to her to recall that not only was she an able editor but one of the city's most attractive assets. No male who knew Miss Anderson in those early days of the century will be able to write of her without mentioning her physical attractions.

Nothing I have said here is intended to minimize the important part played by Miss Anderson in helping to inaugurate and carry forward Chicago's most considerable effort to escape its reputation. It is a pity, I think, that she did not remain in Chicago and, like Harriet Monroe, fight out her "thirty years' war" on the spot; but like so many others of the period she felt the call of the East and later the pull of Paris. It was not enough to contribute to the appreciation of art and the development of creative opinion in a frontier town; she wanted to take the world by storm. Most artists are that way, understandably enough. They are dissatisfied, as they should be, with the deplorable state of a local culture and must seek a greater freedom of expression in older civilizations. But they are wrong, I think. It is their duty to stay at home, at least to stay in America, and help bring about the cultural milieu they dream about. Expatriatism, a selfish but harmless enough exercise of temperament for the most part, in the last analysis is a disguised form of treason.

I am sorry, in view of the present interest in Sherwood Anderson, that my memories of him are so slight. After our casual meeting and exchange of courtesies in the Jackson Park studio I did not see him again for some years, although I knew that Hecht and Margery Currey believed him to be an important newcomer. They talked of him as they talked of all the new talents then being discovered. Then late one afternoon in my last year with the *Daily News*, Anderson came to the office to speak with Hecht, and I was introduced to him all over again. The subject of conversation, as I recall it, although I had the smallest possible part in it, was how best to persuade Llewellyn Jones, then editor of the *Evening Post's* literary supplement, to allow Ben to review a novel that Anderson was about to publish. Presumably the book was *Windy Mc-Pherson's Son* or its successor, *Marching Men,* and why any skullduggery was necessary to bring about the desired end I can't imagine, unless Anderson was afraid Jones would review the book himself and perhaps be stuffy about it. He was insistent that only Hecht must review his novel. The idea seemed to be that only Ben knew what Sherwood was attempting to do in literature and could give the book the sort of review its importance demanded. They settled the matter between them, somehow, and Anderson departed like a successful conspirator. Although slight, the incident is revealing, for Anderson took himself and his work with great seriousness then and later. At that time he was a writer of advertising, and he hated his job—a good-looking, heavy-set man with patent leather eyebrows and a square face that was as impassive as a mask. Only his dark eyes were alive and humorous. He was not a particularly humorous man, however; he was a deeply troubled and confused man who strove all his life to explain himself to Sherwood Anderson (and the rest of the world), never with complete success. Thereafter I met him only occasionally at cocktail parties or at Schlogl's restaurant, and to my regret I never got to know him. Perhaps nobody did. His friends told me he was a vain man and there was some evidence of this in his socks and neckties, which were on the exhibitionistic side. His suits seemed to me always one size too big for him and his hats one size too small. Dressed for a party, whether formal or informal, he looked a bit like a reservation Indian to whom the Great White Father at Washington had just issued a new outfit.

Although I read his *Winesburg, Ohio* with prurient enthusiasm when it appeared, and some of his short stories still seem to me as good as any produced in their time, there is little of his work I now read with pleasure. His sex-ridden, small-town yokels give me the creeps. Like most writers, he was troubled by intimations of mortality and immortality, and I think he mistook an obsession with sex for a philosophy of life. Nevertheless, I wish I had known him better. It is one of my embarrassing regrets that I knew him scarcely at all. I had a box seat for the famed Chicago renascence, but unfortunately I didn't always occupy it. I might have run around between the acts and visited the principals backstage, and no doubt I shall be accused of neglecting my opportunities. I accuse myself. But it is to be remembered that I was only a minor figure in the movement if, indeed, I was that. At its beginning I was a newspaper reporter with "literary ambitions" and later a hard working penny-a-liner. Of the big-name writers of the period, only Sandburg and Hecht were close friends or colleagues. I knew the others and occasionally met them in interesting circumstances; that was all.

Anderson's considered opinion of the period, voiced years afterward, may not be out of place here, although it is a thin tribute, interesting principally as a line of autobiography. "It was the time of a kind of Renaissance in the arts, in literature," he said; "a Robin's Egg Renaissance I have called it in my mind since. It had, perhaps, a pale blue tinge. It fell out of the nest. It may be that we should all have stayed in Chicago."

My relations with Harriet Monroe were not much happier than my relations with Margaret Anderson; that is to say, I failed utterly to convince her that my verse deserved a place in *Poetry*. Heaven knows, I tried hard enough but, as it happened, I was not to see my name in the famous little magazine until some years after her death. I am not blaming her for rejecting my verse, not now anyway. Little of it was then worth anybody's serious attention, and that little I managed to place with the *Smart Set* and similar journals more popular with the thundering herd. At the time, however, I was considerably annoyed with her for failing to find the merit in my verse that Mencken found. I could sell Mencken good sentimental verse or good ironic verse, but I could not sell Miss Monroe verse of any kind. My muse, she once told me, kindly enough, was "too pedestrian," and maybe she was right. It was a useful criticism, at any rate, and I bore it in mind.

On one other occasion we bandied words lightly on the same subject. A bit loftily I told her that I thought the poet, the artist, must be the final critic of his own work. "Criticism," I said, "is important only to the extent that one agrees with it." "Yes," she said, and added with a sharp glance, "or *comes* to agree with it." She was right. I came in time to agree that my poems of the period should not have been published in *Poetry*. Many of them should not have been published anywhere.

I attended a number of parties in *Poetry's* rooms in Erie Street, always with profit to myself. There I met dozens of poets of the day, among them Edgar Lee Masters, Vachel Lindsay, Arthur Davison Ficke, Witter Bynner, John Gould Fletcher, Alfred Kreymborg, Emanuel Carnevali, Mark Turbyfill, Eunice Tietjens, Marion Strobel, Jessica Nelson North, to mention only a handful. At such times a lot of poetry was read and nothing stronger than coffee was served. A pleasing and inspiring feature of the proceedings, for those acquainted with the topography of the area, was a glimpse of Miss Monroe herself, a small black figure, brewing the coffee over an open fire in a back alley. Harriet Monroe, then in her early fifties, liked her job as the high priestess of American poetry, and I think liked her own parties better than other people's. Once she fell asleep in the middle of somebody else's party while somebody was reading a poem. I didn't blame her; it was a dull party and a dull poem. She pleased me enormously, too, one night at the Fortnightly Club, when Vachel Lindsay was the principal guest, by her response to a request that she recite a poem.

179

Others had recited poems. Lindsay had recited several, chanting one of them sonorously as he ran around the room in a circle to show us how he had done it in England to astonish the natives. The air was thick with poems. It was at this juncture that Miss Monroe was asked to contribute. Her eyes were closed and for a moment I thought she was asleep again; but suddenly, without opening her eyes, she began to speak. What she said was:

> *When in disgrace with fortune and men's eyes*
> *I all alone beweep my outcast state,*
> *And trouble deaf heaven with my bootless cries,*
> *And look upon myself, and curse my fate . . .*

and so continued, gloriously, to the end of Shakespeare's great sonnet, reading it from memory as admirably as, I am sure, it ever has been done in this world. It was the last number on the program. Anything further would have been an anticlimax. There was nothing left for us to do but go home.

An old clipping reminds me that I sat beside her at a luncheon given for Richard Le Gallienne by the Society of Midland Authors, at which she presided and I introduced the guest of honor. This would be sometime in January, 1924. In thanking us for our introductory words, Le Gallienne took occasion to observe that Miss Monroe reminded him of Rhadamanthus, then knocked me cold by saying, "Poets are, as a rule, not good to look upon. But I have now met one young man who not only writes beauty but himself personifies it. As the old Narcissus, I salute the young Narcissus!" Thereafter he said some gracious words about a thin volume of verse I had recently published; but it was the more personal tribute that Harry Hansen chose to quote in his account of the luncheon. It may be imagined what a time I had with my rowdy newspaper friends living *that* down. But the older poet's tribute delighted me and did me no harm in the community at large. If Miss Monroe was impressed she gave no sign of it; I continued to knock on her door in vain.

Harriet Monroe's pre-eminent part in the Chicago renascence

180

need not be labored and it can scarcely be exaggerated. First and last she was a Chicagoan. She remained when other lights of the movement fled to New York and Hollywood and Paris. Her idea of a magazine wholly devoted to poetry, which should pay the poets for their work and be hospitable to new names and new methods, was as revolutionary as any idea of its time. She was a tiny little thing, as I remember her, a bit prim looking and a little demure too, with neat gray hair and gold-rimmed spectacles. I think she looked like Miss Marple, Agatha Christie's perspicacious little spinster detective, and I would have told her so if I had met Miss Marple early enough in the century. Witter Bynner hit her off very well in the couplet he composed about her for his poetic portrait gallery, *Pins for Wings*, in which he ironically characterized the leading poets of the day. Of Miss Monroe he wrote:

> *The Mother Superior*
> *Considers lingerie.*

Two other "little magazines," it should be noted, contributed to the Chicago movement, each in its own way. *Art*, edited by Howard Vincent O'Brien, made its modest bow in October, 1912, the month that also saw the first issue of *Poetry: A Magazine of Verse*; and *The Lantern*, edited by Curtis J. Kirch (with Milton Fuessle as associate) appeared in January, 1913, anticipating *The Little Review* by fourteen months. Neither offered much competition to their more dedicated rivals, yet both were typical of their time. O'Brien's little magazine, which survived until May, 1916, when it was absorbed by the *Dial*, was at first only the house organ of the O'Brien Art Galleries. Suddenly in May, 1914, it began to call itself *The Trimmed Lamp* and to publish original poems and criticisms by Amy Lowell, Vachel Lindsay, John Gould Fletcher, and other poets associated with the new movement. It was a handsome little journal, ably edited by a young man destined to comparative failure as a novelist but to long popularity as one of Chicago's best loved columnists. The *Lantern* was quite another kettle of fish. It was a self-serving, ultra-Bohemian periodical, by intention a weekly but actually published whenever Kirch was in funds. I first heard of it from Fuessle, then my colleague on the *Daily News,* who was soliciting contributions for it in the office. Early issues contained stories by Guido Bruno and drawings by Wallace Smith, and Bruno's contributions continued to the end of the dispensation in July, 1913, for the simple reason that he and Curtis J. Kirch were one and the same person. I believe this was the first time Kirch used the pseudonym he later made famous in Greenwich Village.

All that need be said about the *Lantern* is that it was a nondescript miscellany made up of whatever odds and ends its editors could obtain without cost to themselves. Its literary content was pitiful. Kirch, a Serbian (or so he told me), was an amiable creature obsessed by the decadent English "Nineties," sentimental about prostitutes and money-lenders, most at his ease in the fly-blown old hostelries and rathskellers of the Near North Side; and in his own way he was genuinely devoted to the arts, on the fringe of all of which he was a small but interesting figure.

In such fashion, or something like it, our Chicago renascence began. Everybody wanted to get into the act and nearly everybody did. It inflated beyond all reason a great many essentially trivial developments and it endowed with momentary greatness any number of essentially unimportant persons. It was a gaudy and stimulating moment in time and the memory of it is still stirring—and amusing. It should be added that the important writers who gave it significance were not part of the sensationalism and bohemianism that gave it color. The big-name writers went their way much as usual, working hard as always, occasionally lending their presence to miscellaneous gatherings; but the smaller fry were active from sundown to sunup (*sic*) in all manner of fantastic projects and recreations that added piquancy to the spectacle. Exotic cultural centers sprang up on all sides of the city in restaurants, rathskellers, studios, converted coach houses or garages, and similar dives, as well as in private homes and club rooms. Maurice Browne's Little Theater in the Fine Arts Building was not the only "little theater" in the city; nearly every neighborhood had one and the more experimental companies produced some lively and exhilarating programs that caught the new spirit admirably. Although my personal commitments kept me busy much of the day and sometimes part of the night, I witnessed performances in barns and basements, in the back rooms of taverns and printshops, that compared very favorably with those going forward in Michigan Avenue, and they were on the whole more interesting. Certainly they were more daring. I did not myself take part in any of these divertissements, but at one time it seemed that an inspiration of mine might give the suburban township of Austin, in which I lived, a toy theater to end all such phenomena. My idea was to present a series of Grand Guignol shockers in the show room of a local undertaking parlor or, better still, in the embalming room downstairs. It was received with wild acclaim by half a dozen young writers of the township when I broached it late one night after a social evening at the home of Anthony Rud, and I think the undertaker (a handsome fellow) could have been prevailed on to head the company; but by morning we had all begun to question the validity of the inspiration and the project came to nothing.

As I say, it was a lively and stimulating stretch of time. Mencken's recognition of the phenomenon continues to be a good springboard for reminiscence, although I have never believed he intended anything more than an exaggerated compliment. Possibly he was pulling New York's leg. There was occasion for his remarks, however. Serious or otherwise, he was thinking of a particular group of writers when he called Chicago the literary capital of the nation. I think I could tick them off on the fingers of my two hands. They were Sherwood Anderson, Carl Sandburg, Edgar Lee Masters, Ben Hecht, and Maxwell Bodenheim among the creative workers, and such almost Chicagoans as Theodore Dreiser and Vachel Lindsay, who were frequently on the scene and were for sufficient reasons regarded as part of the movement. But Mencken was thinking, too, of a little group of editors and critics, and of one publisher, who were in the forefront of the battle and not the least important part of it. The editors were Margaret Anderson and Harriet Monroe and possibly Henry Justin Smith of the *Daily News* —who was, however, more of an influence than a participant. The literary crickets were Harry Hansen, Burton Rascoe, and Llewellyn Jones. The publisher was Pascal Covici, later an editor at the Viking Press, who established the Covici-McGee bookshop and turned it into a publishing house. I omit Floyd Dell from this line-up only because he had left Chicago some years before the sage of Baltimore made his flattering accusation. Dell's importance as a forerunner is not to be minimized.

Undoubtedly the liveliest book critic in Chicago during the first years of the renascence was the late Burton Rascoe, who became the *Tribune's* first reader in 1917. It is not too much to say that then, at that certain moment, and always excepting H. L. Mencken, he was the most influential book critic in the country. He had an alert and discriminating intelligence. He was young, brash, enthusiastic, and knowledgable. No more unbridled and, withal, scholarly and effective cultural force ever was loosed on a lethargic and complacent community. If Chicago was then the center of the most exciting literary movement in the country, it was so in no small degree because Rascoe occupied one of the editorial chairs and rode it, cavalry fashion, with spurs. Almost from the first, the snap and crackle of his critical whip was heard across the land. His pages in the *Tribune* sparkled. He held important, if proprietary, opinions about books and authors and aired them with a gusto and recklessness that was as stimulating as it was diverting. He was the first to hail Mencken adequately, and among the first to sound the tocsin for T. S. Eliot. He it was who blew the first great trumpet blast for James Branch Cabell which made that obscure Virginian a classic almost overnight. The book he celebrated was *The Cream of the Jest*; and a little later he went all out for *Jurgen*, a masterpiece which, without his original fanfare, might have dropped as quietly from the press as had its predecessors. It was his enthusiasm for *Jurgen* that sent first editions of the book to forty dollars in the antiquarian market in its first year of

184

publication. It brings somewhat less than that today, but that is another story: Rascoe was right about its importance to American literature, as he was right about most of the other books he championed. Parenthetically, I would like to say that I seconded him as energetically as I could in his slashing campaign for Cabell, in reviews contributed to the *Herald and Examiner,* which just then was attempting to establish a book supplement of its own.

Frequently there was a lively controversy going on in the *Tribune* book pages between rival ideologists, for Burton liked nothing better than a full-dress row. Once Rupert Hughes attacked Cabell's æsthetic tenets as expressed in *Beyond Life,* and the letter touched off an exchange of compliments that lasted for several weeks before Cabell had the last word. It was one of the bitterest literary dog fights of memory. Later a minor "international incident" occurred when Conrad Aiken wrote a bitter poem about Robert Nichols, a British poet then visiting America, and Rascoe printed the poem. That sort of thing was always happening in Burton's pages. There has been no such forum in Chicago since. The record of his belligerent adventures in criticism is set forth in his autobiography, *Before I Forget,* not too modestly, and it is still excellent reading. Ultimately he was fired in a blaze of glory and went on to New York, where he was equally disturbing to stuffed shirts and complacent adherents of the genteel tradition. You will catch his flavor best in *A Bookman's Daybook,* edited from his newspaper columns by C. Hartley Grattan. Although good reading, and a storehouse of information about Burton Rascoe and the Chicago scene, his autobiography is tumultuous and wordy and, unfortunately, lacks an index.

The book pages of the *Daily News* were quieter, except when Ben Hecht contributed one of his adjectival causeries. In my time on the paper, by whose decision I do not know, books were relegated to the sticks in a series of "notes" written by Stanley Faye; but just before or just after I went away we got a full-time literary editor, Henry Blackman Sell, and suddenly books became news.

Moreover, they attracted advertising, for Sell had a flair for exploitation and a way with booksellers and publishers. He got out a chatty and distinctive page that quickly became popular. Having established it as a permanent feature, however, he responded to the inevitable call of the East and departed for New York to become editor of *Harper's Bazaar*, and Harry Hansen took over. Hansen inherited one of Sell's most popular innovations, that of rounding up Chicago writers at luncheons given for visiting authors, and thus the famous Round Table at Schlogl's Restaurant came into existence—Sell had taken *his* celebrities to Field's Grill.

For some time Hansen and Henry Smith had been lunching occasionally at Schlogl's, because it was convenient, and soon Ben Hecht and Keith Preston (a little later Pascal Covici and Billy McGee) were eating there too. This would be early in 1920, since Hansen did not return from Europe until 1919. The circle was quickly joined by Dr. Morris Fishbein and others, including the author of these memoirs, and when visiting authors from New York or London reached Chicago they were invited to sit in. Much ink has been spilled by historians seeking to date the Round Table and credit somebody with its inception. I would myself have awarded the credit to Hansen without a second thought, but he has modestly declined the nomination. "Nobody founded the Table," he told me. "If there is any credit in it, I'd say Henry Smith was the magnet that drew us to it." It may be added incidentally that the food was good—although a little above what we could afford—and the atmosphere was just right. In any case, Schlogl's quickly became one of the conversational centers of the movement, and today the Round Table has passed into literary history as one of its symbols. It was our nearest approach to the Mermaid Tavern and ultimately its membership included, with few exceptions, all the men of the Renascence. Among the writers who dropped in weekly, bi-weekly, or occasionally, were Carl Sandburg, Sherwood Anderson, Edgar Lee Masters, Maxwell Bodenheim, Lew Sarett, Gene Markey, John V. A. Weaver, J. P. McEvoy, Lloyd Lewis, Richard Atwater, Robert Ballou, J. U. Nicolson, Wallace Smith, Ashton Stevens,

Sam Putnam, John Drury, John Gunther, Mark Turbyfill, Charles Layng, Gene Morgan, Llewellyn Jones, Charles Collins, and Charles MacArthur—these in addition to the men already mentioned as charter members. The visiting firemen too were a notable lot: Sinclair Lewis, Upton Sinclair, Donald Ogden Stewart, D. W. Griffith, Arthur Brisbane, Raymond Hitchcock, Clarence Darrow, W. L. George, Hendrik Willem Van Loon, Hugh Walpole, Clement Shorter, Gilbert Cannan, J. C. Squire, A. P. Herbert, Louis Untermeyer, Bobby Edwards, Ludwig Lewisohn, are names that come quickly to mind. Most of the talking, as I recall it, was done by Ben Hecht and/or Maxwell Bodenheim, who seldom agreed on anything and were proverbially friendly enemies. They were also the principal interlocutors when British celebrities were reckless enough to sit down with us. Broadly, I would say, the Table was principally a forum for Hecht and Preston. In spite of their seniority, Smith and Hansen were the least garrulous. I used to wonder what impression the visiting notables, particularly the Britons, carried away with them; not that it matters. If their facial expressions were an index of their emotions, they were alternately shocked, pleased, and exhilarated by the genial turbulence of the unique circle.

Most constant of all the many members of the group was Richard Schneider, the "literary waiter" as he has come to be called, who brought us food and drink, then hovered over us like a motherly hen looking after a brood of refractory chicks. "Your order is coming right up," he used to tell us, even before we had seated ourselves at the table; for it was his settled conviction that he knew what was best for us that day and no argument ever moved him. He was called the "literary waiter" because—forgive me!— he had a book. Let me say, rather, he had a Book, and what a Book it was! By 1923 Hansen had published his *Midwest Portraits*, and an early copy suitably inscribed had been presented to Richard. The volume became famous as "Richard's Book" and it was always quickly in evidence when distinguished visitors were among us. Ultimately it was so congested with sentiment and signatures on all its blank leaves and margins that the chirography began to run over into the text. And finally it had been so constantly handled that it had to be rebound. This final gesture of affection was financed by Hansen, I believe, who had presented the book in the first place. I am told that at the last census it contained some five thousand signatures, which must surely mean that some of us signed it a number of times.

It would be difficult to say why we liked Schlogl's. As I say, the place was convenient for the *News* crowd and the food was good, and of course there was Richard; but there was more to it than that. It was comfortable, friendly, and off the beaten trail, and also it was strictly stag—no skirt ever rustled on the fringes of our exclusive huddle—but certainly (except as to conversation) it did not sparkle. It was an unpretentious little German restaurant and barroom, with the usual murky old oil paintings on the walls, and little in the place had changed since its doors opened in 1879. Perhaps that was its charm. Even the old gas fixtures were still there, although they had been wired for electricity. The long black walnut bar and brass footrail had never been moved, the food was still cooked on the original hard-coal stove, and the original round tables stood more or less where they had always stood. The ceiling, once white, was almost black when I knew it, from the smoke of the millions of pipes, cigars, and cigarettes smoked there for sixty years—although Smith's pipe alone could have done it. Our private table, twice as large as any other in the place, stood in a corner somewhat protected from the clutter of politicians and lawyers who also liked to lunch there. As it was a *round* table, nobody seated at it seemed to have the place of honor, but Hansen's chair was generally considered the head of the table. His chief lieutenant, Keith Preston, usually sat beside him.

Preston, later to be book editor in succession to Hansen, had come to prominence in the city quickly. A professor of Greek and Latin at Northwestern University, he began his more public career as a contributor to B. L. T.'s famous column, "A Line o' Type or Two," in the *Tribune*, where over the appropriate pseudonym *Pan* he published some of the wittiest light verse of the day. He became a *Daily News* regular when he established "The Periscope," a weekly column of comment on the book page, which he retained even after he had succeeded T. K. Hedrick as editor of the daily "Hit or Miss" column. If he had cared to, he might have succeeded B. L. T. on the *Tribune* at Taylor's death;[1] indeed, I am told that he was offered the job and turned it down. As editor of "Hit or Miss" and "The Periscope," however, he rapidly became one of the most popular columnists in town. He published a number of slim volumes of verse drawn from both columns, and was acquiring a national reputation when he was struck down by the germ that ended his life. He was a likable little man and his writings, for all their superficial cleverness, reflected the scholarly temper of his mind. He was always the professor at play. Many of his satirical paragraphs and stanzas are as fresh and timely today as when they were written. His posthumous book, *Pot Shots from Parnassus*, is a delightful collection of critical comment that may well stand on the shelves of every bookman. Our personal relations were of the friendliest sort and occasionally I contributed to his daily column. Indeed, our friendship survived my discovery in a second-hand bookshop of his first published work, a doctoral dissertation printed at his own expense. He inscribed it for me handsomely while wondering how many of the "damn things" were still in existence.

But to get back to Hansen: his page was whimsical and chatty, although sufficiently modern, and rather more cordial to all sides of the "lit'ry life," as he called it, than the *Tribune* book page. He was a folksy commentator in his personal journalism, as friendly to the Bookfellows and the Friends of American Writers as to the more glittering personalities of the pen whose exits and entrances he reported. He was a critic all publishers could quote, not just the more iconoclastic and liberal ones. He steered a jaunty middle course between the extremes of modernism and Victorianism with skill and judgment, and of course in time, like everybody else,

[1] B. L. T. (Bert Leston Taylor) was himself a considerable influence on the cultural life of Chicago for many years. His standards were high and his admirably written and edited column printed some of the wittiest prose and verse of the time.

went on to New York. His contribution to the Chicago renascence was considerable and his Round Table at Schlogl's will be remembered when more sensational aspects of the period are forgotten. It is proverbial that revolutions begin in little cafés. And to the extent that the Chicago renascence was revolutionary, history was repeating itself at Schlogl's.

Llewellyn Jones, Chicago's third literary editor, was a survival at the *Evening Post*; that is to say, he was the last although not the least of a brilliant dynasty of *Post* editors. Francis Hackett, who had founded the *Friday Literary Review*, had been succeeded by Floyd Dell, who in turn had been succeeded by Lucian Cary. Under all these editors Jones had served as reviewer; he was the legitimate heir to the berth. He was an easy-going, good-natured Manxman, although a hard worker, and if he was less pyrotechnically brilliant than Hackett and Dell (and than Burton Rascoe at the *Tribune*) he was no less sound in his judgments. He was shrewd, scholarly, conservative, and sometimes heavy-handed. What he really thought of the aesthetic uproar going on around him I never knew, although I used to suspect that he found it somewhat noisy and distracting—his personal enthusiasms were for the British poets Walter de la Mare, Lascelles Abercrombie, and T. Sturge Moore—and by the unassertive nature of his personality he has now all but effaced himself from our literary history. He was not a self-advertiser, but he got out a literary supplement that was better than many readers, debauched by rival attractions, ever realized. He was an early and friendly critic of the new poetry, although he once "got after" Amy Lowell, whom he asserted to be grossly ignorant of prosody, which led to a spirited controversy in the somewhat staid columns of the *Post*. And he was the first critic in this country to hail Joseph Hergesheimer as an important novelist. Jones's best articles and reviews were subsequently collected in a sober volume called *First Impressions*. Unfortunately for his reputation, it was not followed up by later volumes of impressions.

It was through his friendly interest that I became, early in the twenties, a book reviewer for the *Post*. Looking over old clippings of my reviews, it seems to me that I was an adolescent trying to sound like a sophisticated professional; but probably I did no great harm. I used to find "promise" in most of the new novels given me for review and occasionally, to my huge delight, found myself quoted by the publishers on book jackets and in their advertisements. I echoed Rascoe's enthusiasm for Cabell acceptably enough to make Cabell my friend, and when opportunity offered I cheered lustily for my obscure favorites, who just then included Arthur Machen and Haldane Macfall. For these services I received only the books I reviewed—the usual rate of payment for most of the *Post* reviewers— and these I subsequently sold to the old-book sellers, thus adding a trifle to my income, which was meagre at best, for I was still writing short stories and trying to sell them.

Probably it was about this time that I first met Vachel Lindsay, or rather that I first heard his voice, for it was on the telephone that we met. Years before, as early as 1913, I think, when he was still a tramp poet, he had written a letter to the *Post* offering a copy of his privately printed *Rhymes to Be Traded for Bread* to anybody who would ask for it, and I had written at once to ask for it. In his reply, sending me the book, Lindsay called me the "bravest man in Chicago," and confessed that I was the only person who had taken him at his word. He had not forgotten the incident and, finding himself in Chicago one day, had telephoned me at the *Post*. Jones had given him my home number; and thus it came about that I answered a ring one afternoon and heard someone say, "This is Vachel Lindsay. I hope you remember me." We talked for some minutes but were unable to meet, and a number of years were to elapse before I met him in the flesh.

It was at this time also that I came to know Charles Collins, then drama critic of the *Post*, who became one of my closest friends and many years later helped me to establish my own book column in the *Sunday Tribune*. Others whom I met around the *Post* office in those days were Julian Mason, the newspaper's publisher; Richard Atwater, another fugitive from B. L. T.'s famous column, who was conducting his own column in the *Post*; and Robert O.

191

Ballou, a young man of ideas and talent who, like too many others, hurried off to New York at the first opportunity.

Before dropping the subject, I would like to say a word in praise or dispraise, as the case may be, of the little reviewers of that period. Although we received no pennies for our thoughts, we took ourselves seriously and were proud to be part of the movement. We were cocky and pontifical and, ladies and gentlemen, whatever else we were, we sure were *literary*! Even our brief cases seemed to us symbolic. Those of us who could wore horn-rimmed spectacles. We dropped in at the office with empty bags and left with full bags—bags bulging with books the editor didn't want himself—and occasionally we drew something good that made the front page of the supplement. We didn't think of ourselves as reviewers: we were *critics*, like Llewellyn Jones, like Harry Hansen, like even Burton Rascoe himself. In short, we were young and we were part of a literary capital. The Great God Mencken had said so.

Some of the sideshows of the period, so to call them, were more interesting in sheer entertainment values than the main attraction. Under this head I am inclined to place the Covici-McGee bookshop (without disparagement) beside such manifestations of the liberated spirit as the Dill Pickle Club and certain bohemian restaurants of the day, one of which solicited patronage by advertising in large letters: "Our Cook Sings! Our Waiters Dance!" Not that the bookshop was comic; far from it. It was deadly serious in its intention, but its workings were wild and wonderful. Its senior proprietor, Pascal Covici, I have no hesitation in saying, was one of the most important figures of the Chicago movement during the nineteen-twenties. In many ways that movement resembled the English renascence (or decadence) of the eighteen-nineties and like the London development it evolved its own publisher. Covici was our Leonard Smithers. As Smithers published Oscar Wilde, Aubrey Beardsley, and other peculiarly ninetyish figures, Covici published Ben Hecht, Wallace Smith, and a string of peculiarly twentyish figures, including Maxwell Bodenheim, Stanislaus Szukalski, and an ambitious young rebel or reactionary (he never knew which) named Vincent Starrett.

I know nothing about Pat Covici's early history—I think he had been an orange grower in Florida—but when I knew him in the early twenties he was a bookseller. He and William F. (Billy) McGee, a former Roman Catholic priest, had opened a small shop, "three steps down," in Washington Street near LaSalle. Almost at once it became the headquarters of many of the bright young men of the movement, and there on sunny afternoons it was the pleasant habit of those young men and their admirers to loiter aimlessly and let themselves be seen. Particularly it became the headquarters of Ben Hecht and Maxwell Bodenheim, than whom two more picturesque bohemians of literature never existed. Their presence attracted others to the place and for some years the small, somewhat disorderly bookshop was the liveliest den of literature in the city. Not to be secret about it, I did a lot of unnecessary hanging out there myself, with W. C. Firebaugh, J. U. Nicolson, and other cronies. Some day a history of the shop, its habitués, and its publications is going to be called for, and I don't know who is going to write it unless Covici has left a diary of the period. I have no checklist of publications; but the most notable, I suppose, was Hecht's *1001 Afternoons in Chicago* (1923), an important and stunningly produced volume of stories now sought by collectors. It was designed by Herman Rosse, an instructor at the Art Institute, whose spidery black-and-white drawings were in the best modernistic manner of the movement. Another work still sought by bibliophiles is Hecht's *Fantazius Mallare* (1922), illustrated by Wallace Smith, an erotic performance on the part of both men that got everybody into trouble. A federal court found the book objectionable and it was suppressed. As the case was attended by the utmost publicity for everybody concerned, it may be said to have made its own peculiar contribution to the "spirit" of the renascence. Other remembered books published by Covici–McGee were Bodenheim's *The Sardonic Arm*, a volume of verse, and *Blackguard*, a novel, and J. U. Nicolson's *The King of the Black Isles,* a volume of romantic poems in the manner of Swinburne, to which Keith Preston contributed an introduction. For the record, I note that I published three books myself over this imprint and edited several others. My own titles were *Ebony Flame* (1922), a volume of lyrics, *Buried Caesars* (1923), a miscellany of literary appreciations, and *Coffins for Two* (1924), a volume of short stories. The edited works included two volumes of tales and essays by Arthur Machen, publication of which involved me and the publishers in an unhappy literary cause célèbre; but that is a story I will tell in another place.

Covici's printer was a convivial soul named Renshaw—James Lindsay Renshaw—who seemed to embody in himself all the picturesque legends one had read about printers. His presswork was good, although a little on the flamboyant side, which was all right with the authors of the books he printed. It was Renshaw who printed also the *Chicago Literary Times* for Ben Hecht, in establishing which Covici may have had a hand. In this astonishing journal, published semi-monthly from March 1, 1923, to June 1, 1924, Ben applied Hearst newspaper format and headlines to current literature. He and Bodenheim, his associate editor, wrote most of the paper themselves, I think, and sometimes insulted each other in malevolent language for the sake of publicity. I never knew whether Hecht and Bogey really disliked each other as much as they pretended they did, but whether their constant feuds were genuine or simulated they made amusing copy. Few literary reputations escaped criticism at the hands of this precious pair, but they struck a nice balance by praising those writers whose work they conspired to admire. Wallace Smith contributed some of his remarkable black-and-whites to the enterprise and for a few issues I contributed a column of comment captioned "From Hell to Breakfast." Hecht's original intention was to launch this extraordinary journal with a street parade. There were to be brass bands, perhaps a calliope, and half a mile of floats showing the writers and critics of Chicago in action, each identified by a banner; not wax replicas but the men themselves. He asked me if I would take part in this extravaganza and of course I said I would; but disappointingly the sensational project never came to a head.

To get back to the bookshop, Hecht sometimes helped the partners to dress the windows and at such times the display was likely to be unusual. I remember a series of startling black-and-white drawings by George Grosz (reproductions) that held the public attention for some weeks. The drawings themselves, rather like the work of a naughty child of genius, were sufficiently remarkable; but for better understanding Hecht had thoughtfully given them explanatory captions. That the captions did not always describe the drawings was a minor detail. One, a weird sketch of two citizens talking on a street corner, he called simply, and perhaps truthfully, "Two Fornicators." A man and a woman in conversation in what may have been a bedroom became "Fornicators at Play." The word *fornicators* seemed to obsess Ben just then, but as few passers-by knew what it meant, there was no indignant public protest—as Hecht had hoped there might be—and those of us who were in on the joke were disappointed. Szukalski, the sculptor of grotesques, also exhibited his work in this window, I think; and for one reason or another a great many persons came into the shop. Bodenheim, who loved sympathy, used to show up with his arm in a sling, claiming to have a broken collarbone, but it was an old gag and only strangers fell for it. Come to think of it, my first view of Bogey was at Maurice Browne's Little Theater, where the bandaged arm and a huge pipe were conspicuously exhibited as he tramped up and down the lounge with his overcoat collar turned up waiting, he said, for Arthur Davison Ficke to arrive. (P.S. Ficke didn't come.) I remember Bodenheim as a slim, blond genius with blue eyes, pale yellow eyelashes and hair like a mop of wet hemp. His smile was mocking but ingratiating. I thought of him as the François Villon of the period, and indeed he gave a better impersonation of a tavern poet of genius than any other poet I have ever known except Kenneth Fearing.

Poor Billy McGee, who had a bad heart, sometimes enlivened

the conversations that constantly went forward in the shop by collapsing and having to be carried downstairs to a couch in the basement. He was a lovable fellow and everybody's friend, a sort of father-confessor to all who knew him. I never learned why he gave up the priesthood to become a bookseller—he wrote a small pamphlet about it that I didn't read—but I'm sure he was a good priest while he worked at it. After the shop had changed hands a number of times he became a traveling salesman in books and I have heard that he was a Unitarian clergyman when he died in California. I remember him with affection.

When Burton Rascoe returned to Chicago for a visit he added the busy little shop to his ports of call and recorded his impressions in his "Bookman's Daybook" in the New York *Herald Tribune*. I quote a paragraph of his tribute:

"He [Gene Markey] led me to the bookshop of Covici-McGee, where we encountered Markey's only (and hardly relevant) disputant for sartorial distinction among American literary and artistic men—Vincent Starrett. There was Starrett, the eminent Victorian, examining as usual with the eye of a connoisseur, a first edition. His hair is black hair which has turned white with an air; his complexion is pallid and smooth; his features are Stracheyan and bookish; he wears a fur-collared black overcoat with a white muffler; he is the only writer I have ever met who looks like a literary man. That Covici-McGee place is utterly wild and astounding. It has far too much enthusiasm and energy to keep entirely out of jail; it has hired Ben Hecht, Maxwell Bodenheim, Wallace Smith, and Samuel Rudens, and it has retained among its salesmen the good gray dean of Chicago booksellers (William Ramsay); it is issuing an iconoclastic weekly called 'The Chicago Literary Times'; it is publishing a magnificent edition of reproductions of Szukalski's drawings, prose and sculpture; and it has already brought out books by Hecht, Bodenheim, Henry Justin Smith, and Edwin Herbert Lewis."

Unfortunately, my scrapbook clipping retains only that much of Rascoe's article—the part dealing with myself. His characterization of me as "the eminent Victorian," is explained by a dreadful caricature of me in one of Markey's books, in which I was presented as a portly bookman of the old school and called the "last Tennysonian."

Some time in 1916 the Dill Pickle Club opened its doors in Tooker Alley, the heart of what has been called Chicago's Latin Quarter, a congested section just north of the river that for years had been the haunt of artists, poets, and bohemians of every sort. Ostensibly the club was organized for the promotion of the arts and crafts, of literature, science, and oratory; and it did, indeed, promote all these activities after its fashion. In point of fact, the history of the club goes back as far as the year 1907, when it was founded by Jack Jones and Jim Larkin, the I. W. W. labor agitator, as a place where anybody with ideas or opinions might let off steam. Among its early frequenters were "Big Bill" Haywood, Eugene V. Debs, Emma Goldman, Mother Jones, Robert Minor, and other left-wingers of the day. My informant about its early history was the late Dr. Ben L. Reitman, one of its leading figures from first to last. But its cultural history, so to speak, dates from 1916, when it became the nocturnal center—the flaming crater— of the city's revolution in the arts. Its founder (or refounder) at that time was again Jack Jones—John Archibald Jones—an unemployed printer, paper-hanger, interior decorator, and former Wobbly, with a talent for painting and wood carving. Jones was also a cunning opportunist who needed no second knock to urge him to his self-appointed task.

The club was admirably located. It was near Washington Square, popularly known as "Bughouse Square," and was in effect part of that colorful spectacle. The approach to it was interesting: Tooker Alley was a sordid little mews opening into Dearborn on the west, but visitors approaching from the east could slip between two buildings in North State Street, where no passage had been intended, and find themselves within a few feet of the entrance. "Bughouse Square," which serves as a great front yard for the

Newberry Library, was then, as it is now, Chicago's counterpart of Hyde Park in London. The soapboxers of the square and their audiences quickly moved in, and the club became an open forum for anybody with a message to deliver. But the literati came too and members of the fashionable set found it a novel and exciting form of slumming. The radicals predominated, however, and almost took over the place. In theory, Sunday nights were devoted to lectures by university professors, Tuesday nights to poetry, Wednesday nights to lectures by home talent, and so on; but I doubt that this program was scrupulously followed. Often the routines seemed to be inextricably mixed. Some nights were given over to drama and dancing, and almost any night was likely to be more or less of a "whoopee" night. Everybody sat about in a beautiful huddle. Flappers, college boys, visiting poets, university professors, sex adepts, and muggs from "Bughouse Square" jostled one another in reckless camaraderie. From the platform was discussed everything from Nietzsche to sex taboos of the ancients. Geniuses with dirty necks read their poems, atheists denounced God, and wild-eyed pianists played their latest compositions. Rarely, I think, were ideas expressed which, by any stretch of the imagination, could be called moderate. Everybody and everything was *anti*.

Such is my broad impression of the Dill Pickle Club as occasionally I saw it in action. The fact remains that it had its more responsible side. Famous speakers used to go there, once at least, and all the *isms* of the day (including nudism) were authoritatively discussed. Experimental plays were frequently of considerable interest, and on good nights it was possible to hear good poetry read. Carl Sandburg sometimes read his poems there, as more often did Maxwell Bodenheim. Ben Hecht's notorious one-act play *Dregs*, first presented at a studio theater on the South Side, on which occasion some of the audience walked out, was repeated at the Dill Pickle, where I first saw it. Its first line, which had shocked the South Siders, shocked nobody on the Near North Side. Probably hundreds of persons attended that night only to hear the daring words spoken in public. The line was: *"Jesus Christ, I'm a*

198

cross-eyed son of a bitch if it ain't!"—supposed to be uttered by a drunken derelict on catching a bleary glimpse of his own image in a drugstore window one freezing midnight. He had mistaken his reflection for a Miraculous Appearance and thereafter discoursed at length to the figure he took to be the Christ. That was the whole play, plus of course his ultimate surprise when he realized that he had been talking to himself. We all thought it pretty powerful stuff, and nobody at the Dill walked out.

Jack Jones was always present. I remember him as a Jack Londonish figure clad in a blue (or checked) shirt, corduroy trousers, and sandals. Like everybody else at the club he was an exhibitionist; but he was friendly to down-and-outers, and stranded artists or agitators could always stay the night at the club if they had no other place to go. "What we are trying to produce here is facts, not a superior atmosphere," he used to yell furiously when it seemed to him that somebody was looking too critical. As there was usually a fair sprinkling of reporters in the Dill's audiences, many of his utterances got into print. The reputation of the club, however, was out of all proportion to its actual importance to the awakening that called it into being. For out-of-town innocents it was almost a sinister spot; some of them thought they needed a police escort. John Beffel told me he heard a policeman characterize the club for a timid suburbanite who wanted to see some of the city's tough spots. "Tough, eh?" said the amused cop. "Ever been at the Dill Pickle? Say, that's the toughest place in Chicago. They frisk you at the front door to see if you're carrying any concealed weapons." After a thoughtful pause he added, "If you don't have any, they *give* you one."

Maxwell Bodenheim, one of its more talented habitués, called it a rough-house, and that is what it was. Harry Hansen called it "a little audacious circle," which is putting it mildly.

After all the foregoing, it is only fair to confess that I did not often visit the Dill Pickle. It was not snobbishness that kept me away, although I hope a certain fastidiousness was involved. In any case, I was then a married man with a living to make and little enough time to spare for spectacles, however colorful. The Dill Pickle seemed to me phony as far as its expressed purpose of fostering the arts was concerned, while as an entertainment spot it seemed to me even less satisfying. I have never been much of a bohemian and there is no point now in pretending that I was. Now and again I tried to tell myself that I liked such places and the sort of artistic freedom they appeared to stand for; but I never really convinced myself. In my heart I knew I was not cut out for the Greenwich Village type of existence.

Thus in broad outline I remember the Chicago Literary Renascence and the men, women, and magazines that helped to bring it about. In a later chapter I shall describe my own insignificant part in it and my further associations with the writers who made it notable. Just now, for the sake of pattern, if nothing else, a few words about its last days may be in order. The movement ended, as far as Chicago was concerned, simply and solely because most of the writers who gave it significance went away. No sooner had they been made aware of their excellence by Mencken's flattering proclamation than, one by one, they vanished from the scene of their triumphs in quest of further honors and emoluments. With the departure of most of the principals, the movement as a phenomenon naturally ended and the city began to live on its memories. This did not happen all at once, of course, but by 1925 (at latest 1926) the exodus was all but complete.

It should be noted that Mencken himself did not long hold his high opinion of the Chicago group. As early as 1923, when Hansen published his *Midwest Portraits*, Mencken used the book as a springboard for a violent essay on the Chicago writers, including Sandburg and Anderson; and a few years later he inspired an article by Sam Putnam that was intended to be the *coup de grâce*. Putnam, a Paris-minded æsthete, who had been contributing art and literary criticism to the *Evening Post*, was an ideal hatchet man for the job. "Why don't you do an article for the *Mercury*, showing up those phonies out there?" Mencken suggested; and Putnam,

200

nothing loath—he, too, disliked the local cultural scene by that time—wrote "Chicago: An Obituary," which appeared in the *American Mercury* of August, 1926. The uproar that followed this mischievous piece, in which Sam served up the heads of his Chicago colleagues on a gridiron, convinced the brash young man that the city was quite as provincial as he had supposed it to be, and shortly thereafter he too departed—for Paris—on the heels of the "expatriate movement" of the twenties. Mencken was pleased, according to Sam. "You gave all the fakes a salubrious and much-needed shaking-up," he commented.

The "fakes" and "phonies" ordered destroyed by the Baltimore Herod were the more obscure writers who were left to the city after the flight of the Bumblebees. Some of them, notably Keith Preston, who was no respecter of persons, had been guilty of *lese-majesté*, it appears, and Henry wanted their scalps. This is a valuable footnote to the episode that should be remembered when Mencken's praise of Chicago as a "literary capital" is sounded. He that giveth also sometimes taketh away.

We were all outraged by Sam's "obituary," of course, and Preston (when he spoke of it to me) was almost purple in the face. I got off lightly, for some reason, as an amiable dilettante concerned principally with advancing the American fame of Arthur Machen.

"And what good came of it at last?" asked little Peterkin. If I were to be asked what it all meant, what we were trying to do or thought we were trying to do, in all honesty I would have to reply, "I don't know." I suspect nobody knew precisely what the renascence was aiming at, least of all the men and women most conspicuously associated with it. Principally they were seeking individual expression and found it exhilarating to thumb their noses at tradition. Like the people themselves, they were sick of war, sick of the administration, sick of the moral climate, sick of everything. They were against Harding, Coolidge, Victorianism, Philistinism, Puritanism, classicism, prohibition, Babbitry, boobs; a machine-made civilization without spiritual depth or cultural

201

values; middle-class prejudice, smugness, gentility, respectability, and so on—the clichés come readily to mind. Particularly they were against everything that had gone immediately before. Perhaps they were just *against*, period. They stood for greater freedom of expression particularly in matters of sex, and for experiments in technique; that is to say, literary technique. But actually they had little in common except their earnest desire to call attention to themselves, to rise and shine. Their integrity is unquestioned, and the better books of the period—*e.g.*, *Spoon River Anthology*, *Winesburg, Ohio*, *Chicago Poems*—are now American classics. It is to be noted, however, that these books were written by men who worked hard and had no time for posing or for literary shenanigans: the aloof Masters, the puzzled Anderson, the dedicated Sandburg. For the rest, some of their work—for example, the poems of Bodenheim and the short stories of Hecht—are so far from negligible that at their best they may be regarded as minor classics. It takes all sorts of writers to make a renascence, as it does a literature, and all are a necessary part of the spectacle. Leigh Hunt is as essential to literature as Chaucer, Bodenheim is as essential as Robert Frost—not as important, if you like, but as necessary.

It was a day of confused idealism and great creative energy and there was a group spirit, after a fashion, that was helpful to all of us. It manifested itself in the gatherings at Schlogl's, the tea parties at *Poetry*, the informal sessions at the Covici-McGee bookshop, even in the rough-houses at the Dill Pickle. These brought together all sorts and conditions of creative activity, and the contacts were valuable and stimulating. Possibly it was all part of the old quest of art for art's sake which goes underground after each defeat and springs up again, refreshed and vigorous, when the times are propitious. In any case it was a good day in which to be a writer and to be young.

For myself, I have always thought of our Chicago of the twenties as much like Paris in the Middle Ages, the Paris of François Villon, with crime and culture coexisting on different levels, almost in different dimensions; but I have no time for that argument now. I can imagine a day, not in my lifetime, when Chicago will be at once the intellectual and political capital of the nation; not because I have any fears for New York and Washington through military invasion, but because it seems to me a logical development. Today it is an overgrown village ruled by barbarians, a frontier town responding only to stunts and circuses; but we have the makings of another Paris—scenically, architecturally, even temperamentally, I think. I never cross the river at Michigan Avenue on a bus and note the sweep of Wacker Drive that I don't sense the resemblance to the Seine embankment. Some of our prescient painters, too, have noted this and profited by it; their summer pitches, west of the bridge, lend old-world color to the resemblance. I wish the booksellers could be encouraged to emulate them. A row of bookstalls along our own embankment is a civic development that only a politician could find it in his soul to question.

Perhaps Edna Ferber had something of the sort in mind when she said: "I always see Chicago a great, gorgeous hussy dressed in red satin with a lot of jewelry and a swell vocabulary and a heart as big and gaudy as her clothes and her language. She is going to be a lady, or at least her daughters are going to be ladies. There's something unfinished about Chicago, and that's the grandest thing about it."

XV

MY OWN CONTRIBUTION to the "Renascence" was modest. It was a nondescript little magazine called the *Wave*, copies of which I understand are now rare and even desirable. At any rate, they are sought by collectors and by university libraries. The first issue, I note, is dated January, 1922, so I assume the project was inaugurated some time in the fall of 1921. It was not my idea in the first place and, with characteristic apprehension of anything new, particularly if it involved more work for me, I made an earnest effort to avoid the job.

One evening a slim blond young man appeared on my doorstep in Austin and announced that he was Steen Hinrichsen and that he had come to see me about becoming the editor of a magazine he proposed to publish. He was himself an artist and a friend of artists and was in a position to obtain some of the best new art in Chicago, but he needed a literary editor who knew the local writers. I forget who sent Steen to me; possibly Hi Simons or perhaps Sam Putnam. The approach was engaging and disarming, however. I gathered from Steen's confidence and enthusiasm that he had found some financial backing for the magazine and that the matter of money simply did not arise. I was to be disillusioned on this score as time went on. What Steen had was confidence and enthusiasm in quantity, but very little money and very little chance of raising it. At the moment, although flattered by his suggestion, I pointed out that I was a very busy man—which was true enough for I was writing stories furiously in an effort to make a living—and had no time to give to a magazine, even a magazine that promised immediate fame for its editor and a generous division of the profits, if any. Nevertheless the venture pleased me and all too quickly I agreed to edit the "journal of arts and letters" Steen had in mind.

Steen was a persuasive youth, immensely likable, and I am bound to say that I never for a moment regretted a day of our association; although, heaven knows, we passed through all the proverbial difficulties of a little magazine of the period. Hinrichsen, a Dane, was one of a group of young artists, some of whom, notably Edgar Miller and Rudolph Weissenborn, later came to prominence. He was also the center of a lively Danish community on the North Side that supported his plan as generously as possible; indeed, the whole community used to turn out at press time to help us gather the sections of the *Wave* into a book. There were innumerable meetings and parties, both coeducational and stag, before the magazine was announced, however, and I learned more about what I had let myself in for. It was all so completely delightful that many times I wondered why I had not earlier adopted a more bohemian mode of living. For the bohemianism of Steen's group was quite a different thing from that which ran riot at the Dill Pickle. We ate Danish dishes, drank Danish beverages, and turned over more portfolios of Danish prints than I had dreamed existed in the world. Sometimes we sat for long evenings in Danish restaurants and over many cups of Danish coffee discussed the brilliant future of the *Wave*. Now and then the décor of our conferences was improved by the presence and moral assistance of Steen's lovely blonde sister Inger, who, as it developed, was to have a part in the production of the magazine. Our headquarters was Steen's print shop in Lincoln Avenue—he was a printer in his less aesthetic moments—where the community assembled at irregular intervals to gather the sheets that Steen printed. Fortified by strong coffee, we worked sometimes well into the morning hours, and, as the days went by, our enthusiasm mounted. Everything was done in the shop at first, the printing, the gathering of leaves, the binding.

For our first issue I assembled a fairly notable group of writings and there were a number of fine woodcuts by Steen, including a cover design in several colors. Our only advertisements, however, were our own and an exchange ad of the *Double Dealer*, a New Orleans magazine for which occasionally I was writing. We led off with a poem by Haniel Long that is still one of the most delightful things Long ever wrote. This was followed by a fragment of Arthur Machen's then unpublished novel, *The Secret Glory*, which I had been trying to market, and there were short stories by Selma Derry and the editor. The other poems were by Mitchell Dawson, Thomas Kennedy, Edgar Savage, Stephen Huguenot, and W. Clark Russell, the latter piece pilfered from some English journal. Llewellyn Jones gave us an article on "The Poetry of T. Sturge Moore," and somewhere I had found a letter of George Moore's that I tossed in for good measure. Perhaps this is the place to say that Edgar Savage and Stephen Huguenot were alter egos of the editor, who also contributed an editorial department called *"Demi-Tasse."*

Born in a Bookshop

As I turn the leaves of that first issue it still seems to me an interesting gathering.

In my first editorial I said: "The *Wave* is a magazine without a policy. It has an aim of course . . . to obtain and print whatever in the opinion of the editor and publisher is worth obtaining for print, without reference to subject matter. Excellence of form and adequacy of treatment are the only tests. In short, we shall print what pleases us, hoping that it will please you." That was my policy, so to call it, to the bitter end and I still believe it to be a good one.

Long's "Unimportant Dialogue" was not, strictly speaking, the first poem in our first issue. Our half title carried as a sort of text, and continued to carry through all the other issues edited by me, a quatrain by William Saphier, which I quote:

> *I watched two little waves*
> *marching to the shore.*
> *One died with a yawn,*
> *the second with a roar.*

I shall devote more space to the *Wave* than its importance merits, for editing it was a delightful human adventure. Subsequent issues were much like the first. That is to say, they were a medley of original contributions by young writers of the period, pilferings by the editor from obscure English journals, and reprints of lost or forgotten items in prose and verse from the editor's antiquarian files. Some of the other poets who contributed original work were Maxwell Bodenheim, John McClure, James J. Daly, Helene Mullins, William Alexander Percy, Lew Sarett, Harold Vinal, Allen Tate, Nelson Antrim Crawford, Pierre Loving, Rex Hunter, and Witter Bynner. And there was a charming little creature—I always thought of her as little, although I never met her—named Annie Higgins who sent me a handful of poems that I still remember with pleasure. They were fresh, original, and altogether captivating. If they suggested the work of any previous poet, it was that of Emily Dickinson. I printed them all and never heard from her again. [What became of Annie Higgins? I should still like to know.

206

She had the making, I thought, of a fine poet.] I coaxed prose contributions out of Carl Van Vechten, Ben Hecht, Bruce Grant, Paul Eldridge, Paul Jordan Smith, and Anthony Rud. There were some excellent translations by Wilbur Underwood and H. C. Schweikert. My antiquarian researches produced contributions by some very famous people indeed, among them Oscar Wilde, Edgar Saltus, Rudyard Kipling, and Victor Hugo. Our artists were Birger Sandzén, Stanislas Szukalski, Anthony Angarola, Edgar Miller, Rudolph Weissenborn, Asta Ring-Schultz, and even the famous English illustrator Frank C. Papé, who gave us a whole series of drawings he had been unable to sell in England. Ultimately the poets predominated, as always, and we had to print a whole poetry issue to pacify our more pressing contributors in verse.

It was a weird miscellany from first to last, I suppose, but an interesting one, and it was not the fault of our contributors that the *Wave* was ultimately caught in the undertow. It had been announced as a monthly, but actually we were unprejudiced about the intervals. We brought out six issues a year—for one year. The last number, Volume I, Number 6, was dated June, 1923. As Volume I, Number 5 had been a Christmas issue, it is obvious that we were slipping. Then there were two other numbers printed in Copenhagen after the printer and publisher had left Chicago. I had little to do with Numbers 7 and 8.

Our advertisements were an odd lot and can not have brought in much revenue. Too many of them were exchange ads. Now and then we persuaded Covici-McGee to give us a cover ad, and from time to time I was pleased and amused to come upon the cards of local restaurants in our back pages; pleased because I assumed that Steen at least was eating regularly. His methods were naive and entertaining. Once he invited me to dine with him at a Danish restaurant of some repute and I saw him in action. There were four of us in the party, Steen and Mrs. Hinrichsen and the blond Inger and myself. We dined royally with two kinds of wine and thereafter sat for an hour toasting one another with happy impartiality. Then Steen left us with a word of apology and engaged the proprietor, who was also the cashier, in a conversation that I could not follow because it was in Danish. The dialogue began quietly but mounted in volume until it seemed to me that the two were shouting at each other even though, obviously, they were still on amiable terms. I looked at Steen's wife and sister and asked, "Has anything gone wrong?" They smiled tolerantly, as citizens of the world who had passed through many similar scenes, and shrugged. As the uproar at the desk became more alarming, Inger explained the situation to me in English. She said, "Steen is asking the proprietor to accept an advertisement in the *Wave* in payment of our meals." I said, "Good God!" and reached for my wallet, but she laid a hand on my arm. "No, no," she said. "Steen has the money. He'll pay if he has to."

I don't remember how this episode ended, if indeed I ever knew. It is in my mind that Steen ultimately produced a thin pocketbook and paid cash for our entertainment, but it is possible that he effected some compromise. It is only fair to say that this and other rollicking episodes of my editorial career caused me, little by little, to revise my feeling about the bohemian life.

It was fun editing the *Wave*. Amusing incidents keep coming back to me. In Volume I, Number 3, for example, we published two poems by Hi Simons—he told us they were poems—and one of them came out a bit scrambled. That is to say, its last three lines were somehow transposed in type. This is the way they appeared:

> *Loving her.*
> *I shall remain in this night-dungeoned corner,*
> *Vanish utterly, small light.*

We caught this too late for a change in the body of the book, but Steen was equal to the occasion. On the reverse of the contents page he stopped the reader with a word of apology explaining that the last stanza of Mr. Simons' poem should read:

> *Vanish utterly, small light!*
> *I shall remain in this night-dungeoned corner,*
> *Loving her.*

208

Our critics, who by then were fairly numerous in and out of print, were enchanted by this error and its correction. An eastern newspaper devoted considerable space to the incident and argued very plausibly that the last three lines of Mr. Simons' poem, indeed *all* the lines of Mr. Simons' poem, read equally well forward or backward. Collectors will be glad to know that in some copies of the *Wave* for June, 1922, Mr. Simons' poem "Eternally" may be found with corrections in the author's script. When the appalling news was conveyed to him, he clapped his hand against his poetic brow and rushed wildly out of the shop. We learned later that he had visited as many bookshops as possible where the *Wave* was on sale and corrected as many copies as he could in an afternoon's work. The booksellers thought him quite mad, of course, until he explained what had happened and then they were sure of it.

And I treasure a letter from Fiswoode Tarleton, one of whose stories I had accepted for publication. "Dear Starrett," wrote young Mr. Tarleton, himself an editor, "thanks for your letter. *Modern Review* will be out about the first of October and copies will be sent the *Wave*. I'm giving your magazine a full page ad. Concerning my story, will you please change on the first page 'her hips which were enlarged also' to 'her buttocks which were enlarged also.' Faithfully, Tarleton."

Once Steen was unable to finance an issue of the magazine because again he was about to become a father. This was an occasion for one of our conferences, and I remember reproaching him hotly for being so careless at an important moment in the *Wave's* history. But it was nothing either of us could do anything about and in the end the baby won. The *Wave* was delayed for several months. But about all delays and errors our subscribers were understanding and forbearing. They were only a handful in any case, the subscribers I mean, not the errors and delays. One man who had never before troubled to write was kind enough to send us a farewell greeting on the occasion of our demise. "I have now waited six months," he said, "for another number of the *Wave* and can only surmise that this time it is really dead. May I ask whether it died with a yawn or with a roar?"

It died neither with a yawn nor a roar; it just petered out in spite of every effort to save its little life. Steen's happy-go-lucky bohemian existence in Chicago reached its inevitable end and he returned to the land of his fathers where, as I write these words, he is still thinking about publishing another little "journal of arts and letters."

I must go back a number of years to resume the chronological narrative. For many pages the ambitious young man who is the subject of this memoir has been sitting at his typewriter in Austin pounding out his first detective story. He must have been pretty hard up when he and the *News* parted company. It is certain that he had little or nothing in the bank. His salary had never been large and his magazine sales had not been numerous. Quantities of his stuff had been summarily rejected by editors whom he then believed stupid but came in time to know were more than a little perceptive. His wife's piano bench still served him as a desk and he had acquired a second-hand typewriter that daily took a murderous beating. He really worked hard after the debacle at the *Daily News*. He had to. And if his standards were not then high, neither were those of the magazines for which he wrote. Thus a fair amount of prose carrying his signature got into print in some very unlikely places.

To resume the perpendicular pronoun, Lillian believed in me completely, I think. I can still remember the pride and awe in her voice when she called her mother on the telephone one evening and said, almost before she said hello, "Charlie got eighty dollars for a story today!" I didn't hear her mother's response, but it was properly incredulous. The stories I wrote were of many kinds but for the most part they were love stories, mystery stories, and humorous stories, sometimes all three. I seldom attempted realism except as practised by O. Henry, whose surprise endings were at once my delight and my downfall. But my passion for reading and my instinctive flair for the best writers stood me in good stead. Wittingly or unwittingly, I was influenced by the men whose work I most admired, and there is no doubt that Stephen Crane and Ambrose Bierce among others helped to form my style. Then for a time Arthur Machen and James Branch Cabell helped to corrupt it. The better tales I wrote in those days are collected in a volume called *Coffins for Two*, long out of print. As I look them over today I see nearly all my early influences and am surprised to find some of the stories not half bad.

It was my trick of plot that sold my early stories and made it possible for me to make a precarious living for many years as a writer of detective stories and ultimately of detective novels. My mystery tales followed the Sherlock Holmes formula and for a time my fathomers were newspaper reporters, but presently I invented a private investigator who caught the fancy of several editors and paid my rent for a number of years. This was Jimmie Lavender, about whom I wrote some half a hundred stories, only a handful of which have survived. James Eliot Lavender—his full name, known only to myself—was an engaging fellow whose youthful appearance was emphasized by a single plume of white in his thick dark hair. In some of the early adventures he had mismated eyes, I think, one blue and the other brown, but that curious distinction vanished and I find no trace of it in the episodes gathered into *The Casebook of Jimmie Lavender*. His attractive name was borrowed, with the athlete's permission, from my old idol of the baseball field, Jimmie Lavender of the Chicago Cubs. Three editors were particularly friendly to the Lavender stories, Edwin Baird of *Real Detective Tales*, T. C. O'Donnell of *Wayside Tales*, and Harry Maule of *Short Stories*. All lived in shuddering fear that I would get their popular monthly journals into some appalling libel suit, or so it seemed to me when I read their cautious little interpolations; and once indeed I did almost get Maule into hot water by giving one of my criminals the name of a well-known British peer.

I enjoyed writing detective stories and not because they were the easiest stories to write. Nothing is harder to write than a good detective story. And I had some grand ideas in those days before I had really learned *how* to write. I wish I could come up with some half as good today. My problems were ingenious, often fantastic, and Jimmie Lavender solved them very deftly, I think. His deductions were sometimes pretty fuzzy, however, and I can see now that he was very fortunate in bringing some of his cases to a successful conclusion. Once, to my pleased amazement, I sold a story to *Pictorial Review* after it had been refused by all the pulps, and wondered for a few weeks if I had hit the jackpot at last and was on my way to fame and fortune. It brought me a thumping check that all but paralyzed my mother-in-law. But it was only an accident; it was years before anything like that happened again.

Some of my best short stories of the period appeared in the *Smart Set*, and I really had no higher ambition just then than to appear in the *Smart Set*. It was the *New Yorker* of its day and it was the goal of hundreds of young writers with a talent for satire. The word-rate was low but the distinction was high. When my McConnachie was not working well, and I found rejections in the mailbox instead of checks, I wrote without embarrassment for the Sunday School journals. There were days when ten dollars from David C. Cook of Elgin looked like a hundred dollars. Once when my next month's rent was not in sight, I rushed out a number of pious little tales, which Mother might have written, to half a dozen religious publications and all of them came back but one. When I found my last return envelope in the mailbox looking so slim that I knew it must contain a check, I wondered whether it would be for ten dollars or only six dollars. This pleasant speculation engaged me for several minutes and then I opened the envelope. It contained a check for fifty dollars and a pleasant letter from the editor, who sounded like a nice old clergyman. Do you think this an unimportant incident to be reported in one's autobiography? If you do, you have never been a young writer desperately in need of fifty dollars to pay your rent. It is on such little incidents sometimes that

212

a writer's early career is based and their importance is beyond all calculation.

All this time, it should be said, I was writing verse also and selling most of it. There was a good market for light verse in those days, although of course nobody but Ogden Nash ever made a living writing verse. It is difficult for me to appraise my own verse. I still like some of the things I turned out in those salad days, although most of my early work was pretty bad. Perhaps my curse was my facility; but also I was much too pleased with what I wrote. In my verse, as in my prose, I matured late. It was a long time before I cared deeply enough whether my verse was sincere. For a time it was enough that it was smart and salable. And yet I really tried to write *poetry*; I like to think there are evidences of that wish here and there in my early volumes. My best work of the period perhaps was a series of sonnets in celebration of favorite books and writers, and these with certain revisions survive in my best-known book of poems, *Autolycus in Limbo*. About Villon and Falstaff and Don Quixote and D'Artagnan at least I could be sincere, for I was writing with gratitude and affection of people I loved.

Sometimes I showed my poems to Carl Sandburg, but I am bound to say he could never find anything remarkable in them and he used to caution me. "Cut out the fancy words," he would say, "and put some guts into it, Vincent." But when I tried to follow his advice the result always sounded like a bad parody of Sandburg.

All this time, too, I had been writing occasional essays in literary discovery and appreciation and placing them where I could. The first important journal to publish these with any regularity was *Reedy's Mirror*, which printed most of the papers subsequently brought together in *Buried Caesars* (1923). There I paid my first tribute to Arthur Machen and to Sherlock Holmes; and it was Reedy who published my first ejaculations about Ambrose Bierce, Opie Read, W. C. Morrow, Walter Blackburn Harte, and Haldane Macfall. These were the enthusiasms of a very young man, but they were sound and they called attention to some good but neglected writers. Writing for Reedy was fun, for although he paid little for contributions, he was an appreciative fellow and his letters of encouragement were a joy to read. And certainly I appeared in good company, for Reedy was then printing some of the best work of Edgar Lee Masters, Edna St. Vincent Millay, Witter Bynner, and other top-flight poets who had been attracted by the hospitality of the *Mirror*. It was a one-man magazine devoted to politics and the arts. Reedy wrote the politics and the rest of us wrote the arts. I met him only once during the years of our association; that was when he came to Chicago for some reason and visited Lee Masters. He wrote me that he was coming and we shook hands for the first and last time one afternoon in Master's office. I have no idea what we talked about, but after a time we all had a drink together and were merry. I remember riding a short distance in a taxicab squeezed in between the gaunt frame of Lee Masters and the massive flanks of Billy Reedy, and that is all. The last article I wrote for the *Mirror* was a tribute to Reedy himself on the occasion of his death. This too survives in *Buried Caesars*.

Some of the other magazines to which I contributed "critical" articles at this time were the *Freeman*, the *Forum*, the *Sewanee Review*, the *Independent*, and Haldeman-Julius's monthly miscellany, whatever it was called. Ultimately I crashed the *Saturday Evening Post*, a fairly difficult feat, and began to receive red gold instead of pennies for my bookish meditations. My first contribution to the *Post* made a considerable stir in the nation. It was called "Have You a 'Tamerlane' in Your Attic?" In those days *Tamerlane* was the outstanding rarity in the light of which all other rarities were appraised. I had been looking for a copy for a long time without success, naturally enough, since there were then only four copies known to exist in the world. It occurred to me that what was needed to call the elusive item out of hiding was plenty of publicity, so I tried the provocative piece on the *Post* first and it sold the first time out. It may be found in my *Penny Wise and Book Foolish* (1929) precisely as it appeared before the *Post's* enormous public. To say that it attracted attention is putting it

214

mildly. The editors of the *Post* forwarded me literally hundreds of letters from excited householders who had turned out their attics in quest of the book. This interest did not, of course, represent anybody's interest in Poe's second-rate poem, but in something worth ten thousand dollars, the figure I had named as standing for the book's collector value. Everybody who found an old volume of Poe containing the poem was certain he had found the correct first edition and wanted to know where he could sell it for the figure named. I spent a busy few weeks answering letters and explaining why the books offered were not the books sought by collectors. Some of the letters were very plausible and I had to ask for further details before dampening the enthusiasm of their owners.

But my scheme for turning up the rare little book by publicity was justified. A copy did actually turn up in an attic in Worcester, Massachusetts, and its delirious possessor wrote to ask me how to dispose of it. As luck would have it, her letter came one weekend when I was out of town and I had no opportunity to answer it for several days. Then I wrote in hot haste, assuming that she would hold the book until she heard from me. I should have known better. No woman with an old pamphlet worth ten thousand dollars would wait a moment longer than necessary. When she failed to hear from me by return of post, Mrs. Ada Dodd hurried off with her treasure to the public librarian at Worcester, who urged her to communicate at once with Charles Goodspeed, the well-known Boston bookseller. Mr. Goodspeed wasted no time either. He took the next train to Worcester and acquired the book, which he subsequently sold for Mrs. Dodd at a figure considerably larger than the one I had named. He tells the story very fairly (and with a certain sympathy for me) in his entertaining book, *Yankee Bookseller*.

And so, as it happened, I have never owned a first edition of *Tamerlane* and I never expect to own one. The same article, however, did resurrect for me nice copies of the second and third editions of Poe's poems (1829 and 1831) which are almost equally rare although not equally valuable. One came from the little town of Isle of Hope, Georgia, the other from New Orleans, and I was able to buy them both for Walter Hill. I should have liked to keep them but my own funds did not run to such a purchase, and Hill was generous with the owners and with me. Publication of my *Tamerlane* piece in the *Post* did me a lot of good, however. Impressed perhaps by the shoals of letters that followed its publication, George Horace Lorimer subsequently bought a series of articles on old books and book collecting that gave me some standing among bookmen and that became the foundation stones of *Penny Wise and Book Foolish* (1929). Among the friends who mentioned the article to me was Henry Justin Smith, whose comment is worth preserving. We met one day on the street and he said: "That was a good piece you wrote for the *Post*, Charlie. I read every word of it as far as the break."

Incidentally, all my published writings at this time and afterward were signed *Vincent Starrett*, the combination of syllables I had decided to use for my public appearances. Since 1916 or thereabouts I have answered to two names—Charlie and/or Vincent—to the bewilderment of casual acquaintances.

But the life of a free-lance writer was not in the end all I had hoped it would be. It was fun, but it was frightening, too. Almost suddenly, it seemed to me, I was less prosperous than ever I had been in my life. In this situation I was glad to accept a part-time job on a local weekly newspaper, editing and writing copy about suburban events. The work was not onerous; it was just boring. This aspect of the chore was mitigated, however, by my association with Otto McFeely, the editor of the *Austinite*, a whimsical philosopher who had retired some years before from the nervous excitements of daily journalism. McFeely also edited a sister journal, *Oak Leaves*, serving the Village of Oak Park; and I performed the same duties for that valuable tabloid. He was a delightful fellow to work with. Although he took his job seriously and turned out two good neighborhood newspapers, he had an impish sense of humor that made me wish he would write a novel about the suburbanites he treated so considerately in his editorials.

216

Aside from McFeely, my principal interest was in certain of our visitors. Among these was Charles MacArthur, a merry wight, whose brother owned the two papers. This was some years before the younger MacArthur became famous as co-author of *The Front Page*. His conversation was at all times a delight—it was extravagant sometimes to the point of madness—and his only ambition just then was to play jokes on the personnel. Others who came into the office were Edgar Rice Burroughs, the author of *Tarzan of the Apes;* Robert St. John, then an occasional writer for *Oak Leaves;* Dr. William E. Barton, pastor of the First Congregational Church and author of several standard books on Lincoln; Thomas Boyd, who was later to write *Through the Wheat*; Kenneth Fearing, then a sad-eyed unpublished minor poet; and Ward Savage, the cartoonist, one of whose penetrating remarks I shall remember with happiness as long as memory remains to me: "There can never be a revolution in this country," he said one day. "If one were to start, so many persons would hop into their automobiles to go and see it that the whole affair would degenerate into an unparalleled traffic problem."

Although I saw him fairly often, I knew Burroughs only slightly. As any arty youth, I did not think highly of his masterpiece, and so I never asked him about the genesis of Tarzan, later to be a matter of literary dispute. He had no illusion about his books, at that time anyway, and wrote his wild stories with a twinkle in his eye, knowing they would sell prodigiously whatever might be said of them by the critics. He and McFeely were military men of a sort and their conversations were largely about militia matters. McFeely, who had served in the Spanish-American War and had taken a cavalry course at Plattsburg, had organized a battalion of infantry in Oak Park and River Forest when the United States jumped into World War I, and had become a major. Burroughs, who had done a hitch in the regular army, was one of his captains. Strolling down the street together, booted and spurred, after military exercises—Burroughs a huge mastiff of a man and McFeely of the terrier breed—they looked like Texas and Rhode Island taking a walk together.

My last view of Burroughs was on the afternoon of November 11, 1918, when the war ended. That was a wild day even in Oak Park. I was having breakfast with McFeely and Harry McManus in Johnny Hodgson's café when the factory whistles began to blow for the first Armistice Day. Some young women from the office joined us and together we took over the place, including Hodgson's fine supply of alcoholic beverages. McManus and the girls, wearing the chef's cap by turns, took possession of the kitchen and prepared wheat cakes and ham and eggs for everybody who entered the shop; it was all on the house, they said. After a time Hodgson himself showed up and joined the joyous carouse. Printers, bookkeepers, and other employes of the paper reported for duty and, finding the shop empty, joined us in the restaurant. Perhaps no work was done that day anywhere in the United States. Late in the afternoon McFeely and I peeked from the front window of the office to see the remnants of a parade in the street below. What we saw was Captain Edgar Rice Burroughs marching past as if he were in command of a thousand armed men—his only followers two militiamen, staggering under the load of their rifles, and four popeyed boy scouts delighted to be AWOL from maternal authority.

Charlie MacArthur, who went on to the *Herald and Examiner* and then to the *Tribune*, had started with *Oak Leaves*, reporting police news and other sociological phenomena. When I first met him he was working for Hearst, and at the time of which I am now writing he was with the *Tribune*. He used to come into the Oak Park office at odd hours for rest and conversation. He was, as I have suggested, an incurable practical joker and some of his most amusing hoaxes were perpetrated over McFeely's telephone. For some reason he was perenially amused by the name and fame of Henry Wadsworth Longfellow. He was also amused by Maywood's chief of police, a man named Sweeney. Maywood was and is just across the river from Oak Park. Almost immediately on arrival, MacArthur would call up the Maywood police station and ask for Sweeney. "Chief," he would begin, "this is the *Tribune*," a gambit

218

that was sure to alert Sweeney at once, for he had considerable respect for the power of the press and especially for the *Tribune,* which at any moment might shake his complacency by reporting uncontrolled crime in Maywood. "Chief, you have a friend of mine locked up there. I want to get him out. He is innocent. His name is Henry Wadsworth Longfellow."

"Wait a minute," Sweeney would reply hurriedly. "I'll look in the book." And then in a minute he would report back. "We ain't got nobody of that name here."

"Yes, you have," Charlie would insist. "Mr. Longfellow is an influential citizen and if you don't book him at once, it will go hard with you. The *Tribune* will not stand for any such high-handed incarceration of an honorable and distinguished citizen."

This would go on until MacArthur had Sweeney sufficiently tangled up in words like *incarceration,* and then he would shout: "Well, Sweeney, go your way, but you have been warned!" and slam down the receiver. Sweeney never seemed to remember this routine, occasionally varied by MacArthur, and Charlie never failed to give him a bad ten minutes.

Longfellow never ceased to amuse this remarkable playboy. His extraordinary effort years later, as public relations counsel for a cemetery, to have the bones of Longfellow brought from Massachusetts to New York, is one of the great stories of the MacArthur legend.

It was during my time in the village that *Oak Leaves* published MacArthur's first book, *A Bug's Eye View of the War* (now a rarity), based on his brilliant letters from the front to friends in the office.

Carl Sandburg visited Oak Park frequently, sometimes to sing his folk songs at the women's clubs and sometimes to visit friends at *Oak Leaves.* He lived in Maywood, just across the river, and liked to stroll in Oak Park where no saloons were allowed, and Forest Park where there were more saloons than churches. I remember a cold afternoon in late autumn when he and McFeely and I walked for miles, discussing the shortcomings of mankind and laughing so often that passers-by stopped to look at us. Few people laughed in Oak Park in those days and never in public. Ultimately we found a comfortable place in Forest Park and stopped in to get warm. There was sawdust on the floor and a big-bellied stove was throwing off heat in a way we liked. We ordered beer and carried it to a corner table. "After prohibition," said Carl in his slow drawl, "we'll be ordering Coca-Colas again." Then almost without pause he added, "I've been telling the kids some stories lately that I sort of like. Maybe they'll be in a book some day—I don't know—but I'm not ready yet to let them go out; and whoever gets them will have to pay for them."

He began to tell us one of them; and there, in a bar-room in Forest Park, with the big stove glowing beside us and winter coming on, I heard for the first time the story of Henry Hagglyhoogly who played the guitar with his mittens on. It was like hearing Hans Anderson tell me about the dog with eyes like saucers and the shirt collar that fell in love with a garter. I heard also that cold evening the story of how Bimbo the Snip's thumb got stuck to his nose when the wind changed, and the wonderful story of the two skyscrapers that decided to have a baby; when it came, you remember, it was a railroad train—the Golden Spike Limited. These and others that I heard later at Schlogl's or at Dr. Jacob Buchbinder's were the tales that went into *Rootabaga Stories*, on the flyleaf of my copy of which the poet wrote: "To Vincent Starrett, poet, fellow ink fish, may the zizzies be good to him." It is still my favorite among all Carl Sandburg's many books and I still read it, as the little girl said, with prickles of feeling.

Carl's poems in free verse were still being widely parodied in those days, but if he was disturbed by the humorists he didn't show it. Once he said, drawling the words like a cowboy, "A man was building a house. A woodchuck came and sat down and watched the man building the house." That, or something like it, was his invariable retort to his critics.

And then there was Kenneth Fearing, like Ernest Hemingway an Oak Parker born, who was threatened by his father with a

220

career in the law. He came into the office frequently to talk with McFeely and me, and sometimes he showed us his poems. But those early poems were not at all like the poems we now associate with the name Kenneth Fearing. They had to do with "silver dragons in the rain" and suchlike fancies. It was after he went to New York, at McFeely's suggestion, and became a Greenwich Villager that he began to write the vigorous satirical verse by which he is now remembered.

In his *History of American Poetry*, Horace Gregory asserts that I was Kenneth's first teacher and the first literary influence in his life. It may be true; I don't know. If so, Kenneth never mentioned it to me. Possibly my influence was too subtle to be noted at the time and became apparent only in retrospect. Certainly we had many long talks together; he used to sit up half the night with me talking poetry. As his other influences, according to Gregory, were Whitman, Hemingway, Dostoevsky, and a dozen other writers of international repute, it still tickles me to think that I may have been the first. Incidentally, Kenneth Fearing is one Chicago expatriate whose work benefited by his migration to New York.

XVI

THE STRETCH OF YEARS between 1917 and 1927 was certainly the busiest period of my life, not so much in the number of words pounded out of a typewriter—although it ran into the millions— as in the number and variety of my activities. "Once a newspaper-man always a whore," as James Huneker wrote me about a similar situation. At one time I was editing the *Wave*, helping to edit *Oak Leaves* and the *Austinite*, reviewing books for Llewellyn Jones, writing a monthly letter to the *Double Dealer*, and conducting a short story class at the Medill School of Journalism at Northwestern University. All this in addition to my weekly effort to turn out something salable for one of the dozen or more magazines, mostly pulps, in whose pages I was then more or less welcome. I tried, too, to keep in touch with my colleagues at Schlogl's and the Covici-McGee Bookshop, and occasionally found time for a visit to the antiquarian bookshops, although my books were all but pushing me out of the apartment. They were in every room in the place, and Lillian had warned me that she would leave me when I began to keep them in the bathtub.

My first two books in covers belong to this period. The first, *Arthur Machen, A Novelist of Ecstasy and Sin*, was a revised reprint of an essay of the same title which had appeared in *Reedy's Mirror*. It was published by Walter Hill, the friendly antiquarian bookseller. The author of *The Hill of Dreams*, then a journalist in London, had been greatly pleased by my ardent essay; but its most relevant reader had been Guy Holt, editor for the Robert M. McBride Company, who had been moved to get in touch with Machen and sign a contract for one of his books. This was the beginning of the Machen vogue in America. Thereafter others wrote about him with an enthusiasm that rivaled my own, notably Carl Van Vechten and James Branch Cabell, and ultimately we had a first rate Machen boom going that lasted for nearly a decade. However, that was all in the future when my little book appeared in 1918 and made me for the first time, as it seemed to me, an author.

My second book, *Estrays*, was a collaboration. It appeared late the same year under the imprint of the Camelot Press, a poetic invention of my own. Actually, the ugly little pamphlet was printed on the *Oak Leaves* press in Oak Park. It brought together a number of my early poems and poems by Thomas Kennedy, George Steele Seymour, and Basil Thompson; and perhaps the less said about it the better. Printing costs were not high in those days; we were glad to pay twenty-five dollars each to see our stanzas in covers.

Whatever else I was accomplishing in those too-busy years, I was making my name known locally. When I was asked to teach a class in short story writing at the Medill School of Journalism the idea frightened me, for I have always hated public speaking and this seemed to me public speaking at its worst. However, a sizable check was involved for a semester's teaching and a bit recklessly I accepted.

I have never since been frightened by an audience. I still dislike speaking in public, but I know now that it makes very little difference what one says. I told my students what books to read, what stories to study, and read their own stories back to them, thereby inaugurating altercations that sometimes lasted half the period. On the whole, I probably did them no harm. I turned out no Hemingways, no Stephen Cranes, no Sherwood Andersons, no Scott Fitzgeralds. A number of the women subsequently wrote short stories that sold to the popular magazines, and one or two of them wrote novels.

I survived the experience for two winter semesters, a year apart, and had a thoroughly good time. I think my students had a good time too, on the whole, for they are still my friends; but in the end I gave it up. By that time I was involved in too many enterprises and the reading of class papers was taking too much of my time.

All this time, as noted, I had continued to collect the books of other men, possibly to the detriment of my own, and much of my monthly check from Medill was royally invested at Walter Hill's and Frank Morris's alluring bookshops. Collecting was now a disease with me, albeit a pleasant one, as imperative as the drink habit. The booksellers made it very easy for me; I owed all of them money without shame. Eugene Field had always been in Morris's debt, Frank said, so why not I? In point of fact, the handsome old gentleman liked to have me around and finally gave me desk space in his back room just to have somebody to talk to. I returned this kindness by writing introductions for his catalogues, a service that I performed also for Walter Hill.

Among the bookmen of the day who frequented the Morris book rooms was W. C. Firebaugh, the translator of Petronius, who later wrote *The Inns of Greece and Rome* and *The Inns of the Middle Ages*, which Morris published. When his Petronius was published by Boni and Liveright, in 1922, Morris and I played him a scurvy trick. As he strode into the shop one afternoon, happy as only an author can be who has just published a book, we told him a federal detective had been inquiring for him and we were afraid it was about his unexpurgated *Satyricon*. He looked serious, smiled a lopsided smile, and said he would make himself scarce for a few days. We didn't see him again for a week. Some time later his translation of the *Satyricon of Petronius Arbiter* did get into trouble in New York.

Walter Hill's Bookshop was of another sort. He was an Englishman who had lived in America for many years and, when I knew him, was already one of the famous booksellers of America. A dozen millionaires were among his regular customers, and his attractive quarters were bursting with such rarities as millionaire collectors like to acquire. He was a courtly, handsome man, white-haired and dignified, who in moments of enthusiasm lapsed into pure Cockney. It was in his wonderful establishment that I first saw and handled the great books of the world in their costliest form, in the editions in which they first had made their appearance among men. He was a generous man, and what I learned from him about books is beyond my ability to assess. As already noted, he was my first publisher; and for years afterward he continued to bring out little books of mine in limited editions, usually at Christmas, when we could dispose of the volumes among our friends without pain or profit to anybody.

My introductions to his catalogues, incidentally, almost got me a job in New York which, if I had accepted it, might have changed the course of what I like to call my career. Mitchell Kennerley was then head of the great Anderson Galleries, and it was he who offered me the position one day while visiting at Hill's. My duties would have included the preparation of the gallery's catalogues and would undoubtedly have been pleasing. I declined the dazzling offer, however, and stuck to journalism and story writing.

But Hill's and Morris's were not by any means the only bookshops I frequented at this time. Two well known names in the antiquarian field were then just becoming known to book enthusiasts. In 1923 Ben Abramson and Jerrold Nedwick had

224

opened a small shop in Wabash Avenue near Congress Street that attracted all the impecunious collectors of the city. Small and dark as was their first establishment, some attractive finds were made there, and some of the choicer spirits of the "renascence"—among them Lee Masters—were frequently to be seen among the researchers.

This was the beginning of the bookselling careers of two alert young men who went on to distinction. They dissolved partnership at last and Abramson went onward and upward, in the Alger tradition, until he became the proprietor of the famous Argus Book Shop, with wide rooms overlooking the lake in Michigan Avenue, where on good days one might encounter such visiting celebrities as Christopher Morley and Somerset Maugham. Nedwick continued to cater more modestly to the street trade and for some years occupied premises in Clark Street, north of the river, that Sandburg found a fruitful hunting ground. Already the poet had begun to collect material for his gargantuan life of Lincoln; it was early Lincoln material for the most part that he sought and found in old bound volumes of *Harper's* and the *Century* that Nedwick offered at twenty-five cents a volume. There was a trough of these outside the door and one of the historic sights of the time, for prescient citizens, was that of Sandburg sitting cross-legged on the sidewalk beside the low trough, looking for reminiscences of his hero. Sometimes he found a number of them at a sitting, so to speak, and ripped the relevant pages from the old books, leaving the bereft volumes behind. It is only fair to say that he paid for his discoveries at full-volume rates.

Other booksellers of the period who attracted the book collecting fraternity were Alexander Greene, who occupied a quaint old house in Cass Street, said to have been once the home of Charles Dickens's brother Augustus; Fanny Butcher (nationally known as the literary editor of the Chicago *Tribune*), who operated a small shop in a corner of the Pullman Building; and George M. Chandler, who greeted customers in his Van Buren Street shop looking more like Arthur James Balfour than Arthur James Balfour himself. Kroch's famous bookshop was then in Michigan Avenue, and two fine bookmen—Lewis Galantiére and Will Solle —were employed there as clerks; and Marshall Field's great book section was in charge of that extraordinary bookwoman, Marcella Burns Hahner.

One visited all these places meticulously, earnestly, prayerfully, in quest of the absolute, as it were; at least of the pot of gold at the rainbow's end. Chicago was a good book town in the twenties. I have never known a better.

Coincidentally with these activities, the literary renascence, of which it pleased me to think myself a part, sailed bravely on and, whenever possible, I added my presence to whatever collection of enthusiasts was calling attention to itself. Generally, this meant dropping in at Schlogl's at the relevant hour, or visiting the Covici-McGee bookshop, where I was pretty certain to find somebody with thrilling tidings to report. At both places the principal orator was likely to be Ben Hecht. I have already suggested that the Olympians of the renascence who gave it stature were not the bohemians who gave it color; but this is not strictly true if Hecht is to be considered one of the godlings. He gave it so much color and sensation that there are times when I see him as pretty much the whole movement. If he was not the most important figure of the renascence, he was by all odds the most picturesque. He sensed the resemblance of our noisy movement to the *fin de siècle* literary uproar of the eighteen-nineties in London and tried to duplicate that spectacle in Chicago. Anderson, Sandburg, and Masters provided the big names and the big books; but Hecht, with the enthusiastic complicity of Bodenheim, provided the sensations and excitements.

Harry Hansen has called Hecht the "Pagliacci of the Fire Escape," and it is a good phrase. Possibly it had its origin in Hecht's first full-length play, *Under False Pretenses* (later *The Egoist*), written for and delightfully played by Leo Ditrichstein. The comedy contained a fire-escape scene in which the inhibited

226

hero contrived to escape from a lady's bedroom by means of that useful apparatus. I attended the premiere as Hecht's guest. What a night that was for all his friends! Nothing scandalous occurred in the drama; it was always just *about* to occur. At the end of the second act, after Ditrichstein had exited down the fire escape, there were wild shouts for the author, who appeared without reluctance. He had been waiting for that moment in the wings. Suddenly, and somehow simply, he was there, leaning against the edge of the proscenium arch, smoking a cigarette. What he said went something like this: "I thank you, Ladies and Gentlemen, for your very kind applause. I'm glad you like my play. I like it too. Probably you heard the rumors branding it as a scandalously immoral play. Now you see that it is not immoral at all—and it gets moraler and moraler as it goes along."

Bodenheim was there, I think, sucking at an unlighted pipe and wearing his arm in a sling. In the audience were all the big-name writers of the day and, I should imagine, all the little-name writers who could obtain tickets. It was an entertaining comedy, as the critics testified, and it pointed the way to Hecht's ultimate success in Hollywood. In spite of his literary conscience, for he really had one, there was always a lot of box office in Ben's make-up.

This, as I recall it, was just before the suppression of *Fantazius Mallare*, parts of which I had heard in manuscript. That was another Hecht sensation, but of a different sort. Although its author claimed a notable morality for that production also, it was in fact a morbidly decadent work in the manner of his admired French diabolists, and I was not surprised by the government's action. Nor was Hecht, I suspect, or anybody else concerned in the venture. The book was published by Covici-McGee, in 1922, with illustrations by Wallace Smith that were intended to be phallic symbolism but were, as Burton Rascoe expressed it, merely phallic. Nevertheless, the drawings were remarkable; they were finer works of art than Hecht's sophomoric narrative. They were weird, distorted, savage, diseased, diabolical, powerful, and magnificent. It seemed to me that the influence of Aubrey Beardsley was clearly visible in them; but when I suggested this to Wallace he opened his eyes wide and asked, "Who was Aubrey Beardsley?"

Between the publication of *Mallare* in 1922 and its suppression early in 1924, Hecht fitted in his literary newspaper project already described, and the Chicago *Literary Times* blossomed and faded and died. Its last issue appeared a few months after the uproar about *Mallare*, if my chronology is correct, and not long afterward the sensational showman himself vanished from the big tent on the shores of Lake Michigan, taking his fireworks with him. The biggest meeting of the old gang in the history of the Round Table was held in Schlogl's one day to wish him goodbye and good luck.

The next sensation was of my own making, although not by intention. For some time Pascal Covici had been eager to publish a book by Arthur Machen, and I had no difficulty persuading him to bring out a selection of Machen's uncollected tales and essays aimed at the Machen collectors, who were then fairly numerous. I typed madly for weeks, copying out the contents of the volume I was to edit, drawn from my personal collection, as I had no notion of trusting my originals to the printers. The result was a formidable volume called *The Shining Pyramid*, taking its title from one of the essays it contained. It was a handsome volume, well printed and well bound, with a stunning frontispiece by Wallace Smith—in all respects a well-intentioned production—but somewhere along the line there had been a slip-up, for when the edition was delivered to the publishers it was discovered that the spines were blank. In this pass Stanley Szukalsky, one of the company's aesthetic advisers, suggested a green paper label and that is the way the book ultimately appeared some time in 1923. The weird confection sold at ten dollars, a prohibitive price, and did no business worth mentioning. It had been my intention to surprise Machen with a handsome check, knowing it would be welcome, but in the circumstances no check was forthcoming, an embarrassing situation. Undaunted, I tried again and in 1924 Covici published another collection of tales and essays called *The Glorious*

Mystery, which similarly failed to make the author any money. I had Machen's full permission to edit and publish the materials brought together in both volumes; but naturally he expected to be paid for them.

Precisely what occurred thereafter I have no idea to this day, but presently an appalling thing happened, or so it seemed to me at the time. Alfred Knopf had begun to publish Machen's earlier books in America; had become, indeed, his authorized publisher. He had, I think, no slightest inkling of the letters Machen had written informally appointing me his agent and encouraging me to publish what I could of his uncollected early work. Machen himself, I am willing to believe, as his fame mounted in America, completely forgot all he had earlier written me. For the first time in his long career as a professional writing man he was a resounding celebrity, and no doubt it colored his thinking. He had little use for Americans in any case; he had paid his respects to the "United States of Gehenna" many times in his satirical essays, and he was anesthetic to the collector's fever for first editions, tall paper copies, and suchlike foolishness—save as it put cash into his pocket. Whatever happened, Covici and I were astounded one day to read an open letter to the book trade, circulated by Knopf, accusing us of piracy. It appeared that we had helped ourselves to Machen's property without his permission and must be regarded as reckless fellows unworthy of the trade's support. Machen was directly quoted in this surprising document, and it was clear that his opinion of *me* was very low indeed.

We hurried into conference, Covici and I, with Billy McGee, Frank Hyman (who was about to take over Covici's interest in the publishing house), and Philip R. Davis, the firm's attorney, and drafted a reply. It asserted the simple facts, quoting at length all the relevant parts of Machen's letters to me, and so completely refuted the charges against us that newspaper columnists who had hurried to report the tidings of our dereliction were moved to correct their paragraphs in equal haste. A lot of correspondence ensued between Knopf's barrister and our own and for a time threats of damage suits filled the air, but in the end nothing whatever came of the episode.

It shook me considerably and, although Machen and I made up our quarrel when I visited him in London, it was long before I was able to think of him as anything but cynically ungrateful. I had introduced him to American readers and, in effect, found him an American publisher for his books; I had been mainly responsible for the Arthur Machen vogue that began with the publication of those books; I had never at any time received five cents from anybody for my services in his behalf; and his clear statement that I was taking money out of his pocket angered and hurt me. I have no wish to revive the episode now, but it is not the least part of my story and occasionally I still hear echoes of the old canard.

Not all my enthusiasms, I am happy to remember, ended as catastrophically as this one, nor did the Machen episode diminish my passion for discovery. With most of the men I had resurrected for my volume of *Buried Caesars* I entered at once upon a joyous correspondence that continued for years. Or, if they were no longer among the living, I inaugurated a copious correspondence with their widows and their sisters and their cousins and their aunts. Obscure writers who had done good work, or work that I believed to be good, were quite sure to hear from me sooner or later. My passion for discovery was the occasion for many jokes at my expense. Burton Rascoe pretended to believe that I had a strongbox full of literary masterpieces in manuscript that I doled out at regular intervals in the *Wave*; and it was his theory that I was disappointed when the writers I championed emerged from their obscurity as a result of my enthusiasm. There was something in this, I am afraid. It is what comes of being a collector; one likes to boast about his treasures in print, but is reluctant to share them with the thundering herd.

After Machen, my principal "discovery" was Haldane Macfall, whose picaresque novel, *The Wooings of Jezebel Pettyfer*, is quite certainly one of the great books of the world. After reading it, I began a campaign in its behalf similar to the one I had started in

230

Harriet Monroe
Founder and First Editor of Poetry

Carl Sandburg

behalf of Machen; and in this, too, I was successful. So great was the interest I managed to create in the Barbadian Negress and her lovers that this book, too, was published—i.e., republished—by Alfred Knopf as the first volume in a series of forgotten masterpieces.

The year 1924 ended for me, on the publishing side, with the appearance of my first volume of short stories, *Coffins for Two*, and another volume of rather feeble verse; but it seemed to me that I was getting on.

That summer I accepted a cordial invitation from Richard Le Gallienne and had a few days with him at Woodstock before leaving for England. For years the English poet had been one of my minor enthusiasms, and I hoped to produce a bibliography of his writings; there had been a lot of correspondence between us. I had begun to express myself on the subject as early as 1915; and my appreciation reminded him, he said, of his own hero-worshipping youth in London, when every goose was a swan and every poet a king. One of his letters is worth quoting for the delightful story it tells.

My Dear Irrepressible Vincent: though I never, or seldom, answer your charming fly-by-night epistles, you mustn't think that I don't value them; though I can't, for the life of me, understand why you, keeping such fashionable literary company as you do, bother with the likes of me. Your kindly interest in me, however, is none the less welcome to me—"whom there are very few to love, and none at all to praise," or Wordsworthian words to that effect. But why, holding me in such flattering regard. . . . well, I'll tell you a story.

Once in my early, so to speak, Vincent Starrett days, I called on George Moore in his chambers, in the Temple, and humbly brought him the tribute of my praise: the which G. M. —knowing that I was then doing the log-rolling for various London journals—thus acknowledged: "All very charming, my dear Le Gallienne—but—why not in a newspaper?" How often in the intervening years has that shrewd remark come home to me, as my friends have brought me their appreciation, after the fashion of Nicodemus, by night! *Dictum sapienti sat est!*

The old poet stood for something important in my life just then. Except for Max Beerbohm, who was not available, he was the sole survivor of that brilliant period in English literature that brought to prominence such men as Oscar Wilde, Aubrey Beardsley, Ernest Dowson, Lionel Johnson, and Francis Thompson; that made the *Yellow Book* famous as a symbol of decadent romance, and that gave the world some of its most charmingly produced volumes of prose and verse; a period that was regarded as vaguely "naughty" and which I, at least, and some others, believed to be the prototype of our own æsthetic movement. Le Gallienne had been a spearhead of that renascence and I was eager to hear him talk of men and events that were at once near and far, at once legendary and immediate. In desultory fashion I was collecting *all* the men of the nineties, as a matter of fact, and it was a fascinating task; for whatever the merits of their work, their books were delightful confections—limited editions on handmade paper, with wide margins and deckle edges—exquisitely produced. I even meditated for a time a monograph on the whole *fin de siècle* development and hoped that Le Gallienne might contribute secrets of his youth never before published.

As it happened, I was not to write that particular monograph, although the secrets were duly forthcoming. We sat for hours one afternoon on a rail fence in the Catskills while he told me the wonderful story of the nineties and its most memorable figures, all of whom had been his friends and colleagues in that almost mythical London of the gas lamp, the green carnation, and the hansom cab. Beardsley, Dowson, Johnson, Wilde, Beerbohm, Stephen Phillips, Leonard Smithers, John Davidson, Arthur Symons—the names rolled from his tongue in sonorous procession, with crisp characterizations and sparkling anecdotes of each; and always in the center of the pictorial moment glittered that most romantic

232

figure of them all, Richard Le Gallienne himself, living, loving, drinking, wenching, writing his facile poems about "golden girls" and poets dead and gone. He looked and spoke like a genial old satyr, retired and living on his pension, dreaming back to his lost youth in Arcady. I thought of Bernard Shaw's question to Holbrook Jackson: "Did all these things happen or did you invent them?" It was a remarkable recital and I think he may have been quoting it, for not long afterward I found it all, very much as he had poured it out, in the *Saturday Evening Post*. Nearly all; I missed a few savory anecdotes that apparently he felt he could not put into print—and neither, alas, may I! These were the articles that became his entertaining book of memories, *The Romantic Nineties*.

"Richard," I asked him, when the flow of words had ceased, "did you ever find your Golden Girl?"

He was silent for a long time, looking off into the purple shadows deepening around the mountains; I was afraid I had brought to mind some memory that was still poignant enough to distress him. At last he spoke. "The book says I did," he answered; "but perhaps I didn't. Does one ever? Of course I thought I had found her many times, and very charming she was, too, every time. But—do you know—no sooner did I begin to plume myself on the discovery than along would come another golden girl—with a little redder hair—a little more perfect breasts—you know?"

I recalled him to the twentieth century with a question about his daughter. Did he know Eva at all well and were they admirers each of the other's work?

"Indeed, yes," he said, "but it only happened recently. It seemed a bit silly that we should not know each other, in view of our *Who's Who* relationship, so I wrote and said I would like to meet her. She was only a babe in arms, you know, when her mother went away. I suggested a meeting at a quiet restaurant in New York and she was good enough to accept the invitation. I was there first, as you may suppose. I can't begin to describe my emotions; there were too many of them. I thought of my first meeting with her mother, but I thought also of my first meeting with a number of other women, and the picture became a bit confused. I felt like a young lover meeting his sweetheart, and I felt like a stage door johnny who had sent a mash note to a musical star. The only thing I *didn't* feel like was a father meeting his daughter. When at last the lovely apparition came through the door, I was as fussed as I'd ever been in my life. I said, 'Can this be my famous daughter?' And she said, 'Is this really my famous father?' After that we got along splendidly. 'How is that beautiful creature, your mother?' I asked her; and she said, 'Oh, Mother's fine. You know, Richard, I never blamed you for that. You don't mind if I call you Richard, do you? Somehow, I can't think of you as my father.' And I said, 'Darling, believe me, it is not with parental eyes that I am now seeing you for the first time.' And, indeed, it was not," he concluded. "It was simply humanly impossible for me to think of her as my daughter. All in all, a unique and delightful experience!"

That night some of the neighbors came in—Aline Kilmer among them—and he read some of his poems to us, and poems by other poets too. He read poetry exquisitely and, I give you my word, his own sounded every bit as good as Keats' and Swinburne's, there in his candle-lighted living room; but I suppose we both knew better. Today, years removed from his personality and the influence of the period he adorned, I know that his verse is pretty and sentimental, as is much of his prose. He was frequently an excellent critic, however, and his judgments on literature were sound and pungent usually.

His novels, I regret to say, seem to me precious almost beyond endurance, although no doubt *The Book Bills of Narcissus* and *The Quest of the Golden Girl* will continue to be read as typical specimens of their time. Every romantic reader has his Le Gallienne period, I think. "Le Gallienne is a shrine at which I too have worshipped," wrote James Branch Cabell in a letter of confession that I cherish; "but four or five months ago I made the disastrous error of rereading the *Golden Girl*. For to do that was really an error. Ormus and Kimberley could not combine to bribe

234

me, now, into re-reading *Narcissus*; that much at least I mean to keep in memory just as it never was."

After that summer I did not see Le Gallienne again. In the following year I dedicated a volume of verse to him in a sonnet that pleased him, and correspondence went on sporadically for a number of years. Then he went to live in France and all communication ceased. When he died near Mentone in September, 1947, I read the word with a sense of shock and personal bereavement, however, for I felt that the world had lost one of its most picturesque citizens. I still think of him with affection and am happy to have known him. This is what I wrote of him in my Chicago *Tribune* book column:

"Richard Le Gallienne, who died in France the other day, at a fine old age, was a picturesque legend in his lifetime and can hardly be less than that in death. Regardless of his own gifts, which were not negligible, he was one of the surviving symbols of that larger legend, the poetic renaissance (or decadence) of the eighteen-nineties, which has inspired a dozen volumes of critical appraisal. Also, he possessed one of the most magical names in literature, a circumstance that undoubtedly helped his fame. Add to this a notable charm of manner and the well-founded legend of his personal beauty—he is said to have been the handsomest man of his day in London—and Le Gallienne emerges as a romantic figure in the history of letters with whom Time may be expected to deal gently. If I had to characterize him in a sentence I would say, not unkindly, that he was a great poet whose only failing was that he did not write great poetry. But I doubt that he thought himself a great poet; he was too good a critic for that. He knew how few are the great poets; none better. The following lines, which he once gave me in manuscript, are revealing; they are Richard Le Gallienne at his humblest and best:

> *Have you loved the good books of the world,*
> *And written none?*

235

Have you loved the great poet—
And burnt your little rhyme?
'O be my friend, and teach me to be thine!' "

XVII

THAT WAS IN AUGUST, 1924—my visit with Le Gallienne, I mean—and not long afterward I found myself on board the *Arabic*, a nice old-fashioned liner carrying only passengers of tourist class, with Tom Kennedy bidding me goodbye. He had been for some years in New York and we had a day or two together before I sailed. On the day of my departure we celebrated the event in the usual way and Kennedy later wrote a sonnet describing the touching experience. This now becomes part of the record:

To V. S. Going Abroad

The taxicab lurched through a roaring street,
But lifted up with substitutes for wine,
We watched the traffic twist and intertwine,
With kingly nonchalance; and when our feet
Wavered along the wharf, the high conceit
Of genius curved our tongues; in words divine
We spoke of Life—and Love, its anodyne—
And of far places where we hoped to meet.

We parted by the lean ship, quivering
With eagerness to spurn the unwelcome land,
Rushing to meet the strong arms of the sea;
And I could smile—being drunk—and feel no sting
To see you, when your hand had left my hand,
Walking aboard in drunken dignity.

On the voyage I devoted as much time as possible to a friendly American family named Cole. I played chess in the lounge with Mr. Cole, chatted with Mrs. Cole on deck, and danced with Miss Cole in the ballroom. No thought of our subsequent relationship entered my mind, of course, as we danced; yet within a few years she was to accept for publication one of my most popular books. May I introduce her as Lois Dwight Cole, later the well-known Macmillan editor and author of books for children?

One of my reasons for visiting France had been the hope of meeting Anatole France, greatest of living French masters, long one of my principal literary gods. Unhappily for this project, the grand old man died a few days before I arrived—we read the news of his death in the ship's daily newspaper. And so I was able only to attend the great public funeral he was given in Paris. I kept full notes of the event and after my return to America wrote an account of it. Because it is the only full day of my life of which I have a complete record, and because it may have some historical importance in itself, I reproduce it here as it appeared in Edwin Valentine Mitchell's *Book Notes:*

OCTOBER 18, 1924

Saturday afternoon—a gray day with rain threatening and yellow leaves dropping from the poplars along the embankment. A gun-metal and cartridge paper day with occasional sunlight dappling the trees and sidewalks and lying coldly on the water. At street corners and in doorways little whirlpools of dust and scudding leaves . . .

"Look out for pickpockets," said my friends at the hotel; and the admonition amused rather than startled me. No one, I thought, would be more joyously entertained than Anatole France by the activities of pocket-pickers at his funeral.

A vast section of Paris seemed to be abroad in the streets. From all sides of the city the people were hurrying toward the Quai Malaquais. The current of traffic everywhere was toward the river, flowing sluggishly beneath its bridges. Taxicabs, carriages and foot passengers were converging toward a central point. Figures shabby and well-dressed, attired for diversion and attired for labor—all classes of French society. Smiling visitors from the hotels and intense men and women of the lower classes; shop girls, messengers, and artisans. A holiday crowd. It was not gay, however; nor was it particularly serious. A throng that came at once to pay tribute and to enjoy itself, to see and to be seen. From every side it came, across the bridges from the long commercial avenues and down the narrow, twisting streets of the Left Side, datted with bookstalls and antique shops for the tourists. Endlessly.

Long lines of infantry and guardsmen fringed the quays on either side, holding back the crowds on the sidewalks. The rain-blue uniforms and the dull-gleaming helmets were of a piece with the somewhat leaden sky. Handsome carriages and disreputable taxis kept arriving and departing, discharging passengers and going after new ones. Officers rode up and down in front of the lines of soldiers. A heavily decorated general clattered past, followed by his staff: at street intersections he halted to bawl hieroglyphic orders and twist his formidable mustachios for the fashionably-dressed women in the crowd.

The air was faintly chilly and the troops looked very comfortable in their long overcoats. They stood "at rest," amicably smoking and joking among themselves or with the citizens who jostled them at the curb. Far as the eye could reach, in either direction, the walks were thronged with people. At strategic points they overflowed into the streets, and from the Rue des Sts. Pères to the Institut they clustered thickly at every loophole. Men and boys climbed out of mansard windows to cling to the narrow gutters of the roofs or sat impudently astride the gables of old buildings along the quay. Near me a tall man with his jacket open to display a velvet waistcoat, his hands in the pockets of his ample trousers, strutted back and forth on a narrow course with solemn absurdity. His raiment and his astonishing beard gave him somewhat the appearance of Mr. Augustus John, the painter, as later I beheld that eminent bohemian in a Chelsea public-house. I concluded that he must be at least a prince of poets; but nobody spoke to him at any time and he continued his abbreviated stroll without interruption. Somewhere in the congestion, I later learned, were the American writers Pierre Loving and Burton Rascoe, but at no time was it my good fortune to encounter them.

238

At the intersection of the Rue des Sts. Pères and the Quai Voltaire a troop of cavalry had been dismounted, and the pawing hoofs of the horses made a constant clatter that drowned out the conversation of their riders. This was, however, both frank and entertaining, concerned as obviously it was with the attractions of the passing girls.

A stone's throw from the Institut, in the shadow of Voltaire's statue—renowned for its cynical smile—a huge catafalque had been raised over-night, upon which rested the coffin. French flags were draped across it, and a purple crepe hung over all. At the four corners stood bronze urns, ten feet in height, in which incense burned throughout the interminable ceremony. Near at hand a line of flags, tied with crepe and extending across the front of an old building, marked the house in which the dead master had been born—the spot where, in 1844, the father of Jacques Anatole Thibault had carried on the business of bookseller. It seemed an appropriate coincidence that he whose body now lay at the feet of Voltaire should first have seen the light in a house only a few doors removed from that in which the Apostle of Ferney had died; and that the Institut should hover over both. It seemed an admirable arrangement that the ceremonies, however long-winded, should go forward before the door of that erstwhile bookshop in which the young Jacques Anatole had spent his childhood. Here it was, in youth, in a neighborhood later made famous by the etchers, that he searched the stalls along the quays; and it was here in later years that he loved to browse on sunny afternoons—the old collector who was the foremost European man of letters of his day.

The crowd flowed almost up to the black-and-silver tribune that had been prepared for the orators; it surged about the base of the catafalque, heaped high with flowers and swathed in purple gauze. The incense burners smoked in the cool air of early afternoon. Streamers of purple crepe hung from the embankment trees to the little book-stands, and beneath them a rousing business went on. For the bookstalls all stayed open. Behind them the barges floated down the stream and optimistic fishermen cast lines into the water. At careful intervals the poplars dropped yellow leaves upon the coffin. Over all loomed the Institut, from which a mournful bell tolled every quarter of an hour.

The notables were still arriving in carriages and in taxis; they made their way through black lanes to the official tribunes. Members of the Academy in their traditional costume, members of parliament, and members of the Paris Municipal Council. The central platform was filling. A sense of import and activity permeated the spectacle. The crowds rustled and pushed. Somewhere a clock struck—twice—and instantly the space about the statue seethed with tribute-bearers and special delegations. Policemen waved back the tardily-arriving taxis and the forward-struggling throngs. Officers rode hurriedly up and down the line of troops. The ceremonies were about to begin.

A breeze lifted the purple streamers and curdled the smoke of the *pots-au-feu*. The sky seemed to brighten. On all sides bicornes floated up—bicornes of beadles, bicornes of ushers, bicornes of coachmen and academicians, hurrying and dodging through the press. Photographers popped out of crannies in the crowd or materialized from the ether; they stood on ladders against the walls of buildings, on rooftops, on ledges of stone. They hung perilously from windows and scurried between the feet of horses. Madame France had arrived; a small black figure, heavily veiled, greeting the premier of the Republic. The shutters of the cameras clicked like castanets. Then the voice of the chairman, flung harshly by the amplifiers to the limits of the waiting crowd. . . . An orchestra from the Paris Opera and another from the Republican Guard. . . . A choir of Paris schoolgirls, one hundred strong. . . . And finally two hours of fervid oratory.

It was a magnificent tribute to the dead prince of letters, a governmental ceremony in which all classes had their part. Certainly, of all nations, France has most impressively the art of doing adequate honor, at the last moment, to her intellectual workers. The elaborate obsequies were less a ceremonial of mourning than an immense national act of homage. Yet, as I listened, or pretended to listen, it seemed to me that the cynical

240

smile of the statue deepened and spread; and under his coverlet of board I wondered if the dead man too was smiling—not cynically perhaps, but with tolerant amusement.

On the whole, it must be admitted, the crowd listened well. And if there were pickpockets abroad, they thought me unworthy of their attention. The addresses, as I read them in the newspapers, next day—in English—seemed to me quite admirable. But long before they were at an end I had quietly slipped away to the bookstalls of the quay and as far eastward as the Pont Neuf view of Notre Dame. It seemed a better thing to be doing; and I felt confident that if the illustrious old fellow was hovering anywhere near—an archangel in spite of himself—he was more likely to be burrowing in the stalls than listening to his own virtues made public. I looked with pleasure at some astonishing nudes in the windows of a small art shop, and thought of Jahel and Madame des Aubels. . . .

When I returned, the ceremonies were all but over. In a little time the procession began its slow parade toward the cemetery at Neuilly, headed by the representatives of student and Socialist groups, with banners furled. But it was dusk before the coffin was lowered into the family vault, and for hours thereafter the citizens of Paris filed past the tomb with wreaths of roses and chrysanthemums. Had I accompanied the cortege I might have witnessed that final remarkable transaction by which an American collector acquired as souvenirs the lanterns that lighted the labors of those who lowered Anatole France into his tomb.

There was no religious ceremony; at no time had there been one. The candles that rumor stood beside the bier of the kindly old skeptic were electric torches. The tons of flowers that covered the coffin were the tributes of his friends, both in and out of the church, many hundreds of whom he had never met. That much I had learned at first hand, only the day before. It had been with the hope of meeting Anatole France that I had voyaged to his country. On the water, two days from Cherbourg, the wireless brought the tidings of his death. I had hastened to the Villa Said as a final duty. There was the casket and the bier; there were the tall torches and the tons of flowers. But the coffin lid was closed—as irrevocably closed as those "malicious, coffee-colored eyes" beneath it. The flowers covered all. It had been his wish that no one should look upon his face in death.

Bitterly disappointed, I joined the stream of silent men and women that flowed through the death chamber, and into the reception hall. A tray, piled high with black-bordered letters, sat upon a carved table near the door, and the uppermost staring signature was that of Gabriele D'Annunzio. On another table was an open volume and a pencil—an invitation to all who came to leave a record of their final visit. I read a page of the names already written there, and there was none I knew.

This was the end of my sentimental pilgrimage. No doubt I should have asked *his* autograph, had he been living. Now, in effect, I thought, he was asking me for mine. It was less immodest than it sounds.

Wherefore, under the Duboises and the Lebruns I signed my name, as I do now, in tribute to the greatest prose master and the greatest humanist of our time.

But I could not remain long in Paris, for my supply of cash was limited and I was eager to see something of England before I was down to my last penny. Crossing from Calais to Dover one afternoon, I reached London in a pouring rain and began my second experience of the great city I had not seen for twenty years. There were a number of persons I particularly wanted to meet in London and by keeping constantly on the move I managed to meet most of them. My first visit, however, was not to St. John's Wood and Arthur Machen. It was to the home of Haldane Macfall, whom I had telephoned shortly after my arrival in London.

The White House, as he called it, a tall white building with red blinds and a green door, was an imposing looking residence in the moonlight, and the thought occurred to me that Macfall must be a writer of means. The place looked expensive. Inside it was the same: everything looked costly, everything was in exquisite taste, suggesting not only a man of culture but of considerable wealth. The living room was a small but important art gallery; among the paintings that covered the walls I recognized the work of Frank Brangwyn and of Lovat Fraser, the famous colorist, who had been Macfall's protegé. We had spoken frequently of Fraser in our letters and here, under my eyes, was Macfall's great Fraser collection spread on a table for my benefit—books, letters, broadsides, sketches, stage designs—a brilliant and astonishing exhibit. Tall bookcases held rare volumes and enchanting association copies for my inspection; the doors already stood open. How delightful, I thought, to have all the money one needed; to be able to buy all the books and pictures one cared to own. Lucky Haldane Macfall!

In the midst of this opulence Macfall, who had opened the door to me himself, stood and talked. He talked volubly and charmingly. He had begun to speak at once and my impression is that he continued to speak with few pauses for the next two hours: a tall man, remarkably handsome, who still looked more like the soldier he had been than the writer and artist he had become. "Well, Mab, here is Starrett, no longer a mystery," he said to the elderly woman who came to join us; and I was greeted by Mab Plumridge, that is to say, Mrs. Haldane Macfall. I felt her sharp eyes probing me from behind gold-rimmed spectacles. After a time it seemed to me that she had decided to like me and somehow, without quite knowing how it came about, I found myself involved in the marital life of the Frasers, Lovat and Grace. "A lovable fellow," sighed Macfall. Mab agreed but thought that "his marriage to Grace" was the worst thing that could have happened to him. "Mind you," she added confidentially, "they were perfectly devoted to each other!" It was all a little naïve, a little self-conscious, and curiously significant, as if some further revelation would shortly be forthcoming. None came, however, and tardily I understood that these were two lonely people speaking awkwardly as children sometimes do on meeting a new friend. Their home was a "regular museum," they laughed apologetically, and tried to show me everything in the place at once. Between bursts of confidential small talk their friendliness, their solicitude for my comfort, was touching; it was embarrassing.

243

After a time the conversation became less unpremeditated and Macfall paid his respects to Arthur Machen. It appeared that our misunderstanding had crossed the Atlantic and reached his ears. "An ungrateful dog!" cried the major heartily. "Why, Fisk tells me that you actually made his reputation in America—actually *made* him! My dear chap, don't waste your time on fellows like that. They aren't worth it." I don't know what I said to that; perhaps I agreed. We got away from the awkward subject at last, however, and spoke of the English literary scene. Mab, a woman of spirit, was vehement in her denunciation of "the Garvices and Walpoles." But Macfall interrupted the philippic. Walpole had done creditable work, he said, and must not be compared with Garvice. "And this man Locke!" cried Mab. "Now, now," said Macfall pacifically, "he isn't that bad." I ventured the unoriginal thought that writers were sometimes good of their kind, that it was possible to be quite good on one of the lower levels, that critics were unfair in condemning a writer for failing to achieve something he had not tried to achieve. Macfall agreed and added that it was "the same in painting." He wandered about the room lecturing, stopping occasionally to comment on some of his treasures. A gay little oil in blues and yellows, a street scene, was "by Ferguson, you remember, Mab? A capital fellow! I had high hopes for him, but he went cubistic. A man who could do *this* sort of thing. Madness!" said Haldane Macfall. The final word was for cubism, not Ferguson.

We spoke of *Jezebel Pettyfer* and I told him again how the book had come to my attention: how Lucius Malmin, a friend, had found a stray copy in the Virgin Islands while serving there as America's first colonial judge, and had brought it to me in Chicago.

"The Virgin Islands," said Macfall. "A strange place for my Jezebel! Do thank the judge for me, won't you? He liked it, I think you said?"

"He was enthusiastic about it," I told him.

"When people do like it they like it a lot," said Macfall. "Did I tell you that George Meredith liked it? His comment was perhaps

244

a bit enigmatic. He said the book was the finest novel of his generation, but that it ought never to have been written."

Ultimately we climbed the stairs to his study to look at more pictures and more books. The house was cold and Mrs. Macfall appeared to shrink. She drew her jacket more tightly around her. Macfall kept on talking. He showed me his own black and white originals for *The Splendid Wayfaring* and a clock he had made himself. "He's wonderful," breathed Mab as her husband left the room to find something else to show me. "He can do anything. And he's the dearest thing! Sweet, kind, good—and helpless as a child. He believes everybody and everybody uses him—his brains—and gives nothing in return. *Brain thieves*!" Throughout the evening she was an eloquent and persistent advocate of Macfall's greatness and his helplessness. Once when *she* had left the room Macfall confided, like a child whispering a secret, "Poor thing! Her first marriage was miserable."

A little later Mab revealed the secret herself. Once she had had plenty of money. "If we only had it now!" she cried. And then I knew what something inside had been trying to tell me from the beginning. The Macfalls were almost in poverty. In this beautifully appointed house, filled with art treasures, with books and manuscripts, the house of an artist, they lacked only one thing— money. Macfall, it subsequently came out, was doing whatever hack work offered in the field of writing or illustrating.

Presently Mab brought in wine and biscuits and Macfall produced a bottle of lime juice of the sort, he said, that he had learned to like while serving in Jamaica. I sensed that they were embarrassed by what they supposed to be the meagerness of their hospitality, and gorged myself with biscuits. After a time we got back to the pictures and the books. A stuffed bird engaged our attention for a time (not a raven); there was some talk of Lord Kitchener and a conference at which the major had been present; then we were back in the living room among the Lovat Frasers. An array of original pen sketches was laid out and I was invited to select one as a souvenir of my visit. "You're not going away emptyhanded, you know," said Macfall, and immediately I felt like a burglar; but there were plenty of pictures he insisted, and he would be offended if I didn't take one. The great Fraser collection was for sale, it appeared. Macfall was sorry to part with it—"but one must live, eh?" He laughed self-consciously.

He left the room, and suddenly Mab confessed their poverty. It weighed deeply on them both and more and more it troubled *me*, too. "I hope," said Mab, "we can sell the Fraser collection for a decent sum. We're stony broke, you know; living from hand to mouth!" I would have liked to buy some of their treasures but my hands were tied. I was too close to the edge myself.

I left at midnight after Mab had filled my side pockets with biscuits and grapes. "I know these hotels," she said. "You'll be hungry tonight and won't be able to get a thing." Then Macfall took me to the Metropolitan station and tried to give me my subway fare. I got away from him just in time to keep from breaking down. Once again before leaving London I saw him. He had insisted on taking me to dinner and there was no talking him out of it. It was a modest dinner at one of the better tearooms. Mab was not present. Macfall was insulted when I reached for the check and in the end it was he who paid.

That was on Wednesday, October 22,1924, and the next day I went to see Arthur Machen. I had not communicated with him since our difficulty; he had no reason to believe that I was in London. Thus it was with some trepidation that I approached No. 12, Melina Place, and studied a small placard that said distinctly, *No Hawkers*. A high wall surrounded the house, pierced by a small door with a peephole in it. At the last moment I discovered that I had no visiting card and scrawled a message on a scrap of paper, which I handed to the maid who answered the bell. Then I waited, with one eye at the peephole, wondering what my reception would be.

Presently I saw the front door open, and a large woman with bobbed grey hair hurried down the path to the gate; she looked a

From left: Vincent Starrett, Robert Cromie,
and Frederic Babcock in the *Chicago Tribune* Book Rooms

FROM THE LIBRARY OF VINCENT STARRETT

FRIDOLF JOHNSON

Sherlock Holmes Bookplate

little like my mother, I noted, and just as formidable. I knew at once what was going to happen. Machen had refused to see me and had sent his wife to drive me from the door. But I was wrong: Mrs. Machen had come to ask me in and to apologize for keeping me waiting. She was so cordial that I began to feel better about the whole episode. I tramped up the garden path in her wake and into the Machen living room. It was old and comfortable and reassuring. A fire burned cheerfully in a wide fireplace; one wall was congested with old books in open shelves; there were big, shabby, comfortable chairs and sofas. Perhaps, I thought, it wasn't going to be so bad, after all.

Mrs. Machen was smoking a cigarette, not daintily but with the careless automatic ease of a man. She was in black silk and was quite stout, I saw. More and more she reminded me of my mother, except for the cigarette; they had the same square face, the same determined jaw. I was still a little embarrassed, thinking of what had passed between Machen and me; but Mrs. Machen chatted busily. Arthur, she said, would be down in a few minutes. He was just putting the finishing touches to something, she laughed; probably an introduction. Then there was a quick tread on the stairs, a door opened, and Arthur Machen came in.

I was immediately disappointed by his appearance: a short stout man of middle age with prominent blue eyes and lank grey hair that was beginning to turn yellow. Parted in the middle, it hung in bangs over his high forehead and covered the tops of his ears. At the back it appeared to have been badly shingled; I had a swift impression of the Machens cutting each other's hair. But his features were bold and distinguished; his eyes were keen and wide.

I said: "Arthur Machen! I hoped you wouldn't turn me away."

He laughed a rich deep laugh in a vibrant actorish voice. "Of course not," he returned. "Sit down, Starrett. Sit down again and smoke."

Then for half an hour we spoke of everything but the one thing on my mind. Nothing at all was said about our quarrel, and at length it became clear to me that nothing was going to be said

247

about it; not immediately, at any rate. I began to relax, and shortly we were talking easily about books and Americans, and Mrs. Machen was telling me of their many visitors from my country, all of whom had mentioned my name. Then for a time we stood before the open shelves while Machen drew down and talked about his favorite books. This meant snaking many volumes of Dickens out of their niches and whirling the pages rapidly to find favorite passages. "Dickens," said Arthur Machen, "is the Great Possession." The last two words were obviously in caps. I asked about his famous "dog and duck" punch, a combination of sauterne and gin, rumors of which had reached me in his letters. John Gunther, I told him, had mistaken its symbolism. Encountering the words in a biographical note, in which Machen's hobby had been facetiously described by himself as "dog and duck," Gunther had assumed it to be a reference to the writer's exploits with a fowling piece.

The anecdote delighted Machen. "I wouldn't know one end of a duck gun from the other," he said. "Do you still favor it?" I asked. "The punch? Oh, yes!" "But it has been improved," interpolated Mrs. Machen; "there's a third ingredient now." "Yes," agreed Machen, "the first secret was divulged in a New York newspaper by Mr. Burton Rascoe, I believe. We have since added another ingredient; but that is still a secret; you shall try it on Saturday night and see what it does to you."

We spoke of Algernon Blackwood, of whom one thinks immediately after one thinks of Machen. "He is very popular in America," I said; "but you are the finer artist. It annoys me that your sales are not greater than his."

"He publishes more than I do," said Arthur Machen. "That is the great secret of success—to remain constantly in the public eye."

"Do you like his work?" I asked.

His answer was a little parable: "I have met him a number of times in certain esoteric circles. He is a most interesting and amiable man. There is some difference perhaps in our approach to our subject matter, although I realize that we are lumped to-

248

gether by the reviewers. Tennyson, you remember, says 'the cedars sigh for Lebanon,' and that is exquisite poetry; but Blackwood believes the cedars really *do* sigh for Lebanon and that, Starrett, is damned nonsense!"

I was surprised by his knowledge of contemporary American literature and by some of the books he liked. He and Mrs. Machen were devoted to Harry Leon Wilson, but thought *Ruggles of Red Gap* greatly inferior to *Somewhere in Red Gap*, which seemed to me a very subtle piece of criticism from a Briton. Neither of the Machens liked their own great humorist, P. G. Wodehouse, for reasons that I have forgotten; they preferred W. W. Jacobs, the historian of Wapping. Greatest of Machen's admirations at the moment was James Branch Cabell, three of whose books, *The Cream of the Jest, Jurgen*, and *Beyond Life*, he rated among the finest literary performances of our time.

I asked him if I was not to see his favorite "pub"—the Clifton House mentioned in *The London Adventure*—about which he had often written me. "It *was* my favorite pub," said Arthur Machen, "but it is so no longer. About a year ago the old proprietor sold out and there came in a woman with bronze hair." He paused, then added tersely, "I left!" There was another pause and he continued, "Besides there was a black and white artist who frequented the place, and his talk bored me. I have another place now and I reach it by a way he does not know. We are going there shortly, you and I."

He talked like an inspired guidebook as we ambled toward the tavern of his choice, pointing out the erstwhile homes of English men of letters. One of the houses had been occupied by the elder Thomas Hood, as set forth on a bronze plate in the wall. "All over London," said Machen, meaning that all over London were similar identifying plates. "What a wonderful city! We must have a bus ride together, Starrett. London is better seen from a bus top than any other way." Among his recent visitors from America had been Theron Cooper and his wife Netta, and they had strolled this way. "I said to him," said Machen, " 'You couldn't have such walls as these in *your* country, Mr. Cooper,' and he replied, 'No, people would wonder what was going on behind them.' " His flow of gossip and anecdote continued for blocks without appreciable pause.

But when we had reached the tavern and were seated with our drinks he was suddenly serious: "About this affair of ours, Starrett. There are three remarks to be made, I think, and I shall make them and then, if you agree, we'll ring down the curtain on that episode. First, it was foolish of me to give you permission to reprint my early things. Second, having done so, it was wrong of me to forget. Third, it was wrong of you to print those things of mine in a book without first submitting to me a table of contents." He raised his eyebrows humorously, interrogatively, and added, "Curtain!"

"Good enough," I said and put out my hand. "I'm glad it's over. I was sorry that a misunderstanding had spoiled a relationship that gave me great pleasure."

"And that's all of that," said Machen decisively.

He brought a second round of drinks to the table and shortly we were returning by the way we had come.

"What are you doing now?" I asked, just before we parted. "I'm writing introductions," he said. "I'm on *Dr. Stiggins* now. It's polemical and of no possible interest now to anybody, but that's Knopf's business if he wants to bring it out."

"Surely you will do one more novel," I said.

"No," said Arthur Machen, "I have finished. I am sixty-one, and I have written all the novels I shall ever write."

"Possibly your son Hilary will write when he is older," I suggested; but the idea seemed to depress him. "Perhaps," he said, "but we must hope for the best!"

We lunched next day at the Cheshire Cheese and Machen appeared to think well of the place. "The food is good," he said, "but don't believe all the nonsense you read about the Cheese. It was never the favorite eating place of Dr. Johnson. In my opinion that legend is a downright lie invented to attract the tourists. The place isn't mentioned in the Book. But it is undoubtedly old and

250

interesting. Of course it has been commercialized for years; indeed, I believe it is kept up largely for visiting Americans."

That day I saw London as I had not seen it before and as I have not see it since. We were together only a few hours, but it was just such a jaunt as I would have chosen for myself. Certainly few Americans can boast that they have had Arthur Machen for a guide. Some of the time we spent on foot and Machen, although years my senior, stepped out briskly. Some of the time we rode the bus tops and Machen's little lectures, punctuated with gestures and quotations, attracted the attention of other riders until at times we had an amused and appreciative audience. It was Dickensian London in large part that he showed me, and it was clear that Dickens was his passion. Dickensians will know the streets we traveled, the bus lines on which we rode, the old inns and houses we visited. We passed up the "Old Curiosity Shop" however; Arthur Machen would have none of it. It, too, he said, perpetuated a "lying legend." Toward dusk we came into Islington, the "almost mythical region" in which a younger Arthur Machen once had lived and dreamed— it is memorably described in *Hieroglyphics*—and saw from the street the rooms in which he had written some of his earliest tales and essays: I think nothing would have induced Machen to pass inside.

Saturday night found me scratching my shoes on Machen's door-scraper. I was a trifle late, or perhaps others had been a trifle early. Warning gusts of voices smote me as I entered the hall; the adjoining living room was grey with smoke. The same fire burned on the hearth; Mrs. Machen was wearing the same black silk dress and, as far as it was possible to judge, smoking the same cigarette with the same careless ease of the habitual smoker. It was not a party: it was Arthur Machen's Saturday night levee, when he kept open house for his friends. Frank Hudleston was there, Machen's brother-in-law, known in America as the author of *Gentleman Johnny Burgoyne* and *Warriors in Undress*, a lean comfortable Englishman smoking a pipe. Henry Savage was there with Barbara Mole; he it was who later compiled Machen's bibliography and

251

wrote the standard biography of Richard Middleton. And D. B. Wyndham Lewis, the great biographer of Villon, was there; I know this because years later he reminded me in a letter that we had met at Arthur Machen's. And others, half a dozen others, at least.

That was the last I saw of Arthur Machen. When Montgomery Evans visited him a few weeks later, he asked Machen about the difficulty between us. Evans, an ardent Machen collector, had a copy of *The Shining Pyramid* with him and Machen inscribed it in the following words:

> Mr. Vincent Starrett called on me in London a few weeks ago. I submitted to him three propositions:
>
> 1. It was very silly of me to say in 1918: "You may do what you like with my old stuff."
>
> 2. It was wrong of me not to recollect this saying in 1924.
>
> 3. It was very wrong of you to make two books of this "old stuff" without consulting me as to the contents.
>
> ARTHUR MACHEN

That was his accurate enough recollection of what occurred between us when I visited him in October, 1924. Evans showed me the inscribed volume in New York, in 1927, and made me a copy of the inscription. But in spite of our reconciliation and his agreement to call our difficulties ended, Machen would appear to have been still a little sore when he published his authorized edition of *The Shining Pyramid*. His introduction to that work, written in 1925, speaks caustically about the young American who had honored him by pirating the book in Chicago. Although he did not mention my name, I was sorry to see that note of lurking hostility.

My third London visit was to Fleetway House to meet William Murray Graydon. The day was October 25, the eve of my thirty-eighth anniversary. My interest in Graydon was no sudden infatuation: I had grown up on *The Rajah's Fortress, The Cryptogram, Exiled to Siberia,* and other sterling works of improbable adventure that I still held in affectionate regard. And I had some unfinished business with Graydon, so to put it; once I had read the first half dozen chapters of a Graydon serial in a boy's weekly and never had been able to obtain the succeeding chapters. The story was *Red Rose and White, A Tale of the Wars of the Roses*, which in my youthful innocence I thought compared very favorably with Stevenson's *Black Arrow*. I had grown up hoping that some day I would find out how that exciting tale ended. Then shortly before leaving America I had learned that my old favorite was living in England—although an American by birth—and would be glad to welcome me if ever I came his way. My prompt acceptance of the invitation must have surprised him almost as much as it pleased him.

He was now associated with Harmsworth's vast publishing empire and was, at the time of my visit, one of the principal writers of "Sexton Blake" detective stories. The scene of our encounter was his little cubicle in Fleetway House, where I was greeted by a small, slight man, possibly in his early sixties, with bright blue eyes and a little waxed moustache—a dapper little man of great charm and friendliness who for some two hours drank in my memories of his early stories and answered the eager questions I put to him.

Happily, I knew something about Sexton Blake, who may be identified for American readers as the English counterpart of our own Nick Carter. It appeared that he turned out a novel a week about Blake; sometimes, indeed, two novels. But of course they were not full-length novels, he added quickly, and showed me a drawerful of them; a drawer containing hundreds of little paper volumes in lurid wrappers celebrating the fantastic adventures of the indestructible detective.

"Those are all mine," said Graydon. "Have you read any Sexton Blakes?"

I said that a few stray copies only had come my way, but that I had read them with pleasure.

"Do you remember Pedro, the dog?" he asked quickly.

I said I remembered Pedro with much satisfaction.

"*I invented Pedro*," said William Murray Graydon, modestly but proudly.

253

He gave me a sketchy history of the Sexton Blake series. Many authors had worked on the tales over the years. A dozen writers including himself were now turning them out, working with the same set of characters. But Pedro was his personal contribution to the legend. I thought of Dumas's fiction factory and risked a comparison. Yes, it was something like that, he agreed; but it was pleasant work, and it was a living.

Before I left him he said he would like to give me a souvenir of my visit, and I said I would like to have a "Sexton Blake" suitably inscribed. Then for some moments he burrowed like a mole in the bottomless drawer, murmuring to himself as he turned over the lurid pamphlets and looked at the titles. He came up at length with a tale called *The Case of the Four Barons*, thumbed its pages anxiously, reading a paragraph here and there, and said, "Yes, I think I remember this one. I remember rather liking it. I'll give you this one."

"And *Red Rose and White*," I hinted. "Would there be a copy of that in the drawer?"

"By Jove, yes, there must be," cried Graydon enthusiastically. "Let's have a look for it. It's signed 'Alfred Armitage,' you know, which is a name I sometimes use. Yes, here it is! I had forgotten that it was brought out in wrappers. It's just a reprint, but if it's any use to you . . .?"

I said I would never go to bed without looking to see that it was safe in my bookcase; and a minute later I was really holding in my hand an autographed copy of the story I had been questing for more than a quarter of a century.

We agreed to meet a few days later at the Trocadero bar and resume our conversation, but unfortunately I had to sail for America on the evening of our engagement, and I didn't see him again. I am told that he is now, some years after his death, something of a legend among English collectors. His writings are widely sought by "penny dreadful" specialists and are hard to find. As few of the Sexton Blake stories were signed with his name, perhaps not any,

254

the search for Graydons offers some pretty problems. But problems are as the breath of life to collectors of detective literature.

I called on one other boyhood favorite before leaving England; no less a favorite than Gordon Browne, younger son of Dickens's "Phiz," who had illustrated so many of my "Henty books" that I always thought of the two men together. No illustrator ever had pleased me more than Gordon Browne, and when a woman's voice on the telephone invited me to visit him at Richmond one afternoon, I was delighted. My admired illustrator turned out to be a very tall, soldierly old gentleman with a cavalry moustache, so I was not disappointed in his appearance. He welcomed me to his home and studio, gave me tea and wafers, and ended by showing me every picture in the house. For two hours, turning over his portfolios of battle scenes and duellos, of gallant horsemen and intrepid naval lieutenants, I was back again in the world of G. A. Henty.

Another day, starting early, I hurried off to Gravesend to call on R. Austin Freeman, creator of the prodigious Dr. Thorndyke, who stood second only to Sherlock Holmes in my pantheon of detectives. I took him by surprise, I am afraid, and interrupted an afternoon of work; but for an hour we chatted over coffee and ultimately I was permitted to see, nay, to explore, the famous top floor laboratory. Yes, there I was, if you will believe me, in Thorndyke's very rooms, quite as if I were Marchmont or Broadribb dropping in for a conference with the Doctor. It was like participating for a miraculous moment in a chapter of *The Red Thumb Mark* or *The Eye of Osiris*.

These, then, were the men I called on in England, a queerish lot, you may think; but they were the men I wanted most to meet, and now they are all gone and only *I* am moved to write about them. They stood for interests in my life that were important to me then, and are no less so now. I am very glad I got to London just when I did, to meet this little group of survivors. Had Ballantyne or Kingston or Henty or David Ker then been living in England, be sure that I should have visited them too. *Calix meus inebrians quam præclarus est*, as Machen liked to proclaim, rolling out the sonorous syllables like his beloved Samuel Johnson.

But I had one important visit yet to make. The day before I knew I had to sail I ate a hasty breakfast and went at once to Baker Street. I had not then written extensively about Sherlock Holmes and Dr. Watson, but already I had proprietary ideas about the immortal twosome and the rooms in Baker Street. So I strolled the length of the thoroughfare from Oxford Street to Regent's Park and back again, and settled ultimately on the wrong house. It was on the wrong side of the street and too close to Oxford Street; but it looked like the house I had carried for years in my mind's eye, and for the time being I was happy.

Next morning, in a pouring rain, I caught the boat train for Southampton. As I hurried down the long platform looking for a compartment that was not too crowded, a solemn face appeared at one of the train windows and sad, owlish eyes peered out at me from under a high bald forehead. They seemed to be meditating on all the ironies and injustices of life. I stopped and looked back at them. There could be no doubt about it: only one such face existed in the world. It was Ring Lardner, my colleague of the old *Inter-Ocean* days. I had not seen him since leaving that newspaper in 1906. I opened the carriage door and stepped in over his feet. "Shove over, Ring," I said, "and let's get going. *I've* got a deadline if you haven't."

"Why—hello," he said, and groped desperately for my name.

"You don't remember me," I said. "I'm Vincent Starrett, once of the *Inter-Ocean*. We were cubs together in Chicago."

"By God," he cried, "so we were! What are you doing in England?"

"I'm leaving England," I said, "just as I entered it—in the rain."

When he had helped me pile my luggage under and over the seats we settled down for a long talk; but of our nostalgic conversation on the journey to Southampton I remember almost nothing. Somewhere along the way, however, my companion made an immortal remark. "How did you like England?" I asked him; and for some moments he looked gloomily at the wet landscape. "They say," he answered at last, "that the sun never sets on the British Empire. *I've—never—seen—it—rise.*"

On the *Mauretania* we were separated by the trifling circumstance that Ring was traveling first class and I second; but this arrangement did not last long. There was no objection to my second class presence in the first class lounge, since it was obvious that I was a friend of Ring's. I used to sneak across the runway between the two areas of the ship every evening after dinner, making a bit of an adventure of it, but nobody ever stopped me or asked the color of my ticket. There Ring and I continued our endless conversation about books and ball players, old newspaper days, and other matters of interest to two lonely and (to be honest) homesick newspapermen.

At this time Lardner was already widely known. Indeed, he was probably the most famous humorist in America. He preferred his own circle of friends on the ship, however; the others of our group were three or four New Yorkers and their wives. Together we made up a coterie that must have been trying for soberer passengers. Ring had taken a fancy to a comfortable lounge amidships that boasted a small upright piano and where hard liquor was served at all hours. To the best of my knowledge he never left it during the voyage. And always there was a highball at his elbow.

There I learned for the first time that Ring Lardner played the piano, if played is the word; he certainly played chords magnificently and they appeared to fit any song that anybody happened to remember. His big hands could span almost two octaves either way and he obtained some really wonderful effects. The little upright was securely anchored in a convenient corner, and even when he was playing Ring continued his rhythmic drinking. He kept his glass on top of the piano, and when the *Mauretania* pitched and rolled in the manner peculiar to that famous liner, it would slide slowly to starboard, sometimes a few inches at a time, sometimes more rapidly, until it was in danger of crashing to the floor; but it never did. Ring always timed its descent to the fraction of a second and caught it just before it went over the edge; and always without missing a beat. Without missing a beat he replaced it at the far end of the piano top, where again it would begin its leisurely slide to starboard. All this was accomplished with the celerity of a magician's trick and never once in the days I was with him was there a tragedy; never once did he miss a word or chord of his song. I think it pleased him to know that all over the lounge nervous old ladies and irascible old gentlemen were waiting for the tumbler to crash; but no smile ever touched his deadpan mask. His own group always joined him in the songs he sang—old songs like "On the Banks of the Wabash," "In the Shade of the Old Apple Tree," "Down on the Farm," and suchlike masterpieces, always so curiously nostalgic to city dwellers. Occasionally we intellectualized the orgy with "The Rosary" and "I Hear You Calling Me," but Ring's chords were equal to every occasion. He took everything in his stride, he never missed a beat, and he never missed a drink either. Sometimes we had as many as eight or ten persons singing, and once at least somebody complained about the noise we made. The chief steward was sent to reprove us; but Ring handed him a highball and persuaded him to join us. He had a very nice second tenor.

These are my last memories of Ring Lardner. We parted when the ship docked in New York and I never saw him again.

XVIII

LATE AUTUMN found me at my typewriter again; but the stuff went badly and shortly I needed more money than was coming in. For years I had been buying more books than I could afford and, while I owned a fine library of modern first editions, my cash reserve was practically nil. In this pass, although with considerable

258

heartache, I sold some of my books. There is only one reason for selling one's books, and that is poverty; there is no other justification. At my elbow as I write is a handsome pamphlet, the title page of which reads in part as follows: *First Editions of Esteemed Modern Authors Mainly in Original Binding. Authors' Inscribed Copies, Autograph Manuscripts and Letters. . . . Including Selections from the Libraries of Vincent Starrett of Chicago, Illinois, and Waldo R. Browne, of Wyoming, New York. . . . To Be Sold on the Evening of Wednesday, November 18, and the Afternoon and Evening of Thursday, November 19, 1925.* I wonder if Waldo R. Browne of Wyoming, New York, still has his copy of that auction catalogue and how he feels when he looks at it. Only Mr. Browne and I, turning the pages, would be able to say which books were his and which mine. But we know, don't we, Mr. Browne?

A number of times in the years that followed I was obliged to sell some of my books, sometimes at auction and sometimes to individual dealers. One such sale was to David Randall, then Scribner's rare book expert in New York. Oddly, and delightfully I think, the catalogue he issued became itself a rarity now sought by collectors. For browsers among old books here is its full title: *A Catalogue of Original Manuscripts, and First and Other Important Editions of the Tales of Sherlock Holmes, as Written By Sir Arthur Conan Doyle, Together with Important Biographies, Pastiches, Articles, Etc., and a Few Extraordinary Association and Unique Items.*

It was made up almost entirely from my personal collection of Sherlockiana, and the prices attached would seem very low today. Randall and I collaborated on the catalogue and spiked it with a number of items that, I am afraid, never existed in this world. For example: *An Inquiry Into the Nature of the Ashes of Various Tobaccos* (Tibet: Privately Printed, 1893. Folio, second edition, half green Morocco, gilt top, other edges uncut). This astounding title was offered at $100. And, for example: *Practical Handbook of Bee Culture, with Some Observations Upon the Segregation of the Queen* (England: Sussex Downs, 1912). This famous work was offered for the ridiculously low sum of $7.50, and described as a common book, "though unusual in fine state."

One wonders how many avid Sherlockians ordered Col. Sebastian Moran's *Heavy Game of the Western Himalayas* at $20. It was described as a "better than usual copy of this book, usually soiled by the handling of innumerable retired Indian officers." On the margin of the title page opposite the author's name, the catalogue noted, somebody had written, "The second most dangerous man in London." What a pity Holmes did not append his initials!

My favorite spoof—and how I should like to have it back!—was Item 156: *Historical Record of the Fifth Regiment of Foot or Northumberland Fusilliers* (First edition, 1838). On the fly leaf appeared, it seems, the following certification of ownership: "John H. Watson, M.D., 221-B Baker Street, 23 February, 1881. . . . I found this history of my old regiment in a shop at Charing Cross Rd. and bought it for 2/6. J.H.W."

I am told that Professor Randall of Indiana University is happy to purchase stray copies of this catalogue, and so for that matter am I.

I was now living in Chicago's Uptown district, far from my old haunts on the West Side. Although a sense of loneliness flooded me at intervals and gave me some melancholy weekends, the change was good for me and I spent five busy years in a snug little hostelry near which Eugene Field once had lived and written. Paul Thorne, author of that good detective novel *The Sheridan Road Mystery*, lived directly across the street, so I was not without companionship in an emergency of the spirit. Marital companionship had gone glimmering by this time, I regret to say, and Lillian and I had quietly separated. Neither of us were happy about it, but at the time it had seemed the thing to do. I had begun to think of myself as a failure; and I recalled Stewart Holbrook's shrewd observation: "Girls should think twice before marrying newspapermen, who usually die leaving them about two dollars." It seemed to apply.

Meanwhile, life had to go on—although sometimes I wondered why. If anyone was to blame for the split, it was I.

It must have been about this time, too, that Mignon Eberhart and other professional writers entered my life, although some years were to elapse before Mrs. Eberhart pleased and flattered me by making me the murderer in one of her entertaining detective novels. She was one of the many Midland Authors who met weekly to talk "shop" in the Hotel Sherman basement; together, we sometimes dominated the conversation with our gruesome talk of murder and its motives. But my happiest memory of the attractive Mrs. Eberhart is of her enthusiastic co-operation on a difficult occasion. As chairman of a large literary gathering one evening, it was my embarrassing task to reprove a speaker who, lecturing on poetry, took occasion to asperse the readers and writers of detective stories.

"Poetry," she concluded pompously, "is the door to another world."

"I think I ought to suggest to Mrs. Colson that murder, too, is a door to another world," I said mildly when she had finished, and Mignon Eberhart, far out in the audience, stood up and cheered.

Yet another friend and colleague of the time was H. Bedford-Jones, to give him the name by which he was known to thousands of readers. I didn't see him often, for he alternated between Illinois, Wisconsin, and California; but whenever he came to Chicago we foregathered for an orgy of shop talk. On his own level, Henry Bedford-Jones was one of the better magazine writers of his period. Possibly he was the greatest of that numerous company who, year after year for two generations, filled the pulp magazines with some of the best fiction of its kind in the world. His name worked a sort of magic with readers; on the vivid covers of the better all-fiction monthlies, it insured top sales. He was in his time the most prolific and, I believe, the highest paid of our pulp writers. And he was the envy and admiration and despair of those of us who labored in the same field for smaller rewards.

He was a prodigious worker, of course. In his admirable book,

This Fiction Business, he poked fun gently at weary scribblers who thought three hundred words a day a fair stint. Under pressure, he had himself written as much as twenty-five thousand words in a day, a complete story. A good day's work for B-J was from five thousand to ten thousand words. He needed an electric typewriter to keep abreast of his thoughts. Indeed, the speed and quantity of his output gave rise to legends such as the one about a friend who tried to get him on the telephone.

"Henry can't come to the phone," his wife is said to have reported. "He's working on a novel."

"I'll hold on until he's finished," said the caller.

I don't know how true the story is; but I have myself seen four typewriters lined up in his rooms with stories going full blast on all of them.

Then the Stirling Parkinsons purchased a home on the Connecticut shore, and I became a chronic summer guest. This convenient arrangement permitted me to visit New York occasionally, and finally I was spending several days a week in the city, visiting editors, publishers, and, of course, the bookshops. Above all, it permitted me to visit the theater, and one day curiosity led me to an old place in Fourteenth Street where Eva Le Gallienne and an excellent company could be seen in repertory. Thereafter for two summers I was one of the Civic Repertory Theater's most loyal supporters. No such theater-going spree had possessed me since my teen-age debauch on Chicago's West Side. I witnessed every play the company produced, at least once, and certain plays I attended several times. One, Chekhov's *The Three Sisters*, I saw almost as often as it was produced, and every time I wept copiously. Once, as a quite small boy, I remember weeping over the death of Little Eva at a tent-show presentation of *Uncle Tom's Cabin*, and in my teens I had been moved to tears by the parting speeches of Prince Karl and Kathy in *Old Heidelberg*; but only *The Three Sisters* had ever shaken my adult composure so completely. Possibly any good

262

company could repeat the miracle for me, but I doubt that Chekhov's tragic comedy was ever better played than it was played by Miss Le Gallienne and her company in 1926 and 1927.

Those two summers and autumns were the background of some wild book-collecting sprees (for although I had parted with many of my books I had begun at once to build another library), and some memorable meetings. There were luncheons with the poets Hart Crane and Ridgeley Torrence, and one memorable afternoon I had tea with William Rose Benét and Elinor Wylie— I mention the flattering circumstance to be able to say that I once saw Shelley plain.

Meanwhile, at Hotchkiss Grove, near Branford, I had begun to write my first novel, *Seaports in the Moon*. The time, I take it, was the summer of 1927, since the book appeared the following year. It was a book of sequels in which I brought together a number of the romantic rascals I had loved in other men's books. Since some of them were centuries apart, I had to find a plausible thread on which to string them, and this I found in the legend of the Fountain of Youth. The result was a historical fantasia beginning in the year 1483 and coming down the centuries to my own time.

If it had been a commercial success, it is possible that, as in the case of Cleopatra's nose, the history of the world might have been changed; at any rate, my history and my world. Unfortunately, although it had a good press, it sold poorly and was never reprinted; and more or less as a consequence of this financial miscalculation, my next five novels were detective stories. Perhaps I would have written detective novels anyway, but certainly the failure of *Seaports* influenced me. That winter I wrote my first detective novel, *Murder on 'B' Deck*, which did so well on the Crime Club list that it determined my writing for the next five years.

Even so, I might not have begun so promptly if Donald Lauder had not been carried off by an ocean liner. Midnight sailings for Europe were popular just then, and Lauder, a friend of my newspaper days, was saying farewell to a pair of departing honey-mooners one night when the mishap occurred. He had wined and dined on board, not wisely and much too well. When the ship sailed at midnight he was still aboard and was obliged to return to New York in the pilot boat. As I listened to his vivid account of the episode, I realized that the first chapter of a mystery novel was being handed to me on a platter; and thereafter the whole book more or less wrote itself in my head. As planned, the tale was to have been the first book-length adventure of Jimmie Lavender; but for some reason I changed my mind and invented a new detective named Walter Ghost who appeared in two further novels, *Dead Man Inside* (1931) and *The End of Mr. Garment* (1932).

Again, in 1935, I created a new detective (Riley Blackwood) for *The Great Hotel Murder*. This time I hit the jackpot—a smallish jackpot—for I managed to sell the novel three times, as a serial, as a book, and as a motion picture. Incidentally, when the picture appeared, I saw a good story presented by a competent cast, and most of the figures of the tale were called by names I had invented; but there the resemblance ended. Nobody was more surprised than the author by the revelation of the killer's identity. It was a humbling experience. So, perhaps, Shakespeare may have felt at a final rehearsal when some of his best lines turned up missing.

I was in my own apartment now, a set of rooms in the depths of a wandering old building, reached by a labyrinth of underground corridors, and for the most part writing at night. Only a few friends found their way through the winding passages to my lair, notably Percy James, a mystery enthusiast who was one of my twelve disciples. I must tell you about my disciples some time. When he had gone away, at midnight or thereabouts, I began to write and wrote sometimes until daylight appeared in the narrow area beyond my windows. It was a lonely life, after a fashion, but satisfying and productive. I used to wonder about the other occupants of the old building. It was so very still at night that small, mysterious sounds filtered through the adjacent passages and reached me in my book-room; it was interesting to try to interpret them. I never saw the young woman who lived in the apartment opposite mine, but I used to hear her coming and going, and it occurred to me that her working hours were similar to my own. By this and by that I formed an idea of her profession that may have done her an injustice. In a notebook of the period I find a paragraph that possibly reveals a little of us both. This is what I wrote early one morning about the time the milkman was rattling his bottles outside:

"Across the corridor from my room-and-a-half apartment lives, I think, a busy little *fleur de mal*. I never see her, but she comes and goes at curious and significant hours—between eleven at night and four in the morning. Our hours are much the same; and so, I often think, are our labors. As I hear her going brightly forth upon her little assignments, or struggling wearily back, sometimes I say aloud, pretending to address her: 'Lady, we're in the same boat, I think, and really should be friends. Just a couple of whores!' And then I would go back to my cent-a-word detective story feeling a little less lonely—a little less *unique*—in my unadmirable state of heart and mind."

There is more than a hint in this of the way I was beginning to feel toward my work: I was becoming heartily tired of it. I wanted to leave behind me a better reputation than any work of mine then completed was likely to win for me. It was a wholesome state of mind and I determined that my fourth detective novel should be my last. Then I was tempted to do one more, and wrote *Midnight and Percy Jones*. Will Cuppy, reviewing it, thought it my best performance.

I have spoken of the loneliness of these years of solitary writing; but in point of fact I had all the social life that was good for me. Chicago continued to be a stopover point for every poet and novelist headed east or west, and parties were constantly being given them by patrons or professionals of letters, including such groups as the Society of Midland Authors, the Cliff Dwellers, and the P.E.N. Even the bookshops were overrun by visiting authors. At Ben Abramson's Argus Bookshop, one met such writers as Somerset Maugham, Henry Miller, Erskine Caldwell, John Steinbeck, Louis Zara, and Christopher Morley; at Field's, Marcella Burns Hahner had begun her series of autographing parties for best-selling authors; and Mr. Greene's Irish poets continued to arrive and depart on all trains. In upper Michigan Avenue flourished *Le Petit Gourmet*, Mrs. William Vaughn Moody's rendezvous for poets.

Only once, to my regret, was it my good fortune to converse for a few minutes with Edna St. Vincent Millay. She had come to Chicago to read her poems and a distinguished audience had turned out to hear her. Although I met her only briefly before the readings began, it pleased me to be able to contribute an item to her program. As it happened, I had brought with me a short satirical poem she had once written for Chris Morley's *Bowling Green* column, where it was called "The Cheerful Abstainer." It had amused me and I had docketed and preserved it. Now I offered her a typewritten copy and asked her if she remembered it. Her eyebrows went up as she began to read. "I had forgotten I ever wrote it," she laughed. "I'll read it tonight."

To complete the record, the last time I saw Miss Millay was at the Chicago Century of Progress in 1933. Idling along one of the carnival highways one evening about dusk, my attention was attracted by a gay party headed in the opposite direction. One, a slim young woman with red hair, was being taken for a ride in one of the exposition's rickshaws. The young man between the shafts looked vaguely familiar; but the light was bad and anyway, I thought, it was unlikely that I knew him. So, I passed on and would have thought no more of the incident if I had not clearly recognized the other member of the party rolling along in the rear. There could be no question about him, at any rate. He was beyond a shadow of doubt the illustrious Alexander Woollcott *in propria persona*.

So I turned back and had a better look at the other pair. The first rickshaw puller, a gallant fellow with a small toothbrush mustache, was paying the utmost attention to his passenger, and suddenly I realized that I did know him, after all. Indeed, I had once introduced him to a Chicago audience as Thornton Wilder.

I didn't eavesdrop and I didn't barge in, although I knew them all, and they would have been polite to me; but one line of Miss Millay's conversation with her companion came to me as she rolled past me for the second time. It has remained with me ever since. She said, quite clearly I thought, "I should have brought the kitten."

That is all there is to the story. They passed, and I had had my last glimpse of one of the best loved poets of America. When I read of her death, a few years later, that last meeting was the first thing I thought of. I thought of her laughing face in the Chicago dusk, and wished I had a livelier memory of her to report to posterity.

It was at one of Burt Massee's "Gold Coast" bourbon parties that I met another poet, John Drinkwater, and almost poisoned him by adding beer to his whisky instead of ginger ale. Oddly, the poet took a fancy to me after this attempt on his life and invited me to visit him in England. I remember telling him a Lincoln story that amused him, and since it is unique—perhaps the only un-hackneyed Lincoln story in the world—I shall tell it here. Clara Laughlin, whose experience it was, had given it to me only a few weeks before. While engaged in writing her fine book, *The Death of Lincoln*, she had so saturated herself with the subject, she said, that sometimes she was troubled with dreams in which she was visited by the two principals in the tragic event. In one dream, John Wilkes Booth, the assassin, had stood at her bedside and addressed her courteously. "Madam," he told her, "you are making a terrible mistake about me. I did not shoot Abraham Lincoln. He committed suicide in that box!"

Drinkwater's comment was, "Good heavens, what if it were true!"

XIX

AMONG THE AMERICAN MEN OF LETTERS whom I have known, Christopher Morley stands first. I knew him longer and better than any other professional writing man of my acquaintance, excepting only the surviving members of the Chicago group in which I grew up. And I was drawn to him more warmly than to most others by the peculiar correspondence of our interests. Whenever I am inspired to write a gay little piece of bibliofoolishness, or shout my appreciation of a forgotten story-classic, I always wonder if I am not repeating something already uttered by Morley.

I don't remember when I first met Christopher Morley unless it was some centuries ago at the Mermaid Tavern. Probably—in this life—it was at one of Burt Massee's colorful brawls or at the Argus Bookshop over Cook's tourist agency in Michigan Avenue; he could always be found at one place or the other when he happened to be in Chicago. Or perhaps it was at Field's, where he used to sign hundreds of books, old and new, whenever there was a new Morley title in the market. It could have been at Schlogl's or even at the Congress Hotel, an old-fashioned caravansary that he preferred to the city's more glittering palaces of sin. I have no clear recollection of one particular time or place: the experience, as a memory picture, is a montage of jovial alarums and discursions, of wistful flashbacks and exhilarating closeups, of 221B culture and three-star Hennessy. We had been in correspondence for some years before we met. I had reviewed his enchanting fable, *Where the Blue Begins*, for Llewellyn Jones when it was first published, and he had written to thank me for a notice that he found "graceful, generous, and perspicatious," that is to say, a notice highly favorable to the book. Obviously this was a good beginning for a literary friendship, and that is really how it all began.

Ultimately, when he began to visit Chicago several times a year (sometimes with Frank Henry, his editor at Doubleday's and/or Lippincott's) we saw a great deal of each other and one of us at least found the association stimulating. When he happened to have a projected play in his pocket—a first act or one or two crucial scenes—we taxied up to Massee's and rehearsed the play, with everybody at the party—(there was always a party going on at Massee's)—reading a part. Sometimes we just rambled about Old Loopy, his name for Chicago, sampling books and Bourbon here and there and talking torrents of nonsense; and if occasionally we missed a barroom we never missed a bookshop. If it were ever necessary to establish my whereabouts on certain days of the irrecoverable past, I could find considerable corroborative data on the flyleaves of old books and old menus and old wine lists signed and dated by Morley. Once we began a collaborative ballade on a romantic subject frequently celebrated by Villon and Herrick, but gave it up after the first stanza; and once we decided to fly to Toronto and visit my aunts, but changed our minds and went to Lincoln Park instead, to lay a wreath on the grave of David Kennison, the last survivor of the Boston Tea Party. Unfortunately, we reached the park so late that, in the darkness, we couldn't find the memorial stone. In many ways, all satisfying to remember, Morley and I whiled away the hours or days of his Chicago visits; but recalling his admonition, when he heard that I was going to write my autobiography—"Don't remember too much!"—I forbear at this time to relate the singular adventure of the *Paradol Chamber* and the curious affair of the policeman, the housekeeper, and the *Light Cavalry Overture*. Suffice it to say that, whenever Christopher Morley came to Chicago, his friends had a lively time.

Of course I attended his lectures before the Modern Language Association, Northwestern's University College, and other congresses of public enlightenment, and applauded dutifully. On the whole, however, I preferred his private revelations to his more expedient public disclosures. He attracted excellent audiences, for he was well liked in Chicago, and the first and last thing to be said

269

about his lectures is that they were miscellaneous and unexpected. It was characteristic of him to reject the subject assigned to him on the program and, like Stephen Leacock's versatile horseman, dash gallantly off in all directions. This engaging habit injected a quality of suspense, not to say mystery, into his talks that kept listeners guessing at his destination. I used to worry about him until he had finished, leagues from where he had started but with everybody happy. Nothing I could say ever shook his determination not to use a manuscript. He preferred to carry his notes in his head and not infrequently he did so. For the most part, I think, he made it all up as he went along.

Morley's services to me over the years were numerous and helpful. He contributed entertainingly to several of my books and anthologies. He compiled an index for *Books Alive* (1940) that was so amusing it had to be moved from the back of the book to the front. His responses in absentio, on occasions when he was unable to attend local activities in my honor, were tributes full of insight and mischief that helped my standing in the community. As editor of the *Bowling Green* in the *Saturday Review*, he gave many of my poems their first chance in print. His own long poem, "Gentlemen's Relish," urging the merits of my verse upon a reluctant world, was the last of his many published expressions of good will. My file of Morley letters is a bulky one; it is difficult to single out any one or two for special attention. They are literary letters in the best sense, crowded with references to his reading, his thinking, his drinking, his wrestlings with the muse, his opinions of the nuisances who interrupt writers at their work; the sort of chit-chat and gossip that bookmen love to read in the letters of Lamb and Fitzgerald. They are signed in many ways and with many names. A typical short note is the following:

> VINCENZIO: Looks to me I'll be in Chicago by cocktail time next Friday and have much to report. How's about coming to Congress for a snort say six pm. I am smiling

at your pseudo-Horatian ode, just received from a discreet
hand. To hell with discretion!

SEBASTIAN MORAN
(Most Dangerous Man on
the Saturday Review)

But the Morley letter I prize most was written to the Friends
of Literature to be read at their annual dinner on May 9, 1942,
when I received that year's award for prose or belles-lettres or
something. In it he seemed to me to catch certain aspects of my
character and temperament that had been concealed from me by
less friendly critics, and as I am eager to preserve so complimentary
an opinion of my talents and inhibitions, I quote the letter in
its entirety:

"The stage lost a great actor" (to paraphrase a remark
which you all will recognize) "when Vincent Starrett decided to
become a specialist in crime." Also the book trade lost a great
bookseller. Mr. Starrett (misled by the dignity of his argentine
poll, I always feel like calling him "Monsignor Starrett") would
have been one of the few Christians to become a bookseller of
the real vintage type, and he would have done so with his own
subtle quietness. That is what makes the world of books, in its
excelsine terraces, the home of diplomacy and noble craft.
Thrilling things happen so softly. For instance, I open the latest
catalogue from Walter Hill of Chicago and see without fanfare
item number 213—a first edition (1863) of Alexander Smith's
Dreamthorp—(and Walter Hill is one of the few bibliophiles in
the world who knows how to spell *Dreamthorp* correctly, without
a final *e*) for only Six Dollars. It is worth, even in dollars,
ever so much more. That quietly beautiful book has attained
one of literature's highest honors, that many people imitate it
without even knowing what they are imitating. It has filtered
through the muddy vestures of several generations just as quietly, subtly, gracefully, bashfully, as our friend "Monsignor
Starrett" has filtered or seeped, like a fine volatile alcohol,
through the porous pottery of a crude Mogul civilization. There
has never been, since Genghis Khan I suppose, a life-and-times

271

more hostile to the delicate and diffident artist than the years from say 1912 to 1942. That anyone with Monsignor Starrett's acute and analytic and dismogrified intuitions is still alive and eager and nourished thrice daily is tribute to his platinum virility and his caoutchouc endurance.

Monsignor Starrett, deceiving you at this very moment, by his demure and dignified demeanor, is as mischievously ironic as Monsieur Blondin of whom he tells (*Bookman's Holiday*, page 104; $3 at any good bookstore) a delightful story. When Blondin was doing the tightrope walk over Niagara Falls, carrying a passenger on a chair on his shoulders, the passenger grew restless. "If you don't keep still," said Blondin, "I'll have to put you down."

Mr. Starrett is a good artist, and he has my love and homage, because like Blondin he knows that the apparently real world of roaring, engulfing physical phenomena is only an illusion; the genuine world of joy and perfection is on the tightrope the artist treads over vast and vulgar forces—sometimes carrying the customer on his back. If I weren't myself balancing on a very strict and narrow tightrope at the present time I'd be with you to say this viva voce. I know he understands. Give him my love. He has it already, but by sending it in proxy some of it will rub off on the rest of you too.

I have several shelves of Morley's books, of course, all suitably inscribed. I don't like them all equally well. My first favorite was *Where the Blue Begins* and I still find *Thunder on the Left* one of the exquisite fantasies of our time. As a sentimental booklover, I can still read *Parnassus on Wheels* and *The Haunted Bookshop* with pleasure, for in doing so I can recapture the spirit of those innocent days before literature turned tough. On the whole, I think I like certain of his essays best, such essays as one finds in *Ex Libris Carissimis*, *Hasta la Vista*, *Letters of Askance*, and *Streamlines*, more especially those concerning Sherlock Holmes and days and nights in Baker Street.

Somewhere along in the early thirties I came to know two

famous Americans: Alexander Woollcott and Dr. Logan Clendening. Clendening, who lived in Kansas City, came to Chicago frequently. On all his visits I put aside all work to join him for an afternoon of boisterous storytelling and bookly reminiscence. He was one of the best raconteurs I have known, with a special liking for Rabelaisian anecdote. He was a great physician, I am informed. He was the sort of physician who believes that all knowledge may be useful to a doctor. I remember his telling me one day that he would not himself care to be attended by a physician who had not read *Hamlet*. As he was an ardent Sherlockian, too, and an enthusiastic Pickwickian, it was not long before we agreed to make a tour of England together and visit the scenes associated with our several fictional favorites. Woollcott was to be a member of the party also, and together we were to compile a volume of Sherlockiana and Pickwickiana that would be forever the standard work for literary tourists of the future.

Unhappily, nothing came of the projected adventure—as a threesome, at any rate. Clendening and his wife ultimately made the English trip alone, confining it to Pickwickian scenes, and the doctor wrote a charming book about it, *A Handbook to Pickwick Papers* (1936), in which Woollcott and I appeared as his invisible companions playing Snodgrass and Tracy Tupman to his jovial Pickwick. I call the attention of bibliophiles to this excellent little book. When the trip it describes was made, however, I was in China and Woollcott in the midst of a Cream-of-Wheat program that could not be abandoned.

I met both Clendening and Woollcott, in the first instance, through a Sherlock Holmes hoax perpetrated by Harry Bedford-Jones. That incorrigible spoofer had invented a number of the singular adventures that Dr. Watson mentioned only in passing, and had sent them to Woollcott with an ingenius cock-and-bull story purporting to explain how they came to be in his custody. Woollcott, considerably excited, thereupon wrote to Clendening suggesting that he put the matter up to his friend Starrett, an authority on such matters—I had just published *The Private Life*

of Sherlock Holmes (1933)—and see what *he* thought. Throughout his tongue-in-cheek correspondence with Woollcott, Bedford-
Jones had posed as one H. E. Twinells of Palm Springs, California,
and Woollcott had no notion of his real identity. Ultimately Clendening acquired the typewritten manuscripts and passed them on
to me with all the correspondence that had gone before. Although
obviously pastiches, the tales were extremely clever. I knew at once,
however, that they were not by Conan Doyle and shortly, by a
series of deductions worthy of the Master himself, I was certain
they *were* by my old friend Bedford-Jones. His letters betrayed
him. I had many letters from B-J myself, all from Palm Springs
and all typed on the same paper by the same typewriter. The
signature, H. E. Twinells, was suspicious also. H. E. Twinells was
clearly the word *Hell* in a not too difficult cypher. By this and by
that, I reached my own conclusion about the stories and wrote B-J
a congratulatory letter, which he promptly acknowledged. "Woollcott had all the clues you had," he said, "and could have unmasked
me without going to all that trouble."

Out of this three-sided correspondence blossomed my acquaintance with Alex Woollcott and Logan Clendening. I met Woollcott
in the flesh, some time in 1934, when he came to Chicago to autograph copies of *While Rome Burns* at one of Mrs. Hahner's sign-
ing orgies. In his wire to her accepting the invitation, he had asked
her to be sure to have me on hand as I was the only man in Chicago
he really cared to meet—a typical piece of Woollcott arrogance intended to please me and insult the rest of Chicago in the same
breath. I met him again in New York the following winter when
he was my guest at the first state dinner of the Baker Street Irregulars, a diverting experience that will be recorded in its place,
and I last saw him in Chicago some time in March, 1935, when
Thornton Wilder and I attended one of his Town Crier broadcasts.

Thereafter our correspondence was sporadic but reassuring.
(One could never be certain of remaining long in Woollcott's
graces.) In the fall of 1937 I received a cryptic note reading: "It's
high time I sent you a present and I hereby enclose a holograph

letter which I have reason to believe you will value." The enclosure turned out to be an autograph letter of Lizzie Borden. And I had one letter from him on White House stationery—he wrote to all his friends during that experience—while he was a guest of President and Mrs. Roosevelt. My file of Woollcott letters is slim and relatively unimportant, but it is consistently friendly and interesting. A. Woollcott, as he usually signed himself, wrote some of the most malicious and insulting letters of our time, but for one reason or another I managed to escape his wrath.

My final story about Clendening is one I like to tell. Once more when financial disaster threatened, I was obliged to sell some of my books. I had brought together perhaps the finest collection of Sherlockiana in the world, which I prized above gold and rubies; but when the rub came it had to go. I was pretty sick about this catastrophe and, for a time, I thought I never would collect books again. Then a beautiful thing happened. My loss had been well publicized by the appearance of Scribner's fine catalogue of my collection, and one other collector at least knew how I was feeling about it. Inspired by my enthusiasm, Clendening had been making a Sherlock collection of his own; and one day I received a letter from him. It was a casual sort of letter. "My dear boy," it said in effect, "I find that I am not getting as much fun out of my Holmes collection as I had anticipated. I have too many other hobbies to do justice to this one. I hear that you have just parted with your own collection, and I think you ought to start another. Why not start with mine? It is small but goodish—it contains a number of the better pieces that you might have difficulty duplicating—and I am boxing it up this afternoon and getting it off to you tomorrow morning. You will really take a load off my mind if you will accept it."

It is unnecessary to underscore the generosity of the gift or of the doctor's fellow feeling. I suppose no finer thing ever was done for one collector by another. The box contained some twenty of the most desirable items in the field, including the desperately rare first printing of *A Study in Scarlet*. It was the nucleus of a new collection and, touched and overwhelmed by the gift, I began upon it at once.

XX

B̲UT IT IS TIME TO SPEAK of Sherlockian matters at some length. I first met Sherlock Holmes on a doorstep in Toronto; perhaps I was ten years old. The story in which I made his acquaintance was "The Adventure of the Speckled Band," which I was reading out of turn in a book discovered in my aunts' attic in Toronto. I was reading at random; but presently with pounding pulse I hurried back to the beginning of the electrifying chronicle to read what had gone before. That afternoon I found a leader I could follow and from that day to the present moment my allegiance has never wavered. *Did he really live?* I know now that he did and does, and that the old house still stands in Baker Street to prove it. It will continue to stand as long as the cold London fog rolls in with the winter and mischief is planned and thwarted and books are written and read.

That afternoon I began a career of Sherlock Holmes idolatry that I am happy to say still flourishes. But a great many years were to elapse before I began to write about my hero. With the rest of the Holmesian world I devoured each new volume of exploits as it came along. It was good, in 1902, to read *The Hound of the Baskervilles* and realize that Conan Doyle had yielded at last to persuasion and given us another story; but the *Hound* was only a "reminiscence" of Sherlock Holmes by the good Dr. Watson. Holmes, himself, as we all knew, was dead. His body lay among the jagged rocks at the foot of the Reichenbach Fall, with that of his arch-enemy Moriarty. Although our souls rebelled at the monstrous denouement, the facts appeared to be well established. The year was 1905 before we learned the glorious truth that Holmes was *not dead*(!), that he never *had* been dead, that Moriarty alone

276

had taken the plunge. Thousands of men and women still living remember the thrill of happiness that swept them when the miracle was made known. After many perils the indestructible detective was back in London, at the old address, and all was as it had been and ever shall be.

That, as I say, was in 1905. Ten years were to elapse before Watson published the next chapter of the saga and twelve years before I myself struck a typewriter key in celebration of my invincible leader. With the publication of *His Last Bow*, in 1917, it occurred to me that the time had come for me to express my life-long gratitude to Arthur Conan Doyle. I reviewed the book for *Reedy's Mirror* in an article titled "In Praise of Sherlock Holmes," my first contribution to the literature of the legend. I have never reprinted that essay precisely as it was written, although I knew when I was writing it that it was the scenario for a longer tribute that some day I would write. Incidentally, I was careful to send a copy of the relevant issue of the *Mirror* to Sir Arthur, who acknowledged it in the following letter:

DEAR MR. VINCENT STARRETT:

It was really very kind of you to write so heartily about Holmes. My own feelings toward him are rather mixed for I feel that he has obscured a good deal of my more serious work, but that no doubt will right itself in time—or if not, it does not really matter. I am so busy with my history of the war, and see so clearly how many changes, additions &c will be needed, that I feel I have mortgaged the rest of my life, but surely I could not have done so to a better cause. To drop a leaf of laurel on our dead boys would be the best top up of my life's work I could imagine.

Yours sincerely,
A. CONAN DOYLE

I met Sir Arthur only once, in the last year of his life, when he toured the United States for the last time, with his sons Adrian and Dennis. Our conversation was brief and in no way notable. A dozen reporters surrounded him, asking fatuous questions about the afterlife, a subject in which I was not interested. Sherlock Holmes was mentioned. Some fool asked him why he had not taken the detective into the field of spiritualism and he replied that he had thought of it. He rather shrugged Holmes off that day; but I was not too disappointed. At least I had seen and talked with Conan Doyle, had shaken his hand and murmured my gratitude for years of incomparable happiness.

My second contribution to the legend was a pastiche. At Christmas, 1920, Walter Hill published my Sherlockian burlesque, *The Unique Hamlet*, in a limited edition for collectors that is now difficult to find. It was, as asserted, a "hitherto unchronicled adventure of Mr. Sherlock Holmes," but it was also a genial satire on book collecting and Shakespearean commentators. Then, between 1930 and 1933, I contributed half a dozen essays to various American magazines, which became the foundation stones of *The Private Life of Sherlock Holmes*, published by Macmillan in 1933, and in a revised and enlarged edition by the University of Chicago Press in 1960. This work, my best known book, gave me for the first time an international audience and made me a decent reputation in England. British reviewers expressed polite surprise that the first biography of Holmes should have come from America. Since that time I have published many other "pieces" about Holmes and Watson, of which perhaps the best known is my introduction to the Limited Editions Club's definitive issue of the early volumes of the saga.

So much for bibliography. On the human side, I must report some aspects of the Sherlock Holmes movement in America and the fantastic career of the Baker Street Irregulars.

The Baker Street Irregulars (as an organization outside the pages of Dr. Watson) were born in the *Bowling Green* department of the *Saturday Review of Literature*, conducted by Christopher Morley, some time in 1933. Morley's column had become a meeting place for the Sherlockian wits of the day and ultimately, out of the interest in the Holmes legend fostered by Morley, sprang the

BSI. The name was Morley's and no happier one could have been imagined; it captured the imagination of Holmesians around the world. The test for membership became (in 1934) a crossword puzzle attributed to Inspector Tobias Gregson of Scotland Yard but in fact composed by Frank V. Morley, Christopher's publisher-brother. Charter membership was thus limited at first to some twenty-five or thirty fanatics in New York and a similar number scattered here and there across the nation.

The purpose of the society was the study of the Sacred Writings, i.e., the sixty tales recorded by John H. Watson, M. D., for it was then one of the unwritten rules of the order that Conan Doyle's name was not to be uttered. His ruthless erasure of Holmes in the last story of the original group of adventures—before the Ressurrection—had not met with our approval and we consigned him to oblivion. Like other learned and scientific societies, the members exchanged notes of research and contributed "papers" to the general knowledge on such problems, for example, as that of the Brothers Moriarty who, it will be recalled, were all named James. This innocent pastime continued throughout 1933 and much of 1934 before the Irregulars became a fact outside the pages of the *Saturday Review*. Then the first formal meeting of the group, as a public menace, was held at Cella's restaurant in New York City on the evening of June 5, 1934, at which time, a high autumnal wind being out of season, every effort was made to create Watson's favorite alternative, an atmosphere of thick yellow fog. Simultaneously the first dinner of the Sherlock Holmes Society of London was going forward in Canuto's restaurant in Baker Street and suitable greetings were exchanged between the two groups. Some months later the honorable secretary of the English society, A. G. Macdonell, the Scottish novelist, visited New York and was a guest of honor with William Gillette, the actor, at the second meeting of the BSI on December 7, a happy occasion of both wind and fog.

I had been unable to attend the June meeting at which the society was tentatively organized, but I journeyed to New York early in December for the first state dinner. In anticipation of a historic event, I wrote to William Gillette inviting him to be my guest. Shortly afterward I had a note from Alexander Woollcott quizzing me about the affair; so I invited Woollcott also to be my guest. I suggested to him that if a hansom cab could be found in New York it would be fun to charter it for the occasion. This was a notion after his own heart, and more quickly than I had thought possible he wired me that he had rounded up the last two hansoms in the world; they would be at our disposal on the evening of the dinner, he said.

When in due time I reported at Wit's End, Woollcott's apartment in East 52nd Street, and found a noisy party in full swing, I supposed he had forgotten the Sherlockian event; but nothing could have been farther from the truth. The cocktail party went on to the last possible moment; then Woollcott prepared to depart, leaving his guests in possession. "The cabs are downstairs, Starrett," he said abruptly. "Come in here a minute."

He dragged me into a bedroom and rapidly outfitted me with a deerstalker cap and a huge reading glass of the sort used by Sherlock Holmes in pictures by illustrators who have no idea what sort of glass Sherlock Holmes used. Thus attired we descended to the street.

The night was fearfully cold, there was a hint of fog in the air, and I was bursting with Woollcott's sidecars; but, nightmarishly, at the curb there really did wait two hansoms, the first of which immediately drove away empty. "Always take the *second* cab," quoted Woollcott, stepping into it, "the first may be dangerous." And to the second driver, urgently, "Follow that cab!"

Thus we set forth. In spite of the weather it was a congested evening in New York; as the two cabs clattered down Fifth Avenue it seemed to me that half the city was abroad to see us pass. Wondering policemen looked hard at the procession but grinned and allowed us to proceed. Here and there we snarled up traffic briefly; but ultimately, on the tick of the clock—Woollcott had been making theater curtains that way for years—we debouched on the pavement at Cella's, pushed through a knot of spectators attracted by our apparel, and climbed a narrow stairway to an upper room where another party was in progress. Except that there were no women present, it looked to me very much like the party we had just left. A roar went up as we entered in costume, and then. . . .

Several accounts of this remarkable dinner have been left to the world and all of them are slightly cockeyed. I did not, as Henry Morton Robinson asserts, enter on all fours disguised as the Hound of the Baskervilles; and I did not at any time, as Woollcott records, read a paper pretending to prove that Sherlock Holmes was a Cambridge man. I reached the dining room precisely at six-thirty, thanks to Woollcott's uncanny timing, was greeted by Elmer Davis with a highball in each hand, and seated myself at the table about seven-thirty, where I snoozed gently between Morley and Frederic Dorr Steele—slightly supported by Steele—until perhaps nine. At this time there was a commotion in the corridor and I came out of my coma with what is described by novelists as a start. The door was flung swiftly open and in the aperture stood Sherlock Holmes himself. . . .

It was Gillette, of course, and when the uproar for him had died away the dinner went forward as planned. My autographed menu reveals that among those also present were Harold Bell, Basil Davenport, Earle Walbridge, Robert Keith Leavitt, W. S. Hall, Frank Henry, Malcolm Johnson, Allen Price, Lawrence Dodge, and bluff old Dr. Gray Chandler Briggs, who had come all the way from St. Louis to receive the homage due him as the first man to identify the rooms in Baker Street. It should be said that ultimately "papers" were read by several of the members and these were later mailed to the membership in mimeograph so that all might know what had been said at this, our eventful first dinner.

In the following summer it was my privilege to work with William Gillette on a definitive edition of his great melodrama, *Sherlock Holmes*, a delightful experience. And what trouble I gave him! He was kindness itself when I urged him to tone down the final scene in which Holmes unbelievably clasps an altar-bound young woman in his arms. In 1899 I had accepted that scene with enthusiasm, but for some thirty years thereafter had realized its incongruity. I didn't quite know what I wanted the author to do about it, but it seemed to me that there should be some way of suggesting that it was just *theater*. He recast his final lines a number of times in deference to my fastidious criticism, but finally we left them pretty much as they were. As it appears in my Doubleday edition of 1935, the play is a sort of composite of three or four manuscript versions; certain early lines are restored and certain late revisions are eliminated. I should have liked to make it a variorum edition but, as the publishers pointed out, the idea was to appeal more to readers than to specialists.

It was inevitable, of course, that BSI scion societies would spring to life in other cities and this development was not long delayed. Boston was first with "The Speckled Band," to be followed quickly by tight little fellowships in Chicago, San Francisco, Baltimore, Detroit, Indianapolis, and other cities, each aptly named after story titles in the saga. There are now fifty or more of these offspring in the field, including half a dozen university chapters. And the university chapters are not, as you might suppose, made up of enthusiastic students; they are made up of enthusiastic faculty members. Our Chicago chapter was founded in January, 1943, with four charter members: Charles Collins, columnist of the Chicago *Tribune*; Stanley Pargellis, librarian of Newberry Library; Horace J. Bridges, leader of the Chicago Ethical Culture Society; and the author of these pages. Later we were joined by such men as Jay Finley Christ, Otto Eisenschiml, Dr. Ernest Zeisler, Robert J. Bayer, Leonarde Keeler, Dr. Eugene F. Carey, William Braid White, Prof. Orlando Park, Clifton R. Andrew, Arthur Lovell, David Borowitz, and Walter Simmons, co-founder of the Tokyo chapter of the BSI.

The BSI is now (1965) a formidable cult and, if the membership continues to increase in the next twenty years as it has in the last twenty, we'll soon have enough weight to swing a presidential

282

election. Our "constitution and buy-laws," as drawn up by Elmer Davis, is a unique document that readers may care to see in full. Here it is:

CONSTITUTION

ARTICLE I

The name of this society shall be the Baker Street Irregulars.

ARTICLE II

Its purpose shall be the study of the Sacred Writings.

ARTICLE III

All persons shall be eligible for membership who pass an examination in the Sacred Writings set by officers of the society, and who are considered otherwise suitable.

ARTICLE IV

The officers shall be: a Gasogene, a Tantalus, and a Commissionaire.

The duties of the Gasogene shall be those commonly performed by a President.

The duties of the Tantalus shall be those commonly performed by a Secretary.

The duties of the Commissionaire shall be to telephone down for ice, White Rock, and whatever else may be required and available; to conduct all negotiations with waiters; and to assess the members pro rata for the cost of same.

BUY-LAWS

1. An annual meeting shall be held on January 6, at which the canonical toasts shall be drunk; after which the members shall drink at will.

2. The current round shall be bought by any member who fails to identify, by title of story and context, any quotation from the Sacred Writings submitted by any other member.

Qualification A. If two or more members fail so to identify, a round shall be bought by each of those so failing.

Qualification B. If the submitter of the quotation, upon challenge, fails to identify it correctly, he shall buy the round.

3. Special meetings may be called at any time or any place by any one of three members, two of whom shall constitute a quorum.

Qualification A. If said two people are of opposite sexes, they shall use care in selecting the place of meeting, to avoid misinterpretation (or interpretation either, for that matter).

4. All other business shall be left for the monthly meeting.

5. There shall be no monthly meeting.

I last saw Baker Street in the summer of 1937 when I stopped off in England after nearly two years in the Orient. Harold Bell, the Holmes specialist, happened to be in London and we walked the length of the old street and back again together, arguing wrathfully about the precise location of No. 221B. As always we failed to agree, but it was a stimulating experience to explore the fabled street and its byways in the company of an informed Sherlockian.

XXI

IGNORING FLASHBACKS and previews, the chronological development of this narrative has now reached the year 1935, an eventful year for me. In September of that year, with money in my pocket and money in the bank, thanks to *The Great Hotel Murder*, it was easy to decide that I needed a vacation. For ten years I had been taking plots out of my head and I was tired. At this juncture opportunity was offered me to join a small party on a "round the world" cruise, and in an adventurous moment I signed up. My intention was to get away from Chicago for about three months—the cruise was a ninety-day affair—but as it happened I was away for more than two years.

As I looked over the passenger list of the Dollar Line's *President Coolidge*, the most interesting person aboard seemed to be the Princess Der Ling, the Manchu princess who had married an American diplomat and written a number of popular books on old China. She looked jolly and attractive and, when presently I came to know her, I found her as pleasing a conversationalist as she was easy to look at. We had, indeed, many delightful little gossips on a variety of subjects before I found her lacking in a proper appreciation of literature. This disillusionment came about as we approached Honolulu, when, standing beside me at the rail, she indicated the first point of interest.

"That great hill," she said, "is called the Punch Bowl."

"The home of Charlie Chan," I said quickly.

"Charlie Chan?" she echoed.

"The great Chinese detective," I said, looking at her hopefully; but it was obvious that she had never heard of Charlie Chan. She was a gracious lady, however, and I read of her death in an auto accident a few years later with genuine regret.

Approximately a week after this disappointing exchange, I was writing my name in the registry book of the Imperial Hotel in Tokyo, where one of the most surprising episodes of my life immediately occurred.

When I had signed up in a bold hand—a bit defiantly, as one does in a strange country—the dapper Japanese room clerk looked hard at my signature and then hard at me. He spoke rapidly in his own tongue to someone who stood beside him, and looked at me again.

"But you are not Mr. Vincent Starrett," he said in English.

"Indeed I am," I retorted, and as if to clinch the fact I added, "I'm from Chicago."

"I beg your pardon," he insisted with a polite hiss, "but I know Mr. Vincent Starrett very well. He stops here frequently. He is an American banker in Osaka."

It was clear that one of us was mad. I had read that Japan was a topsy-turvy sort of land and had been prepared for surprises, but not for anything like this.

"I'm sorry," I protested feebly, "but I really am Mr. Vincent Starrett. Perhaps you are thinking of somebody with a similar name."

"I assure you—," he began in his impeccable English, and I supposed he was going to repeat his asseveration; but happily an interruption occurred. A tallish young man in American garb had been standing near the desk; it had seemed to me that he was

285

listening to our conversation with amused interest. Now he came forward and touched my arm. "Are you Vincent Starrett, the writer?" he asked; and I knew that at least I had found another American. "I'm John Allison of our consular service. I know your books very well. Let me straighten this out for you."

He released a flood of Japanese at the troubled room clerk and the clerk's face brightened. "Very amusing," he said, and laughed nervously, as a Japanese always laughs when he is embarrassed. "There are two Mr. Vincent Starretts, it would appear. Please excuse my error."

Apparently it was true; there really *was* another Vincent Starrett in this world. I was hearing of him for the first time in the lobby of a hotel in Tokyo. My double, if that is the word, was manager of the Osaka Branch of the National City Bank of New York. He was well known in Japan, Allison said, and predicted that there would be further confusion. He was not mistaken.

On the whole, I liked Tokyo enormously. Indeed, I liked Japan enormously. Although Pearl Harbor was only six years in the future, and I knew that our relations with the Japanese were strained, I found the people excessively friendly and eager to please. My flagrant political naïvete stood me in good stead no doubt; I knew little of international politics and cared less. For the most part I was accepted as the friendly visitor I professed to be, and indeed was. Tokyo, just before the war, was a fascinating place. Its color and congestion delighted me, for I like big cities, and this one—I quickly realized—was just another Chicago in masquerade.

My room was searched daily, I could see, but so delicately that I could not have sworn it was not just as I left it. And until I had somehow proved myself a man of good will, queer characters seemed to blunder into my quarters more often than was plausible, disguised as employees of the hostelry. I really didn't care. It was rather fun, indeed, after years of mystery-story writing, to imagine myself involved in a tale more exciting than any of my own. My deliverance from these little attentions came about in entertaining fashion after a week or two in the city.

One morning a big Japanese in American garments called on me and introduced himself as the editor of the *Japan Advertiser*. He wished to interview me, he said. A little puzzled but pleased by the attention, I agreed, and immediately the interview was under way. The editor had brought with him one of his reporters, a youth who spoke no English but who obviously knew all about our American methods. As he sat before me in his American clothes, with his socks rolled down around his ankles and an unlighted cigarette dangling negligently from his lower lip, it was clear that he had witnessed our great screen drama, *The Front Page*, not once but many times. His appearance would have delighted Ben Hecht and Charles MacArthur for he was their Hildy Johnson to the life, save for the minor discrepancy that he was a Japanese. His manner was in no wise deferential. There was a gleam of hostility in his eye. He wished me to understand that he knew all the ropes. He kept his hat on, crossed his knees aggressively, slouched down in his chair, and barked questions at me in Japanese that were suavely translated by his admiring superior. Occasionally the editor himself put a question and repeated my reply to his subordinate. Between them, they interviewed me with a thoroughness that left me dizzy. When it was all over, the Japanese Hildy gave me a patronizing nod and slouched out, leaving his employer to thank me suitably.

I told them everything they wanted to know. Somebody had informed them that I was a well known writer of detective stories, and for the most part the interview followed conventional lines. How had I come to be a writer of detective stories, and what was I doing in Japan? I supposed the last half of the question to be all that interested them; but I explained simply that I had been a police reporter in Chicago, wrote crime fiction for a living, and was visiting Japan on a vacation trip only. They got my age and other vital statistics, the names of a number of my books, and finally my opinion of Japan and the Japanese. As I had not the foggiest notion what use might be made of my revelations, I was guarded in my replies about things Japanese. I was, indeed, flatteringly eulogistic, which was just as well, as it turned out. They asked me about crime in Chicago, concerning which they had read the usual lurid accounts, and I told them I never had met Al Capone personally, or even seen him; and then I added graciously that I doubted whether any such Napoleon of crime could exist in Japan.

All of it got into the *Japan Advertiser* next day, wonderfully garbled, with a photograph of me taken on the spot that certainly did me less than justice. It was, if anything, a more hideous travesty of my spiritual values than my passport photo. The day after the interview appeared, my visit inspired a flattering editorial in the paper. John Allison translated both items for me and I quote them in full. The interview as it appeared in *Ex Tokio Hochi Shimbum* of October 9, 1935, was captioned "Starrett, the Noted American Detective Story Writer Arrives in Japan," and read as follows:

> Vincent Starrett (50 years), the famous American detective story writer, noted for his "Private Life of Sherlock Holmes," arrived in Japan and is now lodging at the Imperial Hotel. This six-foot tall, gray-haired, red-faced writer, who in his youth was a policeman, stated as follows:
>
> "Feeling that as a writer I should once visit Japan, I have finally come to this country. I have requested my friends to give me letters of introduction for visiting and studying the police system, courts, etc. But, inasmuch as the police system of Japan is one of the best in the world, no such gangster as Al Capone is likely to be born here. As a criminal who can commit twenty crimes in America will in Japan be caught before he has done only two, I am not placing much hope in getting material for my stories from the crimes committed in Japan. I am rather interested in the customs and traditions, the studies of Basho and the prints of Hiroshige, Hokusai, etc. Whether I will use Japan as the setting for my next story depends on the materials I can gather here."

288

Editorially, the paper commented:

The recently arrived noted American detective story writer, Mr. Starrett, after giving a word of tribute to the police system of Japan, remarked that inasmuch as a criminal who can commit twenty crimes in America will in Japan be caught before he has done only about two, there is little that he can expect from the crimes in Japan for use as material for his stories. He stated rather that he is more interested in the customs and traditions and the arts and literature of this country. That he can say this much when he has just arrived in Japan indicates that he has more than fully studied Japan before coming here.

My remark about Capone must have made a hit with the editor for, tucked away on another page of the paper, possibly in a gossip column, was a brief note captioned "The Best Police System in the World," reading thus: "A certain American detective story writer guarantees that Japan has the best police system in the world and that it would be hardly possible for any notorious gangster like Capone to get a foothold in Japan."

I mention all this not only because it was pleasing to me at the time but because those newspaper excerpts in Japanese (which I carried in my pocket) proved enormously useful to me all across Japan. Their immediate effect was useful, too, as I have suggested, for thereafter there appeared to be less curiosity about my movements. After my flattering words about the country and its inhabitants, the petty espionage at the hotel ceased; at any rate, I found no more furtive-looking young men in my room searching for clues to my sinister errand in Japan.

Perhaps my greatest piece of luck in Tokyo was meeting Baron Ichigo and his English wife, an attractive redhead. One of the members of our party carried a letter of introduction to this friendly Japanese, who was, I believe, a remote connection of the royal family. We hit it off together very well. When one is a collector in a strange land, ignorant even of the language, it is useful to know a seasoned *native* collector who speaks one's own tongue and is a respected figure in the curio shops. For, needless to say, my habit of acquisition accompanied me to Japan. In a fortnight my room was littered with captivating little golliwogs and gargoyles that had taken my fancy.

But for a detailed account of my collecting in Japan, I must refer readers to my *Bookman's Holiday*, in which the whole sad, glad, foolish story is set forth in an essay called "In the Wiles of Japan."

I will tell one story, however. Adventuring in a Tokyo bookshop one day with John Allison, I acquired a secondhand copy of one of my own detective novels, which somebody had read on a Pacific crossing and then thrown away. It was Allison who called it to my attention. There was a paper band around its middle that fascinated me. The hieroglyphic symbols gave the familiar book an almost sinister appearance. "What does it say?" I asked. "They've turned your title into Japanese," said Allison. "It says here that your story is about the insides of a dead man."

I should have said earlier that Allison is that same John Moore Allison who later came to international prominence when he was slapped by a Japanese soldier in China in the early days of the invasion, and who later became our ambassador to Japan. It is interesting to recall that his secret ambition was to be an antiquarian bookseller when all the wars were ended.

It will surprise nobody to read that my first visit in Shanghai was to the famous bookshop of Messrs. Kelly & Walsh—an odd pair of names to find over a doorway in the Orient, but one finds many odd things in the Orient. Although the shop was only a short distance from my hotel, I went by rickshaw; and thereafter for more than a year, except for train journeys between cities, I went everywhere by rickshaw. It is the most leisurely and delightful mode of transportation now remaining on earth, after one has overcome the psychological disturbance of seeing men instead of horses between the shafts.

Perhaps my first reason for visiting China was to meet and interview Lin Yutang. I had been reading his book, *My Country and My People*, all across Japan after purchasing it in Tokyo. Dr. Lin was editing a magazine in Shanghai; there was no difficulty about meeting him. His reception room might have been an ante-room in almost any magazine office in the world. There was a table with books and magazines and newspapers on sticks, a small settee, an adequate number of chairs. Nothing else until the tea came in; but from the editorial sanctum beyond sounded the whacking noise of a typewriter, and now and then young men drifted past in robes of black or blue or brown, wearing the dark-rimmed spectacles that seem to mark the young intellectual the world over.

I don't know what I had expected to find; not exactly Fu Manchu in satin vestments and with daggers in his sleeves, nor yet an atmosphere of opium and dancing girls. Something more serene and Confucian was in my mind; but also something flaming with Oriental color. As it was, I might have been visiting Mr. Aldous Huxley, apprehended after breakfast in his favorite dressing gown.

We faced each other across a small table in the reception room, Dr. Lin and I. I saw a slim young-looking man of middle height with brown hair and eyes. His brown Chinese robe fell to his ankles; one caught a glimpse of American trousers. He was smiling behind shell-rimmed spectacles.

Early in our interview he struck a note that coincided pleasantly with my own philosophy. "I do most of my work in bed," said Lin Yutang. "That is how I manage to get so much done."

It sounded Chinese and paradoxical but, to a lazy man, at-tractive. I was a trifle short of sleep myself, having risen at the unholy hour of nine to keep my appointment with Dr. Lin at eleven. It seemed a little silly that we should be sitting there drink-ing tea at an hour when both of us perhaps would rather have been in bed.

"You are in good company," I said. "Mark Twain, Stevenson, Anatole France . . ."

"Mae West," he chuckled. "Wasn't she confessing it in print recently? But you shouldn't put me in such exalted company. What I meant was . . ."

It developed that he was not thinking of work in terms of its physical ardors. He meant only that, curled comfortably on his pallet, a writing man may plan the program of the busy day that lies before him. Reaching his desk then, at say eleven o'clock, he is primed and ready for the period of brisk dictation necessary to translate his matutinal cerebration into copy for the printer. I thought of Gilbert Chesterton, who would have liked to work in bed with a colored pencil long enough to draw pictures on the ceiling, and repeated the *mot* to Dr. Lin.

"Chesterton was right," he agreed. "I could use that kind of pencil, too. I am very fond of Chesterton. It takes a Chinese really to understand him."

He gave me further details of his daily activities. "I am a 100-per-cent American hustler," he said severely. "Believe me, I am at this moment editing or helping to edit no less than five magazines."

I was shocked. There was something disconcerting in the sound of those familiar words on the lips of this amiable Chinese litterateur. Then he smiled again and I perceived that my leg was being pulled. There was no doubt about the five magazines, however.

Two local volumes, so to call them, had come out of my overcoat pocket and lay between us on the table. They were Dr. Lin's collected essays gathered from files of the *China Critic*. Lin Yutang picked them up and laid them down again.

"There you have the real Lin Yutang," he said. "I'm really just a silly, sentimental fellow. In these books you have my secret everyday thoughts about toothbrushes, gardens, bedbugs, tobacco! I find it difficult to be serious." He puffed happily at his pipe.

I said that *My Country and My People* could hardly be described as a frivolous book, and he agreed. It had been written in English for English readers, he said, but some day perhaps there would be an edition in Chinese.

"It would be pretty fine to be the Voltaire of China," I said. "Your satire might turn the trick. It's pretty savage sometimes."

He smiled and puffed. "I satirize what I love most," said Lin

292

Yutang; but his eyes gleamed behind the shell-rimmed spectacles. Then he laughed again. "But suppose I should then be required to translate the Chinese version back into English. Good Lord!"

"Three best-sellers instead of one," I told him. "Why not? It is certainly going to be popular in America, even if Woollcott fails to mention it on the air; but one word of praise from him and it will sell one hundred thousand copies over night."

"Holy smoke!" ejaculated the world's most celebrated Chinese author. "I must certainly bribe him to say that word."

I learned that he was happily married, but did not understand women. The chapter about them in his book was its weakest section, he thought. I learned that he greatly admired Stephen Leacock. I learned that he was economically independent by reason of a textbook that had been popular in China for a number of years. I told him that it was his duty to write the Great Chinese Novel.

"I shall bear that in mind," he smiled; and I went out into the rush of races and rickshaws that is Shanghai, greatly pleased with my morning's adventure.

It was exciting to see the walls of Peking in the distance. I looked forward to a fortnight of sightseeing and collecting in the ancient city before returning to Shanghai for the next Europe-bound liner, and would have laughed if anybody had told me I would settle down in old Cambuluc and become a name in the telephone directory.

As it happened, the next year and a half of my life was to center in Peking. Living at first in hotel rooms, then in pensions, I finally rented a house and compound of my own so close to the Forbidden City that I could see its fabulous red roofs from my bedroom window.

Early in my Peking days Frank Smothers, then far eastern correspondent of the Chicago *Daily News*, came to see me, and through him I met most of the other correspondents and writers then living in the capital. It was at a luncheon given for me by

Smothers that I met Owen Lattimore and Edgar Snow and the English correspondents Frank Oliver, Malcolm MacDonald, and H. J. Timperly, all of whom thereafter helped to make my stay a pleasant one. I made a number of trips with them to Chinese temples and other picturesque shrines that gave me a background for mystery stories I was even then planning to write. But perhaps the most valuable friend I made in Peking was Miss Yi Ying, a student at the local university, to whom I had been given a letter of introduction by Lin Yutang. She introduced me to other scholars, guided me on journeys into obscure corners of the old city, translated for me old Chinese mystery stories never before translated, and was companion and counsellor beyond compare for many months.

As for Peking itself, that great centuries-old capital of the East, I can describe it in a sentence: it was a medieval city even to the great walls that still surrounded it. When I had lived within those walls for many months, I knew what Paris looked like, sounded like, and smelled like, in the days of Villon. That is an impression, of course; the rooftops were not the rooftops of Paris, the streets and alleys were more primitive than those trodden by the watch in Villon's day, the people were another race; but the historical atmosphere was much the same, I think—the prodigious contrasts and paradoxes, the splendor and the squalor, the university students and the scabrous beggars jostling in the streets, all beneath one roof as it were, somehow gave me a lively picture of that other time which had so fascinated me in books.

But all the time I knew I would rather be at home quietly reading about China in old books, say the travels of Marco Polo or (for that matter) Livingston Lowes. Palaces, temples, pagodas, sacred mountains, and all the rest of the phantasmagoria left me cold, and I got away from them as quickly as possible. There was more to it than simple boredom; I actively resented it all. As I stood in old courtyards and looked at shabby, fantastic temples centuries old, the weight of time pressed down on me so like a tangible thing that I wanted to run from it.

In my rickshaw jaunts about the city I used to meet strangers whom I can only call *Doppelgangers*. It is curious how the faces of acquaintances repeat themselves in foreign lands. Uncanny, too, for what could be more disconcerting than to encounter an old friend jogging past dressed like a mandarin or selling chestnuts in coolie cloth? No sooner had I reached the Orient than this began to happen. Friends and associates I thought I had left behind in America, sometimes fellows I hadn't seen in years, popped up in Yokohama, Tokyo, Shanghai, and Peking, looking very much as I had seen them last, yet subtly altered by the native costumes they were wearing. It was as if one met them coming from a masquerade. In Yokohama it was an old school friend who had been dead for years. He was running a cigarette kiosk near the docks and I knew better than to speak to him. In Tokyo it was a genial barber who used to shave me in Chicago. And in Peking there were so many that my blood ran cold.

Among the friends I met in Chinese garb (and with Chinese faces) were some pretty distinguished fellows—Burton Rascoe, Ernest Byfield, Christopher Morley, Scott Cunningham, Jay Latimer, Phil Hampson, Logan Clendening, Harry Hansen. I saw Alex Woollcott many times: once he was chirping seductively at a bird he was carrying through the streets in a bamboo cage. Once my dead mother turned out of a side street and gave me a turn that almost bowled me over. Once I met Bob Casey driving a small donkey attached to a two-wheeled cart: he was selling vegetables. After a time it became an amusing game to look for absent friends and sometimes to hail them genially, and no harm came of it for the Chinese were a friendly people, always ready to hail one in return.

But one day I really did get a shock. Rolling down one of the main thoroughfares of Peking in my rickshaw, I came suddenly abreast of another rickshaw rider headed in the opposite direction. He was bundled up in a fur coat and wore a fur hat, rather like a turban, at a rakish angle. He looked exactly like J. P. McEvoy—and for a moment we looked hard at each other. Then I said,

"Hello, Mac," and he stopped his boy and said, "Why, hullo, Vince! What are *you* doing in Peking?"

Samuel Butler, the *Erewhon* man, once wrote an essay called "Ramblings in Cheapside," in which he commented on the great figures of history whom he encountered in disguise in the streets of London—Julius Caesar, Frederick the Great, and others—and worked up an amusing theory of survival or reincarnation or something; but the friends I met in China who were not really there were nearly all *living* friends. I must suppose that, save in the instance of Joe McEvoy, they were all going about their business back home at the moment I was meeting them in Peking.

I have no explanation for any of this; but something interesting, I am sure, must lie behind these extraordinary resemblances, which are not of course confined to members of the human race. Constantly I meet friendly animals who give me a passing glance or smile, or a lift of the eyebrow, that reminds me of friends in human guise. They may not be the friends of whom they remind me, but obviously they are not what they seem to be either.

One of the by-products of my Chinese experience, published after my return to America, was a slender volume in bright firecracker red covers lettered with Chinese characters in gold. I called it *Oriental Encounters: Two Essays in Bad Taste*, and dedicated it to the thirty-one American editors who had rejected one or both of the pieces for their sacrosanct pages. The shorter piece, "New Movements in Old China," is perhaps the only authoritative account in print of China's night soil collectors. The longer piece, "The Passing of the Eunuch," is, as you might suppose, about eunuchs.

My interest in eunuchs was neither Freudian, I hope, nor facetious; it was for the most part entirely literary. Early in my reading career I had made their acquaintance in my expurgated *Arabian Nights*, but at that time I was youthfully ignorant of their place in the scheme of things oriental. They seemed, however, to be sinister rascals who would bear watching. Even when I learned the sorry truth about them, the notion persisted that they were almost mythological monsters of the days of legend. They were still figures in the fantastic tapestry of oriental fiction when I went out to China. That is, until one day I suddenly met one of the creatures on a street corner in Peking. It was like meeting old Haroun al Raschid himself.

"Oh yes," said my guide, who was Ida Pruitt that day, "a few of them survive. You must remember that the empire did not fall until 1912, and this is still a medieval country. Funny old boy, isn't he? He's probably in from the hills for the day to visit friends. They have a temple of their own not far from the Pa Pao Shan golf course. It's a sort of refuge for old eunuchs."

Suddenly the whole subject became as fascinating as a detective story. I hurried to the libraries and bookshops and ultimately to the hills, and there I found the eunuchs, perhaps the strangest group of survivors in the modern world.

All this time I had been collecting Chinese detective stories, so to call them. This research had become the overwhelming passion of my Chinese adventure. It had been a passing mention of the mystery stories of China by Lin Yutang that first inspired me, but it was Yi Ying who assisted most notably in the search for the rare books I needed. Happily, she was herself an ardent if surreptitious reader of this subterranean literature—the equivalent of our American dime novel—and already was well up in the subject. I had also the help of Professor Chen Shu-yi of the local university, who accompanied me to the native bookshops and made known my wants. Sometimes we went away empty-handed and then immediately the "grapevine" began to work. The word went round that a mad American was in town, ready to pay fantastic sums for old books, perhaps as much as eight dollars for those he really wanted. The little dealers consulted together and pooled their interests. And ultimately the books I needed most came out of their concealment and passed into my hands. The result of these activities was "Some Chinese Detective Stories," now in my *Bookman's*

297

Holiday, the first comprehensive discussion of China's numerous legendary detectives. There you may meet old Pao Kung (pronounced Bow-Goong), the Sherlock Holmes of China, who flourished in the ninth century; Di Jen-djieh (pronounced Dee-Ren-Jee), the mighty minister of state in the reign of the Empress Wu T'se T'ien, and other famous justice-doers of old China.

My own last detective novel, *The Laughing Buddha* (later *Murder in Peking*), was written in Peking during 1936. The inspiration was a weekend visit to Helen Burton's rented Chinese temple in the hills, which is faithfully described in the early chapters of the book. It is a *roman à clef* with a vengeance. Friends and acquaintances made up the *dramatis personae* and the fictional murderer was myself. The young woman who was murdered was, of course, an invention.

One further note about Helen Burton. She was an American who made a phenomenal success in Peking. Her fine curio shop, "The Camel Bell," was better than a museum. Her parties, whether at her exotic Chinese temple or in her exotic Chinese town house, were famous. She was, to put it simply, one of the most generous and charming women in the world. No visitor to Peking failed to visit her astounding shop and none ever escaped without writing in her guest book. I have forgotten what Bernard Shaw wrote in that remarkable album, but I remember her story of what passed between them. After looking over her brilliant display of gems, many of considerable value, the Irish playwright said, "How dare you expose them in this way? You don't know but what I may slip half a dozen of them into my pockets. What would you do if I did?"

"We would be proud to say that Bernard Shaw had stolen some of our jades," answered Miss Burton promptly.

"And there'd be lots of people who'd believe it," said Bernard Shaw quickly.

Most of my time in China was spent in Peking, a sufficiently exciting place, participating in the social activities of the foreign colony, giving and attending parties for visiting celebrities (Lin Yutang, Warner Oland, Vicki Baum, Anna May Wong), dis-

298

cussing Chinese folklore with L. C. Arlington and Dr. Hu Shih, casing the bookshops with Yi Ying, visiting the motion picture theaters, and watching the slow advance of Japanese invasion. At tea, one day, I met Pierre Teilhard de Chardin, the famous Jesuit paleontologist, who later sent me two of his little books, privately printed in China.

One of the first things I had done in Peking was to come down with dysentery—"Poor Master," said my No. 1 Boy, to one of my feminine visitors, "all night water closet!"—and later there had been other embarrassments, including sore throat, toothache, influenza, and I think falling of the womb. One of the last things I did in Peking was to come down with some nameless misery and go to a hospital for a fortnight, where I was wormed like a dog and ordered to leave the country. My stay in China was at an end. In any case, my cruise ticket was about to expire. Overhead—flying daily over my Chinese residence, now surmounted by an American flag—were Jap planes in war formation; daily the streets of the Legation Quarter resounded to the marching feet of the soldiers of Japan, the first step in the game of intimidation that preceded the invasion.

The month was March, the year, 1937. I had no wish to be caught by the war, to be killed or interned, or even to be trapped in a last-minute rush of fugitives for the port. I looked up my Dollar Line folder for sailing dates and got the hell out of China.

XXII

ALTHOUGH I SPENT six weeks in Italy, and would gladly have spent six years, I saw Mussolini only twice. Once he appeared at a horse show that I attended and once I was one of a Roman mob that stood under his balcony and listened to an impassioned harangue. With greater satisfaction I remember the white cat that used to appear on a tiled roof, opposite my hotel balcony, and respond amiably to my greetings before settling down to her morning ablutions. She kept me company on sunny mornings while I pounded out my extravagant fictions on a rented typewriter. And I remember the little statuette of Mark Twain owned by my friend Federico Gubinelli of the Café Grecco. It was by Luigi Amici, an Italian sculptor who had been his father's friend and patron, and it pleases me to think that in it I may have discovered an unknown portrait of our greatest humorist.

As I heard the tale from Signor Gubinelli, Amici in his old age lived with the elder Gubinelli and left his friend the contents of his studio, among them the statuette and a medallion portrait of Mark, "both taken from life." Clemens frequented the café "about the year 1870," according to Gubinelli, and made the acquaintance of Amici at that time. I can not reconcile this assertion with any known visit of the humorist to Italy at the time stated; but if the actual year was 1867, the portraits could have been taken during the visit celebrated in *Innocents Abroad* and noted in Daniel Morley McKeithan (ed.), *Traveling with the Innocents Abroad: Mark Twain's Original Reports from Europe and the Holy Land* (Norman, 1958). I bequeath the problem to the specialists.

Ultimately, of course, I visited the Protestant Cemetery to doff my hat at the graves of Keats and Shelley (which were satisfactorily melancholy on a day of rain) and found there an older friend than either. Idling among the other tombstones, I was about to turn away and seek more cheerful surroundings when a name leaped out at me—and suddenly, all unprepared for the revelation, I was looking at the last resting place of Robert Michael Ballantyne, the old master who had written *The Coral Island* and other favorite stories of my boyhood. I stood beside his grave for a long time watching the shadows fall over the Pyramid of Cestus . . .

In a hurry to reach England now, not even the book stalls of Paris could hold me long; within a fortnight I was in London, and the most satisfying adventure of my long life of literary curiosity was just around the corner.

I have said, I think, that one of my favorite books is Washington Irving's *Sketch Book*; but, if I have neglected to do so, I will say it now. And of all the tales and sketches in that delightful miscellany my favorite is, and has been since childhood, the gay Shakespearean research called "The Boar's Head Tavern, Eastcheap." It would be one of the first three essays I would select for the perfect anthology. Probably you remember Irving's quest for Dame Quickly's "parcel-gilt goblet" and the tobacco box depicting the revels of Falstaff and Prince Hal, as set forth in Shakespeare's *Henry IV*. I could never be certain whether Irving invented the whole episode or whether it really had happened as he described it. He found the precious relics, or claimed to have found them, in the custody of a certain Dame Honeyball who kept a tavern in Miles Lane. They were introduced to him as "choice vessels of the vestry" of St. Michael's church, handed down from remote times when the parish meetings were held at the Boar's Head Tavern. This was in 1817, according to Irving, at which time they had been transferred to Dame Honeyball's establishment and deposited in the "parish club-room."

One hundred and twenty years later, almost to the day, I began my own search for the relics, covering as far as possible the ground traversed by Irving. Many times, indeed, I must have been walking in the very echo of his steps. But St. Michael's, Crooked Lane, had vanished and with it the Mason's Arms where Dame Honeyball had simpered and smiled. Only the uproar of Eastcheap and modern London lay around me. "Marry and amen!" I said, as Irving had said before me. "Here endeth my research!"—and I was about to give up my quest when my companion, Miss Ray Latimer of Chicago, pointed out a church spire not far from the scene of our explorations. It was the spire of St. Magnus the Martyr and, as the church was clearly an ancient one, we dropped in to ask questions about the neighborhood. Only to ask questions; no premonition had directed our steps. Yet, within ten minutes, we were looking at the relics Irving had quested more than a century before.

They had been there since 1830, when the parish of St. Michael's had been united with that of St. Magnus.

They were precisely as Irving had described them: the gigantic iron tobacco box with the Boar's Head Tavern painted on its lid, and the "parcel-gilt goblet." But it was the painting that stirred me most. Here at last was the famous inn frequented by Shakespeare and his friends—at least by Falstaff and his roystering companions —and here was the whole convivial group from *Henry IV*. They were in full revel, pictured (in Irving's words) "with that wonderful fidelity and force with which the portraits of renowned generals and commodores are illustrated on tobacco boxes for the benefit of posterity." My final note on this adventure may not come as a surprise. Some years later I married Miss Latimer, the young schoolteacher with literary ambitions who had been my companion that day.

One further literary pilgrimage remained to be made; but, as it happened, I did not make it. For years I had been hoping to visit Rochester, the scene of Dickens's *Mystery of Edwin Drood*. I held certain proprietary ideas about that great unsolved—perhaps insoluble—mystery, and wished to test them on the spot. But it was not to be; even as I was making preparations for the jaunt, I was snatched from London and rapt to Norwich by the inspiration to visit scenes associated with George Borrow and old Sir Thomas Browne. Nothing was added to the world's knowledge of either man of letters by my visit; but for three months I settled down in the fine old city and caught up on my reading and writing.

That was a stimulating experience for I had two exceptional guides to the attractions of Norwich in the persons of Herbert Leeds, the well-known Norwich columnist, and R. H. Mottram, the famous English novelist. It was Herbert Leeds who found for me, through his popular newspaper column, a first edition of *Black Beauty*, with a presentation inscription by Anna Sewell, its all but forgotten author. This discovery in itself was worth the trip to

302

Norwich, for *Black Beauty* in its first published state is one of the rarest books in the world. And it was Mottram who led me about the city in the footsteps of Sir Thomas Browne and told me one of the best literary anecdotes in my collection.

Today the busy uproar of the Haymarket sounds around the site of the old physician's house and garden; but there is a tablet to mark its ancient identity, and not far away sits the old gentleman himself, on a stone pedestal, piously contemplating a broken funeral urn. It may be that he is thinking long thoughts about the curious vicissitudes that befall a person after death, for it was only in recent times that his own skull was rediscovered in a local hospital and decently buried with the rest of him in his grave at St. Peter's. However that may be, this is the story told me by R. H. Mottram about the tablet at No. 12 Orford Place. In conversation with his friend, J. B. Priestley, the first novelist told the second novelist of a curious error in Kelly's directory of Norwich for the year 1929, in which volume, through a misreading of the tablet, "Browne, Thos. M.D." was entered as a living and practicing physician.

"By Jove!" cried Priestley, snapping his fingers, "there's a story for you, Mottram."

"What do you mean?" asked Mottram.

"Don't you see it? The year is 1929, just after the publication of that directory. Late at night, with everything closed solid, a woman is suddenly taken ill and her frantic husband grabs for the directory to look for a physician. There is no telephone, but the nearest doctor is a man named Browne, a few squares away. The husband snatches his hat, rushes out into the darkened streets, and in a few minutes is standing before the tablet in Orford Place. Yes, there he is! 'Thomas Browne, M.D.' He plunges his thumb into the bell and . . ."

"And what?" questioned the first novelist.

"*Gets him!*" said the second novelist softly.

This story, which illustrates the speed at which the literary mind sometimes operates, pleases me as much as any authenticated ghost story I have ever read. And with it I close my European adventure.

XXIII

SOMETHING HAD HAPPENED to the mystery story in my absence. It had been happening for a long time without my being aware of it. What had happened to it was, in large part, an ex-Pinkerton operative named Dashiell Hammett, whose five novels written between 1929 and 1934 may be said to have founded and defined the hard-boiled detective story. For better or for worse, it was now a vogue. I couldn't have written one to save my life. It seemed to me, too, that I had about written myself out as far as plots were concerned. Happily, I was mistaken and presently I was turning out Jimmie Lavender short stories again with all the old enthusiasm, and selling them to the popular magazines. (Some years later I was to publish the first collection of these adventures in *The Case Book of Jimmie Lavender*.)

At this time also I began to write again about what A. Edward Newton called the "amenities of book collecting." Almost at once this led me to a larger subject, the whole history of books, and tardily I knew that I had found my last and best subject. The first fruit of this decision was *Books Alive*. I wrote half a dozen chapters of it for Arnold Gingrich, then editing *Coronet*, placed a few pieces elsewhere, and in 1940 Random House published the book. It was followed in 1942 by *Bookman's Holiday*, a miscellany of bookish essays. During this period also Charles Honce gave my morale a lift by compiling *A Vincent Starrett Library*, an annotated bibliography of my published writings as of that time. Possibly it was this splurge of energy and authorship that enabled me to get my best book of poems published. For some time I had been hoping to bring out a definitive collection, and this was accomplished in 1943

304

with the publication by Dutton of *Autolycus in Limbo*, for which William Rose Benét wrote the introduction.

Needless to say, perhaps, none of these books made me wealthy and there arrived at length a bad moment when I saw clearly that the profession of literature, for me at least, was just a gentlemanly way of making not very much money. Out of this sound reflection was born my newspaper column *Books Alive* in the book supplement of the Sunday Chicago *Tribune*, where it still appears.

It was my old friend Charles Collins, himself a *Tribune* columnist, who wangled this berth for me. I wrote a few specimen columns for Mike Kennedy, then Sunday editor, which he was good enough to like, and soon found myself again a newspaperman. My immediate chief was Frederic Babcock, editor of the *Tribune's* book section, another old friend, with whom the happiest relations existed throughout his long term of office.

One of the most interesting developments of my new situation resulted in the publication of one of my most popular books, *Best Loved Books of the Twentieth Century*, which became a best-selling paperback. The initial suggestion came from an old friend, W. W. Goodpasture, vice president and general manager of Kroch's & Brentano's Bookshop, and I was promptly commissioned by Babcock to write a series of short essays on the outstanding books of the century for the *Tribune's* magazine of books. The feature ran weekly throughout 1954 and caught on so well that the fifty-two articles were published by Bantam Books in a handsome little paperback. Of course I dedicated the book to Goodpasture, and on January 21, 1955, K & B celebrated the first anniversary of their "super bookmart" by giving me an autographing party, the first such party, I believe, in the "world's largest bookstore." Edward Wagenknecht reviewed the book for the *Tribune* and was reckless enough to call me the "Number One American Bookman." And George Matthew Adams gave it a flattering plug in one of his syndicated columns. "I know of no better guide to great books," he wrote, "than this one by Vincent Starrett."

Other books that grew out of my weekly column were *Books*

and Bipeds, published by Ben Abramson, and *Book Column,* published by the Caxton Club of Chicago, with an introduction by Harry Owens. To complete the muster of my books to date, two other titles must be noticed: *Brillig,* a last collection of verse, privately printed by the Dierkes Press, and *The Great All-Star Animal League Ball Game,* published by Dodd, Mead and Company with delightful pictures by Kurt Wiese. This last title, my first and only juvenile, had been lurking in my subconscious for years, perhaps since boyhood. I am glad I got around to it at last, for it continues to bring me delightful letters from small boys, and sometimes girls, in all parts of what H. L. Mencken used to call the "federal union."

Somewhere in this prolific period I was commissioned to write introductions for a dozen or more books, of which the most important were the Limited Editions Club's fine issues of Poe's *Tales of Mystery and Imagination,* Conan Doyle's *Adventures of Sherlock Holmes,* Wilkie Collins's *The Moonstone* and *The Woman in White*; and the Heritage Press edition of Dickens's *Mystery of Edwin Drood.* For the Caxton Club I did an introduction to *John McCutcheon's Book,* which gave me great personal pleasure.

Thus far in my remembrance of things past, this record has been in large part a portrait of the artist as a young man. From now on I am afraid it is a portrait of an aging gentleman known to those who have occasion to mention him as the Dean of Chicago Authors.

It is axiomatic that, in spite of little hints and warnings of impending disintegration and the daily report of the desk calendar, one never quite realizes that one is growing old. Something outside one's self has to occur to call attention to the phenomenon. When not only my friends but strangers began to call me the dean of Chicago authors, I was at first pleased, then alarmed, then indignant. I didn't believe it; I don't believe it now. There are dozens of nice old persons, men and women, among Chicago's hundreds of writers who are *deaner* than I. But there was nothing I could do about it, and when all this friendly misunderstanding began to crystalize in luncheons and other civic attentions for the Grand Old Man, I realized that the accolade was official.

But of my considered thought of Vincent Starrett and all his works I have already written in a newspaper column that I should like to preserve. It appeared shortly after my sixtieth birthday:

"Your commentator celebrated an anniversary recently, if celebrated is the word. Not to be secret about it, he was suddenly sixty (it happened overnight), but instead of carrying on as if the occasion were important to others than himself, he merely sipped appropriate liquids and meditated.

"First, of course, he realized that he would never make another sixty, and wondered if he cared. He decided that he didn't. It had been a happy life, on the whole, and there had been a lot of it; but there was no part of it that he particularly wished to live over. A number of ambitions had gone wrong; but his failures, he knew, had been of his own making. On the other hand, many of his successes had been helped by others, and he was grateful. People in general had been kind. Critics had been more than kind, with the usual stupid exceptions. There was still an appalling number of things he wanted to do; he hoped he would be permitted to get some of them done. He saluted himself gravely, decided that at least he was not frustrated, and quoted Mr. Chesterton's famous line, 'After all, I think I will not hang myself today.' "

As always, I am willing to let Chesterton have the last word.

As I near the end of this long reminiscence, this salute to yesterday, these private satisfactions of an incurable bibliofool, and look back over what I have written, I can imagine someone asking persistently, "But did these things really happen or did Starrett invent them?" A good question; but the answer is simple. They couldn't have been thought out; they could only have happened.

It was good to be a newspaperman again. And again things had begun to happen. For years I had been a member of the Mystery Writers of America, Inc., whose famous slogan *Crime does not pay—enough!* is known around the world. Suddenly my colleagues surprised me by making me the first recipient of a new award. At their twelfth annual Edgar Allan Poe dinner I received one of their coveted "Edgars" accompanied by a flattering citation written by Ellery Queen. Having little humility, I quote it in full:

> This year (1958), for the first time we honor one of the Grand Masters in our field, and by the unanimous vote of the board of Directors of MWA the first recipient of this award is Vincent Starrett. Who among us has a more distinguished record in so many different facets of our work? Vincent Starrett has earned our respect, admiration, and affection as a detective novelist and short-story writer; as one of our foremost historians and critics; as a poet and anthologist; as an essayist and columnist who has made a fine art of writing about books and bookmen; as an explorer in bibliography and a discoverer in book collecting; as a Sherlockophile and connoisseur without peer—as, indeed, the noblest gentleman-and-scholar in our ranks. All honor to his accomplishments and undeviating integrity! [In 1961 I was elected president of the MWA.]

I have saved for my last paragraph a tribute from Carl Sandburg that has always given me great pleasure:

> Vincent Starrett is one of those few men whom I have little difficulty in placing in most any previous era of civilized mankind. His outward look and manner, his wit and ready inner grace, his casual and debonair camaraderie that he can employ on occasion to hide his investitures of wide learning, and his lore acquired by companionship with books great and little, good bad and indifferent . . . You can see him at home and at ease in several former human societies, talking small talk where the easy wisecrack is approved or making conversation on the timeless themes and queries. . . . The snow of winter is on his head, as with others of us. When the time comes that he shall enter Valhalla I can see him sharing confidences with A. Conan Doyle, sharing tobacco and book talk with Charles Lamb, sipping strange green liquers with François Villon, mixing in

pleasant arguments with Walter Pater, Walter Savage Landor, Walter Raleigh, and saying he will have no truck when they arrive with either Walter Lippman or Walter Winchell, though in a pinch he will take Winchell as against Lippmann on account of Winchell having made bold additions to the American language. . . . I join with you in your salutations to Vincent Starrett—a modern—an antique—rather timelessly human.

I didn't say it, Carl, you did. But it's as good a "30" as an old newspaperman is likely to get. And so 30—the close—at least for just now.

Index

314

319

324

The text for *Born in a Bookshop* has been set on the Linotype in 11-point Times Roman, a highly legible type designed by Stanley Morison. The paper on which this book is printed bears the University of Oklahoma Press watermark and has an intended life of at least three hundred years.